LIVING ELECTRON

Living Electronic Music

SIMON EMMERSON
De Montfort University, Leicester, UK

ASHGATE

Published by
Ashgate Publishing Limited
Gower House
Croft Road
Aldershot
Hampshire GU11 3HR
England

Ashgate Publishing Company
Suite 420
101 Cherry Street
Burlington, VT 05401-4405
USA

Ashgate website: http://www.ashgate.com

British Library Cataloguing in Publication Data
Emmerson, Simon, 1950—
Living electronic music
1. Electronic music – History and criticism 2. Performance practice (Music) – 20th century 3. Electro-acoustics
4. Computer music – History and criticism
I. Title
786.7

Library of Congress Cataloging-in-Publication Data
Emmerson, Simon, 1950—
Living electronic music / by Simon Emmerson.
p. cm.
Includes bibliographical references and index.
ISBN-13: 978-0-7546-5546-6 (hardback : alk. paper)
ISBN-13: 978-0-7546-5548-0 (pbk. : alk. paper)
1. Electronic music–History and criticism. 2. Music–Philosophy and aesthetics. I. Title.

ML1380.E46 2007
786.7–dc22

2006032288

ISBN 978-0-7546-5546-6 (hbk)
ISBN 978-0-7546-5548-0 (pbk)

Printed and bound in Great Britain by TJ International Ltd, Padstow, Cornwall.

Contents

List of Figures

Note on the author

Since November 2004, Simon Emmerson has been Professor of Music, Technology and Innovation at De Montfort University, Leicester, following 28 years as Director of the Electroacoustic Music studios at City University, London. As a composer he mostly works with live electronics; recent commissions include works for: Jane Chapman (harpsichord), the Smith Quartet, Inok Paek (kayagum), Philip Sheppard (electric cello), Philip Mead (piano) with the Royal Northern College of Music Brass Quintet. He has also completed purely electroacoustic commissions for the IMEB (Bourges) and the GRM (Paris). He was a first prize winner at the Bourges Electroacoustic Awards in 1985 for his work *Time Past IV* (soprano and tape). A CD of his works was issued on the Continuum label in 1993. He contributed to, and edited, *The Language of Electroacoustic Music* (Macmillan, 1986), and *Music, Electronic Media and Culture* (Ashgate, 2000) and is a contributor to journals such as *Organised Sound*, *Contemporary Music Review* and the *Journal of New Music Research*. He was founder Secretary of EMAS (The Electroacoustic Music Association of Great Britain) in 1979, and served on the Board of Sonic Arts Network from its inception until 2004. He is currently working on a new IMEB (Bourges) commission and two solo CDs for Sargasso.

Acknowledgements

To my students past and present who never cease to challenge accepted ideas and (usually) accept challenging ideas. To my past colleagues at City University, London, for an amazing 30 years (from postgraduate student to professor). To my present colleagues in the Music, Technology and Innovation Research Centre at De Montfort University for such an enthusiastic welcome that I felt immediately at home – and thrilled to be joining such a large, eclectic and stimulating group of creative people. To my friends in the wider music community for whom live performance is life's blood; music was ever thus. To my fellow composers and friends because we know that music is the only thing we could ever do. To my friends and colleagues in the Sonic Arts Network because community is important and so is exchange. To Ashgate Publishing for this golden opportunity to get things off my chest. And, above all, to my wife, Cathy, for her love and support.

Preface and Introduction: 'Between Disciplines'

This book is intended for anyone interested in contemporary music, but most especially in what has often been called *electroacoustic music* – a music heard through loudspeakers or sound made with the help of electronic means. But that definition is extended here to include amplified acoustic music where the amplification changes, in essence, the experience of the sound and is integral to the performance. The discussion draws on literature from acoustics and auditory science, psychology of perception, anthropology and the social sciences, as well as references from literature and the fine arts. But I hope it remains focussed on the *musical experience*. This in turn is a product of *performance* – but extended to embrace all possible spaces and places, personal and public. It is also prompted by the simple observation that more and more music is being made and listened to without any recourse to *mechanical* production beyond the vibrating loudspeaker cone. Most music now heard appears to present little evidence of *living presence*. Yet we persist in seeking it out. From grand gesture to a *noh*-like shift in the smallest aspect of a performer's demeanour, we attempt to *find relationships* between action and result.

When Pierre Schaeffer subtitled his *Traité des objets musicaux* (Schaeffer, 1966), '*essai interdisciplines*' – essay across disciplines – he sought to emphasize that sound and music could no longer be understood through one discipline alone (pp. 30-31). Classical acoustics foundered at the borders of the perception system. An explanation of sound as perceived – for example an explanation of *timbre* – demanded a cognitive science, one of listening and understanding. Schaefer's enterprize was the beginning of a longer chain of integrations and further interdisciplinary projects. Writers from the very different tradition of semiotics, such as Jean-Jacques Nattiez refer to the 'total musical fact' (Nattiez, 1990) within which questions once confined to musicology and musical aesthetics can no longer be separated from a wider net of 'ethnomusicology', social sciences, psychology and history. Writers such as Christopher Small ask further ethnographic questions about the very nature of music (from many genres) and its role in 'culture' (Small, 1998). And then we have even more recent newcomers: ecological and evolutionary science seek to encapsulate all these within the much longer-term development of human capacities. This has led, firstly, to the reframing of our response systems as 'negotiations' between our surroundings and our biological disposition (Gibson, 1979; Windsor, 2000) but also the more risky 'how did all this come about – or, put another way – why is this the way it is'? (Cross, 1999; 2003). Furthermore, some of these writers seek a revolution in approach to where 'the human being' (to be precise the human mind) is situated. No longer an observer of the world 'out there' but a participant in a complex web of relations which define what it is to 'live and perceive' – to which I will add 'and to make music' (Ingold, 2000).

It has proved impossible to construct a straight-through narrative for this book. Each chapter is designed to be a self-sufficient essay, yet all cross-reference and 'need' each other to get the bigger picture. While they may certainly be read in any order I have grouped the six chapters into three pairs. To discuss any electronic music ('live' or 'fixed') we need to start with the 'acousmatic revolutions' of the nineteenth century. From that time, slowly but surely, the production of music started moving away from the mechanical universe with its specific set of causal relationships – all based on well-understood Newtonian mechanics of action and reaction, motion, energy, friction and damping. This cannot be separated from a shift in consequent social relationships. A preliminary look at this era gives us some background.

The first revolution was at the tail end of this mechanical universe: Edison invented a *mechanical* memory for sound – a trace physically inscribed and mechanically reproduced on the cylinder of the *phonograph* (1877). But electricity, as we know from the near simultaneous invention of the telephone (1876), was a newly understood form of energy perfectly able to act as an *analogue for sound*. At first it collaborated with the old mechanical world, extending its capabilities – only later would it increasingly strive for a kind of independence as synthesis arrived at the dawn of the twentieth century. The last 25 years of the nineteenth century saw all the elements of the modern electronic sound world in place: recording, the telephone, synthesis and radio communication.

The telephone introduces us to the fundamental and symmetrical pair of electroacoustic inventions, the microphone and the loudspeaker. For this first purpose the duo remain small and relatively unobtrusive – but that is because they were used at first to just convey sound one-to-one. The need for electronic amplification follows from the two subsidiary demands of greater communication distance and also, crucially, 'to make sound louder' in the one-to-many communication of public address. But wanting *music* louder is not new – Liszt and Chopin drove the market that ended with the iron frame for the piano (Steinway patent of 1859) for greater projection to larger audiences. Orchestras grew in size proportionally throughout the nineteenth century but balance was, of course, through acoustic means – sheer force of numbers: just how many strings does it take to balance the increasing volume of brass and woodwind?[1] Then someone somewhere spotted the potential for the loudspeaker to cross over from re-presentation (recording and radio), to performance.[2] The two ends of the chain drive each other: loudspeakers in performance demand versatile yet simple and unobtrusive microphones, especially when applied to instruments (pickups). The earliest such pickups date from the 1920s at the same time that contemporary moving coil loudspeaker designs were established. The instrument could at last grow a larger sound without a larger body

1 In fact there was a mechanical predecessor – the *Strohvioline* were modified string instruments with horns designed to focus the sound towards the pre-electric recording funnel. Used again in Mauricio Kagel's *1898* written to celebrate the seventy-fifth birthday of Deutsche Grammophon (see the cover of the recording for illustrations) (Kagel, 1973).

2 I suggest it is the public address function that linked the two worlds. It combines information conveyance with oratory.

or playing with additional clones of itself.[3] Its sonic presence could become greater than its physical size suggested. This first generation of pickups amplifies an existing acoustic sound and aims to retain some fidelity to it. Guitars can now balance better with piano, brass and wind – even dare to become more soloistic in mixed ensemble. Then followed voice and the crooners – who could sing intimately and personally to a large hall full of adoring followers, or appear comfortably close from radio or record player loudspeaker.

In parallel there was synthesis – the very first sound to be produced by other than mechanical means. First designed in the last years of the nineteenth, and first heard in the earliest years of the twentieth century, Dr Thaddeus Carhill's *Telharmonium* (1906) celebrates its centenary as I write. Lee de Forest's invention of the thermionic valve (1907), as well as provoking a quantum leap in communication technologies, encouraged a second more realistic generation of instrument inventors. It enabled the electric and optical-electric keyboards; as well as the more experimental *Theremin* and *Ondes Martenot* in the 1920s. Also in this decade, with local and national radio networks came the first major widespread domestic use of the loudspeaker. Shortly after, sound film extended that still further into the public domain as well as introducing the first synthesis through visual (optical track) methods.[4]

The first experimental uses of recording technology for creation and performance – rather than re-creation – start to appear about 50 years after its invention. The third movement of Ottorino Respighi's *Pines of Rome* (1924) demands a pre-recorded nightingale. Representing the 'non-musical' has been a constant theme in music from many cultures but from this time the literal importation of environmental sound through recording will be a recurrent theme. In Berlin, Paul Hindemith and Ernst Toch made preliminary studies in 'made-for-phonograph-record-music' as early as 1930 18 years before Schaeffer's leap into *musique concrète* (Kahn, 1999, p. 127). In all this the 'live' never goes away, but the seeds of a shift in usage and hence meaning have been sown.

These innovations raise questions which are not confined to what is called 'live electronic music' – and we shall see there is considerable disagreement about this term. Yet live electronics confronts and exaggerates issues of personality, presence and performance – and their mirror *absences* – in ways which challenge all our received assumptions from the era of mechanical music. One function of this book is to place questions before composers, performers and listeners about the nature of the performance of contemporary music with technology. To understand something of how contemporary electronic music has evolved in its many forms demands a fresh look at some aspects of its evolution. A first cluster of questions might, for example, be:

- Exactly what does 'live' mean anymore? How do I know you're not just

3 Amplification did not replace increased instrumentation overnight of course – the big bands of the 1930s and 1940s increased instrumental line-ups as well as utilising a first generation of amplification techniques.

4 For example, at the Bauhaus in Germany, Norman McClaren's experiments in the UK and Canada and Yevgeny Sholpo at the Moscow Experimental Studio (Manning, 1993, p. 12).

miming on stage? What clues are there? It's only a laptop and a mouse. You claim you are taking decisions and acting on the result – even based on how I (a listener) am 'responding' to you. Can I hear that?

- Does it matter how you got there or how the music got there? Did you make it? Or did a machine? Based on what? Are you just another icon? What do you and I take away from the performance and bring to the next one?
- Do I have any real evidence that you are not a complete fraud? If icons work and give the audience a buzz, a sense of occasion … does it matter providing I enjoyed the experience?

There are no answers except creative ones for which there is no 'right or wrong' – but there is always a 'game of consequences'. Much of the discussion on 'live' electronic music overlaps with questions on the composition and performance of 'fixed' electroacoustic pieces and there is, of course, no clear dividing line if one believes that performance is the only true instantiation of any music. In fact it is precisely this ambiguity between 'live' and 'studio-created' which is increasingly highglighted in contemporary practice.

The first two chapters might be grouped as a pair. Chapter 1 ('Living Presence') starts with the apparently simple set of questions about gaining useful information from the sounding flow (when visual information is not available). In musical terms this is about 'undoing Schaeffer's *bracketing out*'. A range of works which have challenged Schaeffer's view of the acousmatic are discussed. This is divided into three parts. First there is 'Physical Presence: Action and Agency', a discussion about the interpretation of the acoustic flow in basic 'source/cause' terms. Secondly there is 'Psychological Presence: Will, Choice and Intention' which suggests that we search for clues as to how the sounding agents will behave in the future on the basis of choices we believe they are making now (a one-time survival need becomes a game). Finally, there is 'Personal and Social presence: What you mean to me, Where I am and Who I am with', which draws on ideas from those branches of musicology that have always acknowledged that the work of music does not float independently of its performance and what *all participants* bring to that (Small, 1998). The new music made through technology has need of all three discussions if we are to begin to understand the fundamental shift in 'the live' music paradigm in the last years of the twentieth century.

Earlier writers (notably Handel, 1989; Bregman, 1990) have examined 'auditory scene analysis', but none has focussed on this search for a holistic view of musical context. We produce and receive physical, psychological and social cues continuously – they are not always distinguishable. But the boundaries of 'the live' have been both eroded and extended through audio technology; I can 'play' the sounds of the environment like an instrument. Furthermore the shamanic role of the orchestra conductor has translated to become the DJ, or the laptop artist superstar, all there to conjure up spirits from 'a world beyond' – or perhaps, as some would argue, to put us more intensely in contact with the world around and within. I hesitantly move towards the conclusion that there is no clear boundary between the sentient and non-sentient soundworlds. It is ironic that such a dissolution has been enabled and encouraged through technology.

In Chapter 2 ('The Reanimation of the World: Relocating the 'Live'') the shift outlined above is put in the context of a *two way exchange* between the so-called animate and inanimate worlds. The idea of 'models', apparently non-musical constructions, which generate music becomes increasingly formalized from the 1950s (for example, in works by Xenakis, Berio and Stockhausen amongst many others). Models become increasingly appropriated within the computer music – especially 'live' computer music – paradigms of the late century. I argue that it is as important to see this as a *reanimation* of human-world relations rather than an invasion of dehumanized 'automata'.

Chapters 3 and 4 also form a pair. We talk blithely of 'real world' and 'human presence' in electroacoustic music but it often remains a rather abstract idea: a landscape, an instrumentalist, a singer, a *sounding action*. Some parts of the 'art music' tradition tend to exclude (or at least de-emphasize) individual personality – in the sense of a specific recognisable location, human character or performance act behind the production of these sounds – being generalizations in the name of a 'timeless' art. But of course there *is* music which presents – to a greater or lesser extent – recognisable soundscapes or recognisable human presence, possessing 'real' and individual personality or reflecting the human body and its rhythms. In Chapter 3 ('The Human Body in Electroacoustic Music: Sublimated or Celebrated?') the apparent opposition of 'body' and 'environment' within western music in general and electroacoustic music in particular is examined. Electroacoustic 'art' music has become increasingly environmental in its impulses while its experimental popular music (derived) cousins (electronica and IDM) retain their strong body and dance references. How can these two relate? Interestingly electroacoustic music history has often seen and heard real human presence, though usually fleeting and ephemeral – sometimes these can get too close for comfort. Chapter 4 (''Playing Space': Towards an Aesthetics of Live Electronics') looks at some ideas in live electronics from the point of view of *spaces*, both personal and public. I develop ideas for a live electronics of 'local' and 'field' functions. How can composers and performers 'play' with the spaces that they can both create artificially through electroacoustic means or create literally through the creative 'dislocation' of source and loudspeaker around an auditorium.

The final pair of chapters look at those 'first creations' which helped give birth to the acousmatic condition we inhabit: the microphone and the loudspeaker. In truth separating the two was arbitrary: they must work together – although the chapter on the microphone assumes the loudspeaker more than the reverse. They have both complementary and contrasting functions. Both can be key parts of performance instruments and have developed independent performance traditions; microphones have slowly become smaller while (at least some) loudspeaker systems have become substantially larger. Each chapter is prefaced with a non-mathematical summary of the transducer theories behind the different types. This has crucially influenced their 'character' and the ways composers have approached them as tools. Chapter 5 ('To Input the Live: Microphones and other Human Activity Transducers') starts by introducing the microphone as the key to the door into music made with technology. Recording aside, the microphone entered live performance practice slightly later.

We examine the evolution and functions of amplification in live electronic music.[5] The discussion is expanded to include other 'human activity interfaces', from gesture interfaces which capture physical performance action to visual tracking and biophysical interfaces. Chapter 6 ('Diffusion-Projection: The Grain of the Loudspeaker') suggests that loudspeakers have real performance character and personality. The French tradition of the *orchestre de hauts-parleurs*, other more 'geometric' propositions, the 'total' immersion spaces of clubs and personal stereo, as well as the *polytopes* of Xenakis are compared. But is 'acousmatic music' truly acousmatic? We might *see* the loudspeakers as real instruments – there is a divide between those who look and those who do not. But the loudspeaker – which has hardly evolved in basic design in 80 years – may be set for a radical overhaul with contrasting 'spotlight' and 'wave field synthesis' methods in current development.

No chapter is really first or last and there are no definitive conclusions. I dedicate this book to my many students over the years – especially those who have challenged my 'first generation' definition of live electronics. It is clear this needs a rethink – exactly what is it 'to be alive' in music making? There may be no answer but there is a very real question.

Simon Emmerson
London, May 2006

5 Liberally defined here to include any work *requiring* amplification for its proper performance.

CHAPTER ONE

Living Presence

Introduction

I had originally intended to title this chapter 'Human Presence'. After all live, human activity in music making is a central theme of this entire book. Yet as it emerged, it became apparent that this chapter was not so much about 'live humans' in music as about the *relationship* of the human music maker to other possible sound sources and agencies, whether natural and environmental or human-made and synthetic. Thus while I accord the human being a central position in a discussion of 'living presence', other entities will be identified and contribute to our sonic discourse. It might also have been called 'Real World Presence'; but here, too, distinctions are hard to maintain – just what might a 'non-real' or 'abstract' world be like if it is in my imagination? This question presupposes an 'observer-world' distinction which I wish to play down in this text. My imagination is part of the living and real world. Nonetheless this 'real-non-real' distinction is very important historically. It is clear that there is a transcendental tradition in music which does indeed seek to 'bracket out' most of the direct relationships to what we might loosely call 'real world' referents. Pierre Schaeffer's reaffirmation of the acousmatic and the particular way he established the practices of *musique concrète* continued this aesthetic line. The first part of the chapter examines this approach based on 'reduced listening' and – more importantly – some of the many and various rebellions against, and reactions to, its strictures. It seems that so many composers have *wanted* to bring recognizable sounds and contexts back into the centre of our attention that something more profound is at work. To explain this we need to step back from history for a moment to examine just what 'cues and clues' we are getting from the sound stream to allow us to construct what may be a recognizable 'source and cause' (whether human or not) for what we heard. And we will want to go even further – we may also react and respond to the sounds and search for relationships and meanings amongst the agencies we have constructed.

Presence – something is there. Of course when we hear something we can simply say 'there was sound'. We can describe the sound literally using a wide variety of languages. There can be a scientific attempt to describe sound without reference to actual objects in the world around us – that is in terms of its measurable 'abstract' parameters, spectrum, noise components, amplitude envelopes and the like. But in contrast we have languages of description that use more metaphoric kinds of expression. These might draw parallels with other sense perceptions, colour, light and dark, weight and density, sweet and sour, speed and space, shape and size. We might, in time, learn to relate these two language domains. But description of the sound in these terms is not description of our *experience* of it. We might tentatively move in that direction – we might describe a sound as 'threatening', 'reassuring', 'aggressive' or even 'beautiful' but what we are doing is not so much to describe the sound as to describe our response to it. This response will be based on a complex negotiation of evolution and personal circumstance. It may be that we cannot completely suspend the 'search engine' that is our perception system (even when we sleep). This engine seeks to construct and interpret the environment (perhaps the two cannot be separated). Furthermore the perceiving body – the listener – is part of that environment and not a detached observer.

I intend to approach this 'search and response' in three parts – but these parts are not 'stages': I am forced to address one after the other but they are in practice simultaneous and interacting. First we discuss the search for *Physical Presence: Action and Agency*. The listener can gain basic information on objects, agencies and actions in the world, allowing a tentative construction of possible sources and causes of the sounding flow. But perception does not stop there. The search also applies to a different dimension. Playing games and constructing narratives, our listener also searches for clues on *Psychological Presence: Will, Choice and Intention*. What are the options, choices and strategies open to the (surmised) agencies in the 'auditory scene'. What might happen next and are our expectations met? Furthermore both these two 'presences' are themselves embedded in a third: the listener is somewhere real – not outside the world. There is *Personal and Social Presence*. Where are you? Who are you with? What do they mean to you? How do you relate to them? I suggest that 'style' and genre are not simply descriptions of the sounding features but must include a discussion of venue, social milieu, performance and dissemination practice. A simple comparison of different genres of electronic and acousmatic music which have upset traditional definitions shows this clearly. The 'identity of the work' is not something fixed and unchanging if we compare 'traditional' acousmatic composition, laptop improvisation and 'electronica/IDM'. We can summarize the core of this attempt at a holistic approach in a simple diagram (Figure 1.1).

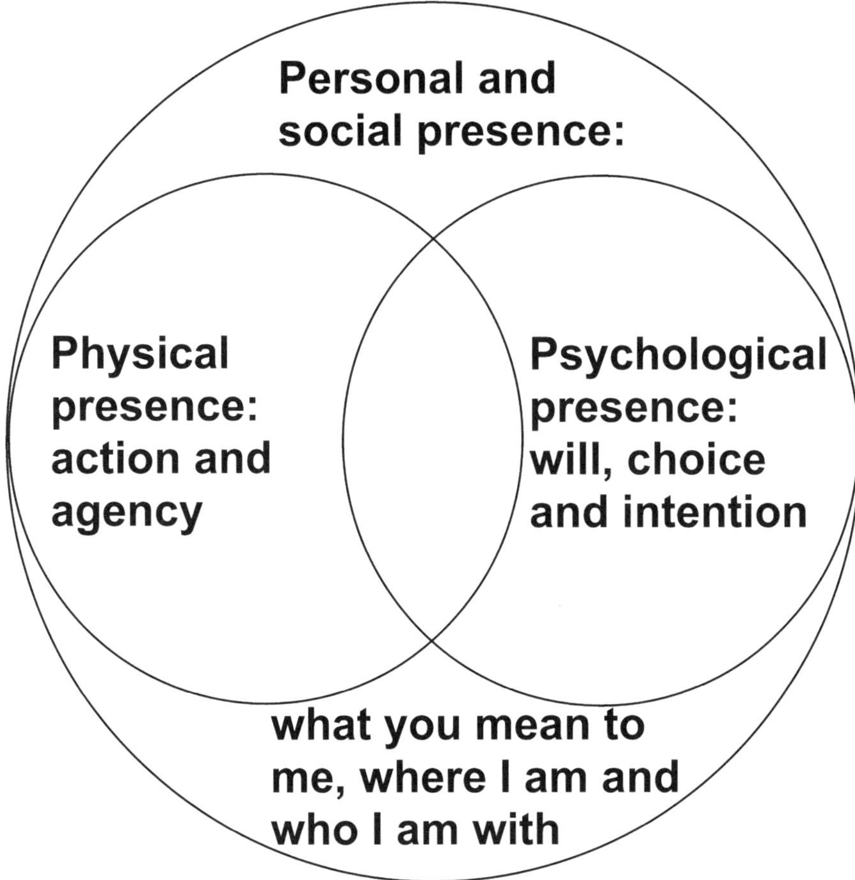

Figure 1.1: Living presence

Can Listening be 'Reduced'?: On not Recognizing Origins

An *agent* is an entity (a configuration of material, human, animal or environmental) which may execute an *action* (a change in something, usually involving a transfer of energy). We will be mostly concerned here with the causes of actions by agents which result in *sound*. In most music before recording the need to search for and identify the source of sounds was minimal if not non-existent. Occasionally musical results might be surprising (Haydn) or even terrifying (Berlioz) but the field of sound-producing agents for music was limited by conventional mechanical instrumentation. This itself was perpetually evolving and adapting to meet a complex of musical, social, economic and technological demands. Thus developments and additions were incremental, and could be seen, heard and understood relatively quickly.

Consider a piano concerto or symphony of the early twentieth century compared to one of about 1800. The immense additional volume of sound would be delivered from an iron-framed piano; violins, wind and brass which had been redesigned to be louder, more versatile and with extended range (tuba, bass trombone); possibly entirely new instruments (saxophone) and newly imported instruments (percussion).[1] But all were recognizably from the same stables as their predecessors. A knowledgeable ear might pose and then hazard answers to questions of inventive orchestration. But this was not a necessary prerequisite for appreciation of the music – although when Wagner deliberately hid the orchestra in his design specification for the *Festspielhaus* in Bayreuth, he clearly intended the mundanities of physical production to be 'bracketed out'. Wagner suggests a kind of acousmatic listening to 'absolute music':

> … I hope that a subsequent visit to the opera will have convinced [the reader] of my rightness in condemning the constant visibility of the mechanism for tone production as an aggressive nuisance. In my article on Beethoven I explained how fine performances of ideal works of music may make this evil imperceptible at last, through our eyesight being neutralized, as it were, by the rapt subversion of the whole sensorium (Wagner, 1977, p. 365).[2]

But aesthetic argument is complemented by acoustic consequence; luckily the two here reinforce:

> Although according to all that Wagner published on the sunken pit the main purpose was visual concealment, it has the secondary effect of subduing the loudness and altering the timbre of the orchestra. The sound reaching the listener is entirely indirect (that is, reflected), and much of the upper frequency sound is lost. This gives the tone a mysterious, remote quality and also helps to avoid overpowering the singers with even the largest Wagnerian orchestra (Forsyth, 1985, p. 187).

Even when confronted by an entirely new instrumentation – the gamelan ensemble at the Paris Universal Exhibition of 1889 for example – generic vocal, metallic or bowed string timbres could quickly be related to source. Western music has often appropriated these sources, which are always absorbed with an apparent amnesia, later to include the African xylophone and other percussion instruments from pre-Columbian cultures of the Americas.

But the ability to *identify* instrumental timbres was not really an issue – it was not part of the *game* of classical composition. The landscape of classical music (as

---

1 Steinway's iron frame patent dates from 1859. Theobald Boehm's rationalized flute was developed over 20 years up to 1851, while the clarinet action named after him (in fact designed by Hyacinthe Klosé) dates from 1839. Most Stradivarius violins had new 'improved' necks added at some time in the nineteenth century to allow greater tensioned and more massive strings. Adolphe Sax invented the saxophone in the 1840s. Low brass were added progressively throughout the nineteenth century. Compare the bass drum, side drum and triangle of the 'Turkish music' of Haydn and Mozart's time with the battery needed for Mahler's sixth Symphony (1904).

2 In *The Artwork of the Future* Wagner writes that ideally '… for all our open eyes, [we] have fallen into a state essentially akin to that of hypnotic clairvoyance' (1977, p. 186). Following the quote given above, however, he goes on to replace this with the 'picture' of the drama on stage – with attendant contradictions that might entail (see discussion in Chapter 2).

Trevor Wishart has described it) is 'humans playing instruments'. The 'search engine' of our perception system is only minimally engaged. However, the *acousmatic* condition that recording emphasized (but did not strictly invent) slowly reengaged this faculty as part of an aesthetic engagement with a new 'sonic art' not based on any agreed sound sources. But it did so in a way which was to produce tensions and contradictions within the music and amongst its practitioners. The unresolved question in short – do we want or need to know *what causes the sound we hear*?

Pierre Schaeffer's answer is clearly 'no', and in developing the ideas of *musique concrète*, he placed this response at the centre of his philosophy, calling it *écoute réduite* ('reduced listening') which is encouraged by the *acousmatic* condition. As paraphrased by Michel Chion:

> Acousmatic: … *indicating a noise which is heard without seeing the causes from which it originates*. … The acousmatic situation renews the way we hear. By isolating the sound from the "audiovisual complex" to which it initially belonged, it creates favourable conditions for a *reduced listening* which concentrates on the sound for its own sake, as *sound object*, independent of its causes or its meaning … (Chion, 1983, p. 18).

Not only (according to this view) was source identification (and any associated 'meaning') unnecessary, it was misleading, and distracted from the establishment of a potential musical discourse: carefully chosen *objets sonores* become *objets musicaux* through studio montage (their *relationship* to other sounds) guided by the listening ear. The necessary skills were developed in a thorough training combining research and practice (Schaeffer, 1966).

But there remains a niggling doubt about the premiss. Michel Chion (whose paraphrase of Schaeffer (quoted above) is that of a sympathetic insider, as a member of the *Groupe de Recherches Musicales* (1971–76)) expresses it simply:

> … Schaeffer thought the acousmatic situation could encourage reduced listening, in that it provokes one to separate oneself from causes or effects in favor of consciously attending to sonic textures, masses, and velocities. But, on the contrary, the opposite often occurs, at least at first, since the acousmatic situation intensifies causal listening in taking away the aid of sight (Chion, 1994, p. 32).

This doubt opens the door to a vast range of acousmatic musics, as we shall see.

Throughout the history of the post-renaissance western arts many revolutionary practitioners have appeared to set out to overthrow and replace a particular world view while in practice becoming part of a renewal process which would in time be absorbed into the mainstream.[3] Yet, paradoxically, in some ways Pierre Schaeffer's was a mirror position to this. His intention was to renew and revitalize from the inside, yet in many ways his work has turned out to be more revolutionary and universal in its consequences than he ever intended.

---

3 The classic theory of the avant-garde – itself a product of romanticism and western modernism – is explicit in the writings of Wagner, Schoenberg, Boulez, Stockhausen and Schaeffer – but not Cage. See also Poggioli (1968) and Nyman (1999).

> If one admits that it is necessary to be a musician to enjoy well the classics, that it is necessary to be a connoisseur to appreciate suitably jazz or exotic musics, then it is necessary to hope that the public will not claim entry at first attempt to the *concrète* domain. That is because this entry is so new, renewing so profoundly the phenomenon of musical communication or of contemplation, that it appeared to me necessary to write this book (Schaeffer, 1952, p. 199).

His attack on *notation* (in the sense of the manipulation of *symbols*) as the central means to produce music (which he called '*musique abstraite*') and its replacement with *sonic quality* (the manipulation of *sound as heard*) as the driving force ('*musique concrète*') remains a monumental shift of focus. Yet it was intended to renew and revitalize the western tradition not replace it.

At heart his insistence on reduced listening means that *musique concrète* was intended to refine and accelerate the development of a primarily timbral discourse which had already had a long history within western music (most especially within the Russian and French classical traditions).[4] If the search for source or cause is to be bracketed out then the *field of play* of such timbral music is made much richer by the materials of *musique concrète* but is in principle not changed in its aesthetic aims. But this extension into recorded sound acted as a Trojan horse containing another world altogether – one which Schaefer did not accept – where the temptation to *refer to things apparently outside 'music'* would be hard to resist.

Interestingly, as Kofi Agawu has emphasized, there are plenty of 'extra-musical' references in what is often considered 'abstract' classical music (Agawu, 1991). For example, we might give 'trumpet or horn call motif = military or hunting' (even when played on the piano) as an obvious case, but such a relationship might be extended to the timbral domain of the kind 'trumpet or horn *sound* = military or hunting'. Then there is the age-old association of wind and reed instruments with the pastoral. Originally rooted in their material construction, where place and function meet, such associations may progressively fade in a post-pastoral urban environment. But these may be replaced with a new set of associations – and certainly sounds of the environment often bring strong associations with them. We can go even further perhaps risking the assertion: *sounds inevitably have associations*. So perhaps while the 'source/cause' search might be suspended, the 'association' of the sound, bracketed together with it by Chion (after Schaeffer), is certainly not. Some of these responses may indeed be automatic and we may not have sufficient conscious control to 'bracket them out'. The unintended consequences of Schaeffer's puritan position[5] were to be profound.

---

4 Mussorgsky, Rimsky-Korsakov, Stravinsky and Berlioz, Debussy, Ravel, Varèse, Messiaen.

5 This is the first of many 'exclusions' which this approach articulated and is the most fundamental; other chapters will discuss aspects of pitch argument and rhythm which are also largely 'bracketed out' within the modernist phase of the development of *musique concrète*.

Source Recognition Regained

One key idea of this book centres on a regaining of a relationship to the sonic resources around us (both on- and off-world). As I shall be taking the argument considerably further than in previous writings, I need to revisit certain landmark steps in the development of electroacoustic music within and beyond the *avant-garde* of the 1950s.

The explicit notion that recorded sound should not only retain an identifiable link to source and cause but that such links should be developed into narrative threads is made explicit in a series of post-Schaefferian developments of the 1960s and 1970s. I will summarize these in a cluster of references and works. This group is not exhaustive but designed to summarize the wide range of approaches which have evolved. Some assume more or less common perceptions and declare their aims to be a wider communication and dissemination; others aim to elicit more personal responses, dependent on individual memory of personal or historic details.

'Nature Photographs' (Luc Ferrari)

There were, of course, many even within the *Groupe de Recherches Musicales*[6] who came to doubt Schaeffer's initial premises. Luc Ferrari's invention of what he termed *anecdotal music* was seen as a major act of dissent and rebellion. He wanted to restore a dualism to our sound perception:

> I thought it had to be possible to retain absolutely the structural qualities of the old *musique concrète* without throwing out the reality content of the material which it had originally. It had to be possible to make music and to bring into relation together the shreds of reality in order to tell stories (Pauli, 1971, p. 41).

He goes on to describe such work as '... more reproduction than production: electroacoustic nature photographs ...' (p. 58).

There are two strands of development in Ferrari's anecdotal compositions. *Hétérozygote* (1964)*[7] and *Music Promenade* (1969) present fragmented shots of the 'real world'; cutting between scenes and snapshots and using multi-channel

---

6 The *Groupe de Recherches Musicales* was founded in 1958 as the successor organization to the variously named sequence of studios and groups for *musique concrète* within Radio France.

7 Luc Ferrari is not properly credited with major influence on Stockhausen's move to use of 'anecdotal' sound (in, for example, *Telemusik* (1966) and *Hymnen* (1967)). Ferrari taught '*musique concrète*' [sic] on the Cologne New Music Courses 1964–66; *Tautologos II* was broadcast by Stockhausen on the WDR in 1964 and *Hétérozygote* in 1966 (with extensive discussion of its 'musical photography') (see Emmerson, 1986b, p. 35).

* Throughout this book a date given immediately after a work title refers to the accepted date of completion of the work. However its reference will be made in the standard way using the composer's name and date of publication of the specific media (score, LP or CD). Thus Luc Ferrari's *Music Promenade* (1969) can be found on Ferrari (1995).

techniques to differentiate these in space. The later series of *Presque riens*[8] are generally cast in longer scenes; any edits are deftly concealed and the whole evolves smoothly through a clearer journey-like evolution. Whether reconstructed from fragments or reinterpreted from continuity Ferrari declares: 'My anecdotal music brings to the public the pictures of its own reality and its own imagination' (Pauli, 1971, p. 47).

'Sound Symbols' (Trevor Wishart)

While Luc Ferrari makes no assumptions about the listener's interpretation of the anecdotal sounds in his works, Trevor Wishart seeks to build on firmer, more commonly held responses. In fact the near-automatic response (for example to the horn call mentioned above) is the kind of association which Trevor Wishart suggests contributes to the creation of *sound symbols*. These are recognizable sounds that clearly convey a feeling, idea or concept to the listener. This he develops into the idea of a musical 'myth' – something capable of carrying an unequivocal message beyond aesthetic abstraction, clearly rooted in the discourse of the material world.

> In order to build up a complex metaphoric network we need to establish a set of metaphoric primitives which the listener might reasonably be expected to recognize and relate to, just as in the structure of a myth we need to use symbols which are reasonably unambiguous to a large number of people (Wishart, 1986, p. 55).

In *Red Bird – A Document* Wishart elaborates how these sound symbols derive their significance:

> (i) An example of the general archetype of which it is a member (e.g. Birds)
> (ii) Conventional symbolism (e.g. Birds…to Fly, Above, Transcendence, Freedom…)
> (iii) Its articulation in relation to (ii) and the other symbols, in the context of the piece (Words..TO…Birds, Well-water….TO….Birds, etc.) (Wishart, 1978, p. 4).[9]

Yet the work has an open intent, intended to challenge 'closed' conceptions of the world: '… entire landscapes (such as the GARDEN and the UNIVERSAL FACTORY, the POET etc.) act as dynamic symbols in that their underlying principles of organisation symbolize conflicting models of realities' (Wishart, 1978, p. 4). However, Wishart's claim that such symbols are part of a shared archetypal set has subsequently been challenged. Birds may very well be a symbol of freedom to some but represent a more predatory, instinctive and unfeeling life form to others (for example Alfred Hitchcock).

---

8 There are four explicit *Presque riens*: *Presque rien no. 1* (*Le lever du jour au bord de la mer*) (1970); *Presque rien no.2* (*Ainsi continue la nuit dans ma tête multiple*) (1977); *Presque rien avec filles* (1989) (all on Ferrari, 1995); and *Presque rien no. 4* (*La remontée du village*) (1990–1998) (on Ferrari, 2005).

9 '…' as in original (not omissions from text).

The World Soundscape Project (R. Murray Schafer)

The date for the formation of the World Soundscape Project is formally given as 1971, although it progressively emerged from the work of its founder R. Murray Schafer in the late 1960s. Originally intended to combine 'education and research' subsequent development of soundscape studies shows two clear trends emerging. At first, in Barry Truax's words:

> ... the basic aim was not to further exploit the environment as a source of musical material but rather to exploit the knowledge base of musical design in order to re-design the soundscape, and to reawaken people's perceptual appreciation of its importance (Truax, 1996, p. 53).

To this end the group developed a useful descriptive – and evocative – vocabulary. Three of their earliest[10] and most important keywords were *keynote sound* (a near ubiquitous 'ground' against which foreground sounds may be set), *sound signal* (a sound which carries significant information for the community) and *soundmark* (a unique sound of cultural or historical significance, deserving of preservation). An evangelical streak comes directly from the ideas of its founder as expressed in his pioneering publications *The New Soundscape* (1969) and *The Book of Noise* (1970). His original intention was for the WSP to act as a critique of the urban environment and its increasingly 'lo-fi' soundscape within which sensitive discrimination (and hence the creation of perspective) was increasingly difficult.

> The hi-fi soundscape is one in which discrete sounds can be heard more clearly because of the low ambient noise level ... In the hi-fi soundscape, sounds overlap less frequently; there is perspective – foreground and background ... In a lo-fi soundscape individual acoustic signals are obscured in an overdense population of sounds. The pellucid sound – a footstep in the snow, a church bell across the valley ... – is masked by broadband noise. Perspective is lost. On a downtown street corner of the modern city there is no distance; there is only presence. There is crosstalk on all channels ... (Schafer, 1977, p. 43).

Subsequent sound artists have accused him (and the movement) of an anti-urban nostalgia.[11] The fact that Schafer was himself a composer and gathered several other composers into the WSP group meant that the original 'from musical design to environment' arrow was also (and inevitably) reversed in a parallel stream of work which emerged in the 1970s (most notably from Hildegard Westerkamp and Barry Truax).

Zoom Lens (Hildegard Westerkamp)

Of course much soundscape composition is more than 'mere' representation. Referring to both animic and totemic depictions in so-called 'craft' or 'art'. Tim Ingold argues:

---

10 See for example Schafer (1978) and Truax (1999).

11 David Toop discusses some of these in his book *Haunted Weather* (Chapter 2: 'Space and memory') (Toop, 2004).

> In a word, they are not representational … Whether their primary concern be with the land or its non-human inhabitants, their purpose is not to represent but to reveal, to penetrate beneath the surface of things so as to reach deeper levels of knowledge and understanding (Ingold, 2000, p. 130).

This revelatory aspect of image can also be made explicit in sound and especially in soundscape works. Hildegard Westerkamp's *Kits Beach Soundwalk* uses the real filters of electronic technology to enhance the psychological filters of perception. At one moment she filters out the ambient city noise (still dominant at a distance) to foreground tiny beach sounds. These techniques are added to her already extraordinary sense of perspective and detail gained through using the microphone as an acoustic lens:

> I like to use the microphone the way photographers often use the camera, searching for images, using the zoom to discover what the human eye alone cannot see … I like to position the microphone very close to the tiny, quiet and complex sounds of nature, then amplify and highlight them … Perhaps in that way these natural sounds can be understood as occupying an important place in the soundscape and warrant respect and protection. I like walking the edge between the real sound and the processed sound … But I abstract an original sound only to a certain degree and am not actually interested in blurring its original clarity (Westerkamp, 1996, pp. 19–20).

Confronting/Provoking (Luigi Nono)

It might seem that an almost exactly opposite view is taken in some of the electroacoustic works of Luigi Nono. Far from wanting to preserve and respect, Nono heard many aspects of soundscape reality as articulating the oppressive relations of industrial capitalism. Nono remarked after his first experience of the symphonies of Gustav Mahler that they showed him:

> ... that art, and therefore also music, is not metaphysical, nor abstract, distant and remote, also not what merely falls into aesthetic categories, but a means of getting to know a historical situation, a reality, or from the point of view of the artist, of presenting knowledge of reality (Pauli, 1971, pp. 106–7).

His works which present stark reproductions of the sounds of war, protest and industrial processes and relations are intended to pull the listener up short and place unavoidable questions on the table.[12] *La fabbrica illuminata* (1964) pits the humanistic lyricism and anger of a solo soprano against the factory sounds of the Italsider factory in Milan and crowds chanting slogans. Nono presented a performance of the piece[13] in the factory:

---

12 In a manner clearly the descendant of some aspects of the theatrical techniques of Bertholt Brecht (*Epic theatre* and associated 'alienation effects').

13 I have examined the dialectical relationships of this work more fully in Emmerson (1986b).

> Quite directly the workers wanted to know how this was composed, how factory din and wage contracts could become music. What they heard they immediately related to themselves. And then they reproached me, that the noises in my piece, in 'La fabbrica illuminata', were not as strong by far as those they were accustomed to (Pauli, 1971, p. 120).

Thus sound is a product of an activity that has been reified by capitalist industrial production. It is both oppressive in itself – damaging to those in its vicinity – and representative of an oppressive system of production. Philosophy, ethics and aesthetics are allied in this critique.

'Real-World Music' (Katharine Norman)

In her essay 'Real-World Music as Composed Listening' (Norman, 1996), Katharine Norman has described her ideas for a music involving recognizable sounds yet one which is distinct from soundscape composition as such. Her emphasis rests strongly on the 'music' in this phrase. She describes a kind of musical argument 'sounded off' the memory of reality constructed through sound and our very personal interpretations of it:

> I contend that real-world music is not concerned with realism, and *cannot* be concerned with realism because it seeks, instead, to initiate a journey which takes us away from our preconceptions, so that we might arrive at a changed, perhaps expanded, appreciation of reality (Norman, 1996, p. 19).

The journey she proposes is strongly internalized and imaginary, the metaphors human-centred, subjective, ambiguous but transforming. Using her work *People underground* as an example:[14]

> The sounds of people walking in foot-tunnels, and interacting spontaneously with these unusual surroundings, are used as the starting point for an imaginative, inner journey, one weighted towards emotional rather than intellectual perception. Although framed by a simple 'narrative' – a descent from above ground, a journey underground and re-arrival at the surface – this musical underground journey descends beyond reality, and beyond temporal narrative (Norman, 1996, p. 24).

For as the 'author' remarks in Marcel Proust's *Time Regained*:

> … for in order to get nearer to the sound of the bell and to hear it better it was into my own depths that I had to re-descend. And this could only be because its peal had always been there, inside me, and not this sound only but also, between that distant moment and the present one, unrolled in all its vast length, the whole of that past which I was not aware that I carried about within me (Proust, 1983, p. 1105).

---

14 Katharine Norman's work *Trying to translate* (piano and tape) (Norman, 2000b) is discussed again in Chapter 4.

Each individual carries a unique memory trace which will resonate in different ways to 'real world' sounds and music.[15]

Animals and Myths (François-Bernard Mâche)

François-Bernard Mâche (1992) has suggested the establishment of a new science of *zoomusicology*. Mâche takes an intensely universalist line, more rooted in biology and neuro-psychology than the cultural myth construction of Trevor Wishart:

> If we had at our disposal sufficient studies of the neuro-physiological links between biological rhythms and musical rhythms, I would probably have been able to draw up arguments which reinforce the conception I am defending, that of music as a cultural construct based on instinctive foundations, with myth functioning as a substitute for, or as a mental projection of instinct (Mâche, 1992, p. 95).

Nature (he argues) has always provided models for music. Firstly at a very primeval level, animal sound and song imitation has had a variety of practical and ritual functions, from hunting to more spiritual relationships. These have been sublimated in subsequent music history but have never gone away. Mâche draws detailed parallels between the forms and repetitions of birdsong (various species of warbler) and two of the 'Russian period' works of Stravinsky (*The Rite of Spring* and *Les Noces*) (pp. 116–24). Conscious or not these reflect universal *models*[16] for musical syntax. Finally he suggests the conscious re-application of such models in contemporary composition. Citing Messiaen and Xenakis in support, he describes applications in his own music. But unlike Messiaen who transcribes birdsong for traditional instruments and Xenakis whose models are not literally 'sounding' as their original sources, Mâche often uses animal-produced (and other natural) sound recordings as his source. For example, in *Korwar*[17] (harpsichord and electroacoustic sound) (1972) his fascination with the classical Greek elements covers sounds of the creatures of *earth* (boar, wild boar), *air* (bird calls, wings rustling) and *water* (whale, shrimp) as well as the 'element' rain itself (Mâche, 1990).

Nature in her Manner of Operation (John Cage)

> I have for many years accepted, and I still do, the doctrine about Art, occidental and oriental, set forth by Ananda K. Coomaraswamy in his book *The Transformation of Nature in Art*, that the function of Art is to imitate Nature in her manner of operation (Cage, 1968b, p. 31).

---

15 The poetic relationship between Proust's novel *A la recherche du temps perdu* (Proust, 1983) and Pierre Schaeffer's *A la recherche d'une musique concrète* (Schaeffer, 1952) is complex: both are narratives of discovery (sometimes painful). Yet Schaeffer brackets out Proust's key to unlocking his own creativity – the memory and its associations.

16 This use of the term 'model' is identical to that elaborated in Chapter 2.

17 This work is discussed further in Chapter 4. See also the analysis in Emmerson, 2001b.

But Cage's famous dictum can be misunderstood here: nature's 'manner of operation' does not imply that the results need somehow to be perceived as 'real world sounds'. However, such sounds, although a relatively small subset of the sonic universe for Cage, did have a central importance in his work. Well before his visit to Paris in 1949 Cage had been interested in sound enabled through technology. This had covered a wide range of sound types. *Imaginary Landscape No.1* (1939) uses phonograph test recordings (of sine waves) while *Credo in US* (1942) demands a prerecorded phonograph record (chosen by the interpreter). The classification of sound Cage uses in *Williams Mix* (1952) shows an interesting emphasis on origin rather than sound typology and behaviour (Schaeffer's preference).[18] Environmental and studio recordings sit side-by-side in many of these categories and there is also a lack of any real distinction between 'nature' and 'culture' sounds. What becomes clear in listening to the work is that Cage's philosophy of sound removes (or at least undermines and minimizes) any such distinctions. This will re-enter our discussion of 'reanimating the world' in Chapter 2. The sound categories are there for production not perception.[19] Cage had little to say on any referential functions for environmental sound and, although he never wanted to dictate what could or could not be included in performances of his indeterminate works, he 'had little use for' any music which was based on the performer's memory (whether classical, jazz or popular references). This could not, by definition, lack intention.

> [RT] *The basic message of* Silence *seems to be that everything is permitted.*
> [JC] Everything is permitted if zero is taken as the basis. That's the part that isn't often understood. If you're nonintentional, then everything is permitted. If you're intentional, for instance if you want to murder someone, then it's not permitted. The same thing can be true musically … I don't like being pushed while I'm listening. I like music that lets me do my own listening (Rob Tannenbaum talking to John Cage in 1985, in Kostelanetz, 1989, pp. 208–9).

In the final analysis he did not rule out the listener's right to interpret how they pleased.

> It's not that I intend to express one particular thing, but to make something that can be used by the person who finds it expressive. But that expression grows up, so to speak, in the observer (John Cage in conversation with Birger Ollrogge (1985), in Kostelanetz, 1989, p. 215).

However it would be wrong to assert that Cage does not acknowledge 'action and agency'; it is just that these need exhibit *no expressive intention* and need not even be apprehended or understood. In this sense Cage mirrors and extends the 'bracketing out' of Schaeffer's *écoute réduite* – only here (for Cage) all *objets sonores* become

18 Cage's six first stage categories were: city sounds, country sounds, electronic sounds, manually produced sounds (including the literature of music), wind-produced sounds (including songs) and small sounds requiring amplification to be heard with the others.

19 Strict rules of categorization and combination (for example using the *I Ching*) are designed to encourage the suspension of judgements based on personal taste.

potential *objets musicaux*.[20] In indeterminate scores such as *Fontana Mix* and most of the *Variations* series Cage sets up situations where agencies are indeed established for the *possibility* of action but neither agency nor action is completely predictable:

> Reserve as many triangles as there are loud-speakers available, as many half circles as there are sound sources available, as many bisected short lines as there are components (exclusive of mixers, triggering devices, antennas etc., inclusive of amplifiers, pre-amplifiers, modulators and filters) available, as many of the straight lines as exceed by one the number of sound systems practical to envisage under the circumstances … Let the notations refer to what is to be done, not to what is heard or to be heard (Cage *Variations VI* score instructions).[21]

The listener is free to 'search for origins' or not, although Cage himself declared:

> Hearing sounds which are just sounds immediately sets the theorizing mind to theorizing, and the emotions of human beings are continuously aroused by encounters with nature. Does not a mountain unintentionally evoke in us a sense of wonder? … And sounds, when allowed to be themselves, do not require that those who hear them do so unfeelingly (Cage, 1968a, p. 10).

Thus, for Cage, sound can invoke feelings (and 'theorizing') but through no intention of possible human producers or enablers.

Aural and Mimetic Interpenetration

In 1986 I described this essential tension in terms of a simple axis of materials from 'aural discourse' (abstract and not obviously source-referential) to 'mimetic discourse' (imitative of, and referential to some aspect of the world not 'normally' found in music) (Emmerson, 1986b). In subsequent discussions this has become elaborated. Music does not just refer mimetically to the world through such simple means as re-presenting recognizable sounds. More complex dimensions of metaphor and reference have been identified. Denis Smalley's idea of *indicative fields* (Smalley, 1992a) suggests that even within an 'abstract' discourse where no sounds are directly *identifiable* as the result of real world sound events, there may remain direct reference to the behaviour characteristics of such events.[22]

We have two strands of thought evolving here – *both* with a degree of reference to the greater sound environment. One captures and works with material which possesses recognizable source/cause reference, the other creates and develops non-referential[23] sound in ways that relate more or less directly to real world *behaviour*

20 As, for Cage, there is to be no judgement of their suitability.

21 Original entirely in capitals. *Variations VI* (1966) is subtitled 'for a plurality of sound-systems (any sources, components and loud-speakers)'.

22 Indeed (he suggests) these should be present to maintain a communicable discourse.

23 More exactly 'not necessarily referential' sources. The opening of Jonty Harrison's *Klang* and *Et ainsi de suite* (Harrison, 1996, 2000) both present sound objects which are recognizably struck or bounced real objects (for example, casserole, ping-pong ball) but 'real

characteristics (as described in Smalley, 1992a).[24] The closeness of this relationship possibly explains the strong presence of works composed in recent years (in the post-Schaefferian tradition) which mix these two worlds (aural and mimetic). Superficially we might expect a stark contrast (even incompatibility), yet the two worlds not only sit happily side by side but can strongly reinforce. In Jonty Harrison's *Unsound Objects* and *Hot Air* (Harrison, 1996), the sudden intervention of a firework display, seaside waves and other clearly real-world scenes is not suddenly interpreted as 'narrative'. The scenes seem to function almost 'outside of time' giving us images from the vast to the close and intimate which adds depth and resonance to the indicative fields of the rest of the work's more abstract sounds:

> Where this initial material is drawn from recognizable sounds, the sounds of our everyday experience, then the purely musical, spectromorphological relationships between sounds are complemented by a wider frame of reference: alongside Schaeffer's *écoute réduite* we can perhaps also experience 'expanded listening' (Harrison, 1996, p. 16).

This interpenetration and mutual support of real and imaginary – or perhaps that should be outer and inner reality – is a characteristic found more or less across a range of composers to have studied with Jonty Harrison.[25] In Andrew Lewis's *Four Anglesey Beaches* (1999–2004),[26] the 'real pictures' stand both as morphological archetypes – sea, air, beach pebble (single and mass attacks), bird – and as resonant memories of atmospheres and places. In Adrian Moore's *Study in Ink* and *Foil-Counterfoil* (Moore, 2000) you can sense the fricative materials in an extraordinarily tactile way. As we shall discuss later in this chapter the perception system does not construct an image and *then* interpret it. We can *feel* the sounds directly.

But this is not at all confined to a single stream or tradition. We see a wider network emerging, for whom this aural-mimetic interpenetration is a major force, for example, many composers from the French Canadian tradition (centred on Françis Dhomont)[27] as well as from Sweden (such as Åke Parmerud). Even Denis Smalley's *Empty Vessels* (1997) (Smalley, 2000) is unique in his output in the degree to which a clearly environmental recording forms the core of the material and the leading driver of the work's evolution. The atmosphere, birds, slow decent of aircraft, rain and bees are all filtered (mechanically) in the 'empty vessel' of a large ceramic pot, suggesting their further (electronic) development. Extraordinary, too, is the way that – although beautifully layered and spatialized – the original is never far from the surface. Natasha Barrett's work starts with this same aural/mimetic dichotomy (Barrett, 2002).[28] But the integration of the two worlds has become a fantastic balancing act. Sometimes

---

world' associations are immediately minimized through transformation and extension 'away from' this reference.

24 A different approach to this same division is taken in Chapter 2 in discussing models and metaphors.

25 And worked with the BEAST diffusion system (see Chapter 6).

26 Unpublished; available from http://www.AndrewLewis.org (consulted May 2006).

27 Such as Christian Calon, Robert Normandeau, Giles Gobeil and Yves Daoust.

28 Natasha Barrett's *Isostasie* (2002) is a remarkably integrated group of works dating from 1999–2001. The following remarks apply to a consistent extent to all the individual

a kaleidoscopic helter-skelter mix of fast changing recognizable/not-recognizable sounds, at other times the perfect placing of isolated sounds in environments both 'real' and imaginary – integrated by perfect balance. In Barrett's work, the expressive aspect of the recognizable sounds (their triggering of memory and association) seems to cross over into the more processed and abstract soundworld, assisted by an extraordinarily detailed use of spatial placement and movement.

Thus these streams are not at all dialectical, contradictory or incompatible. In *listening* the differences may be transcended and even reversed. I may hear the perfectly recorded soundscape as an abstract pattern of extraordinary sound shapes. Soundscapes often contain 'local knowledge': I do not know *a priori* the sounds of sheep shearing in the Hebrides, nor the difference between morning and evening cicada sounds in the Mediterranean.[29] It may be that urban sounds are more uniform throughout the world, possibly thereby more reassuring. What we respond to in the sound will be a near instantaneous negotiation with our experience and current situation (I will discuss this further below). I may simply not recognize many of the sounds in an otherwise well-known environment. Furthermore in the more 'aesthetic' listening environment of my front room or personal stereo, I may, after all I have argued, *choose* to 'bracket out' any source–cause information.

On the other hand I may hear the complexities of a noise artist, electronica group or experimental solo DJ as an 'urban jungle' of systemic noise streams. Here there is a mirror image 'bracketing in' of the real-world noise-scape. Probably encouraged by the acousmatic condition, this approach to sound perception is often written off by sophisticated listeners as 'naïve' listening – 'that sounds like something from the real world'. But a more developed form of this can emerge in complex musics. 'Bracketing in' pushes sounds which are not (when considered dispassionately) of real-world origin into the arena of 'environment': encouraging and provoking the construction of apparent origins, sources and causes. These need not be explicit or programmatic. I do not mean these sounds become, somehow, *good imitations* of real-world sound events. We have suggested elsewhere that in the acousmatic condition, if a sound *appears to be* from a particular recognizable source, *then it is* (for our artistic purposes). But no, here I refer to sounds whose *behaviour* (often in intense and dense conditions) suggests that real-world origin so strongly that disbelief is once again forced into suspension. We shall return to this more fully in Chapter 2.

The Ear/Brain Responds

Luke Windsor has adapted the ideas of James Gibson to music perception in adopting an 'ecological' approach. Gibson has challenged what we might call the 'classical

---

pieces: *Three Fictions*, *Displaced: Replaced*, *Red Snow*, *Viva la Selva!*, *The Utility of Space* and *Industrial Revelations*.

29 Gregg Wagtaff et al. TESE project recordings of Lewis and Harris communities (TESE, 2002); Apostolos Loufopoulos has pointed out that an experienced listener from the region can estimate time of day and season from cicada recordings [personal communication].

sequence' of perceptual analysis: first the data gathering, then its representation and finally its interpretation:

> According to Gibson (1966; 1979), perception does not require the mediation of mental representations of the external world … Rather than assuming that the sensations passed from the sense organs to the central nervous system represent a chaotic source of information that mental processes organize and store in the form of meaningful percepts and memories, the ecological approach assumes that the environment is highly structured and that organisms are directly 'sensitive' to such structure … However, he [Gibson] is keen to distinguish between perception itself and the symbolic systems that facilitate the mediation, storage and communication of perceptions … (Windsor, 2000, pp. 10–11).

Taking this one stage further traditional music (and sound) analysis has to abandon the traditional sequence also. The direct perception and effect of the sound is *followed by* the conceptualization and symbolic representation needed for communication, further investigation or analysis:

> Moreover, the dynamic relationship between a perceiving, acting organism and its environment is seen to provide the grounds for the direct perception of meaning. Gibson's term for this kind of meaning is 'affordance' (Windsor, 2000, p. 11).

Luke Windsor's application of these ideas to sound interpretation places a holistic umbrella over the process we wish to examine. This emphasizes the interpretative function first and foremost – what does the sound or the object that produced it *afford* the listener? This suggests that how we perceive many of the sounds around us is a real negotiation of our needs as organisms and what we believe to be the agency producing the sound.

In stone-age societies no one had heard the sound of a metal tool, sheet or anvil. There could be no template for such objects against which sound data might be matched. Confronted with a struck metal sound for the first time it might appear to possess 'magical' qualities. These would only slowly be integrated through a complex learning process involving visual, tactile and sonic perceptions to construct the fuzzy entity 'metal object' or even, when sounding, 'metallophone'.[30] But here our ecological re-think is fundamental. We do not hear a sound, construct the image of 'a metallic sound' and *then* 'respond to it'. We need make no 'mental' representation of the quality but have an immediate response. The crude identification of sources is not usually the issue – acousmatic music plays with a pre-identificatory element, maybe even pre-linguistic. The irritation of many listeners with an intellectualization of music hinges on this crucial point – we shift from the feelings associated with these sounds to a description of them, inevitably if we are to discuss them at all. Many people find scraped metallic sounds frightening (or at least irritating) and it is this response that is felt immediately and only in later consideration (and optionally)

---

30 In post-iron-age societies we have been surrounded by metallophone sounds from anvils, through sword play, to factory metal formers, scaffolding, jangling keys and cutlery. The sound of a Javanese gong heard for the first time in the west, will thus be relatively easily cross-referenced. But we may only very recently have developed a sense of (literally) 'plastic' sounds which in 1900 would not have been recognized.

might an explanation be sought. This conceptualization is rarely made consciously in the 'run time' of the experience unless the listener disengages from the continuing soundstream. Most listeners respond first, describe and analyse later.[31]

But we do analyse later; such analysis is at the basis of communication, learning and experience. Not knowing the cause of a frightening sound is (in the first instance) a severe disadvantage if we feel it poses a threat, though one substantially reduced in the 'cultural' confines of a concert hall or in private listening. In the penultimate scene of *The Wizard of Oz*, Toto the dog pulls back the (acousmatic) curtain to reveal the wizard talking into a microphone which had been used to amplify and project his voice to fill the gigantic space of his castle.[32] His magic, being revealed and explained, collapses. Of course, in acousmatic concerts we are asked to suspend *this* cynical disbelief and to allow our imagination to reinstate the magic. With that proviso in mind we can look again at what kind of information forms the basis of that response, and what aspects of the soundstream suggest that information.

Physical Presence: Action and Agency

Undoing Schaeffer's Bracketing Out: Clues to a Reconstruction of the World

The acoustic events of the world we live in are absolutely determined by the forms, shapes, materials and energy fields of its component parts. In the ecological view our perceptive capacities have evolved to identify affordances relevant to our particular needs, clearly related to our circumstances (in the broadest sense). Let us review basic acoustic theory with this in mind.[33]

In the mechanical universe sound results from two (or more) objects[34] that touch in some way. Energy is transferred and – assuming a medium (usually air) surrounding the objects – the resulting motion sets soundwaves in train to any listener. This process of excitation may be one off or repeated (sometimes appearing continuous). This energy transfer results in the *onset* (initiation) and possible *continuation* of the sound. These two terms are worth distinguishing but of course are part of one continuous process. The object-systems in this relationship interact to a greater or lesser extent. The percussion player feels the resistance and compliance of the drum skin for single or repeated strikes. If the interaction continues the two systems tend

31 I accept that for the trained listener, possibly a composer at a concert or a tracker in the outback, it might be possible to think consciously through some of the contemplative questions about the soundstream while it is happening, but I suggest this is a rare and specialist skill.

32 Interestingly an image of his face is also projected, suspended in space and similarly enlarged, but clearly as 'dislocated' from any real body as the voice.

33 Such theory remains anchored in Aristotelian logic: what causes sound? What materials ('material cause')? What shape or form ('formal cause')? What agency ('efficient cause')? But the fourth ('final') cause ('why?') will be left to the following section and is not traditionally part of acoustics.

34 'Objects' interpreted in the broadest sense to include fluids and solids, perhaps not always clearly bounded – this can include the air itself – for example, the 'bull roarer' which creates turbulence in the free air as it is swung around.

to coordinate; this is known as 'coupling'. Woodwind and brass players adjust their reed or lip vibration to match the resonance vibration of the air tube of the instrument. The string player learns to bow at the correct pressure and bow velocity for the slip/grip of the frictional bow to coordinate perfectly with the string vibration.[35] Such coupling usually takes some amount of time to establish over the period of the onset. Indeed the player often 'attacks' the sound with a noise burst[36] designed to contain and initiate the necessary resonant frequencies – the process of coupling preserves these and progressively loses most of the remainder.

The possible continuation of the sound beyond this noisy onset depends on the nature of the body set in motion. All vibrations lose energy due to friction both inside the object and between objects. This results in 'damping' and the steady decay of the vibration. A wind column decays very quickly when energy input ceases (it is 'highly damped'). A stretched violin string decays more slowly; the bass notes of a piano or a low gamelan gong, decay very slowly (they are 'lightly damped').

So with a wind column we need a continuing energy input after the onset to sustain the sound at all; for a string instrument we may (bowed violin, rebab) but need not (piano, guitar, sitar). The difference between continuous and repeated excitation methods is one of degree. The paradidle of the drummer is obviously a repeated action. But in fact continuing friction excitation – bow on string (or metal), finger on wine glass rim or hand rubbed across membrane, is a series of repeated 'grip then slip' cycles between the two objects. And a player may appear to blow continuously into a wind instrument but the reed vibration or lip buzz repeats the 'open then close' cycle of a valve converting this power to pulsed air pressure bursts.[37]

The *decay* of the sound has two components. First reflecting how the vibrations of the object itself decay effectively to nothing when energy input is stopped (as described above). This decay tells us more about the nature of the sounding material itself and also, perhaps, the way it is supported – suspended from above or supported from below, stretched between relatively rigid boundary 'edges' which all to a greater or lesser extent externally damp the sound vibrations. However a second decay characteristic is that caused by reverberation which reveals clues as to the nature and disposition of surrounding surfaces, objects and their material. This is important enough to warrant a separate discussion (which is given below).

Literature on acoustics is, to a very large extent, based on traditional instrumental models and I have used such examples above. Too often texts have fallen into the trap of reducing acoustic descriptions to an idealized form, clearly derived from Platonic models.[38] Strings and tubes of air are reduced to models based on 'simple harmonic motion' from which they 'deviate' and have 'errors'. In this world view 'noise' is

---

35 A good parallel is pushing a swing in a children's playground; we must coordinate the regular input of an impulse of energy to the right part of the swing's cycle – mistime it and we would be removing energy. The two (swing action and energy input) are coupled.

36 The 't', 'd', 'k' tongue attacks of woodwind and brass; the initial 'extra bite' of the bow action. The pluck and strike have the same function.

37 Both 'slip/grip' and wind reed or lip vibrations are coupled to the resonance frequencies of the string or air volume to which they are attached (as above).

38 Helmholtz (1954 (original 1863)) sets the approach for most texts right up to contemporary times.

seen as such an 'error' in the real instrument; pitch is thus rationalized and idealized. In a more ecological model, however, noise is a fundamental source of information about the world and pitch can only indicate a single dimension (a length). So-called 'errors' and noise components have the potential to give us extensive additional information on other dimensions, materials and actions, and their relationships. We have need of an acoustics of all sound, unconstrained by (though not ignoring) that of the traditional musical instruments of the world.

The emergence of an acoustics of the environment will most likely come from the concerns of acoustic ecology and soundscape studies but will make its most important point of contact with the small subset of sounds produced by 'traditional' musical instruments through the study of percussion. The word 'percussion' is a convenient simplification: the acoustics of a garden water feature (let alone its environmental equivalent, the waterfall) is easy to describe but difficult to explain.[39] The traditional distinctions of instrumental families disappear in a richer mix of materials and excitation types (including water and stone).[40] The existing literature on the acoustics of percussion is a small doorway into this new world.[41] Immediately we see that the theory of 'simple harmonic motion' must be sidelined in favour of a more holistic and empirical approach – *this is what is*, let us try to describe it and, if we are lucky, begin to explain it. Idealized membranes, plates and bars are clearly inadequate and give way to the reality of tablas, gongs and zanzas. The acoustics of idiophones is little researched, yet the statistical impacts of dried seeds within a resonating enclosure (maracas, rainstick), the extraordinarily controllable characteristics of some African drums (used significantly in 'talking drum' exchanges) fill out the range of sounds to something more approaching the environmental soundworld itself. Models for all our instrumental families are to be found within a pre-industrial sound environment. The principle of woodwind instruments is present in the sounds of birds; brass instrument production less ubiquitous in the trumpeting of elephants (and other similar species), and stretched strings the likely product of certain plant growth (and certainly the regular production of traps, fishing lines and hunting bows of human creation).[42] Understanding the acoustics of the entire soundscape helps us come to grips with acousmatic listening in general; the fact that that soundscape now includes sounds of electronic origin will be a continuing part of our discussion.

Space: Reflections off and of the World

First we must be clear on the meanings of two words commonly confused in some literature and in everyday talk. We should make a clear distinction between the terms

39 David Toop gives an excellent phenomenological description of a Japanese water feature (*suinkinkutsu*) of which he heard only a recording (Toop, 2004, pp. 89–90).

40 Rock and water are still rarely used even in the 'extended percussion battery' of the twenty-first century but are commonly found in acousmatic music.

41 Backus (1977) and Campbell and Greated (1987) are two standard texts to have basic coverage of percussion instruments that suggest a more empirical approach.

42 Music bows resemble hunting bows closely and are found in nearly every part of the world.

'echo' and 'reverberation'. Both are products of sound *reflection*. If we stand 50m from a solid brick wall and clap our hands we will hear an echo about 300ms later. This sound is clearly a repeat of the original (although sometimes slightly changed in colour and always at lower sound level). Now the ear perceives these as *separate events* quite clearly only if they are separated in time by greater than about 50ms.[43] If a sound is repeated within a shorter time it is not clearly discriminated from the original.[44]

Imagine we are in a cave with many reflecting surfaces like the previous wall, but the shapes are completely irregular, some near to us some further away. There are a vast number of reflections and re-reflections of our hand clap arriving at our ears at random times[45] and with very short time between each one. No discrimination is made, no separate hand claps are heard – instead we hear a 'blur' we know as *reverberation* which seems to be a kind of frozen hand clap decaying to silence over some time.[46] This pattern of reflections carries the 'mark of the world' in which the sound is produced and is inseparable from it.[47] There are two phases here, too. In any space the earliest reflections to be heard are single reflections off the closest boundaries. Even in a large space these reflections are usually still too close together to be heard as echos, yet they are not yet so dense as the multiple reflections that form reverberation. While we are not normally consciously aware of it we decode this 'early field' to give us a sense of the size and shape of the space we are in – or at least the location of the nearest surfaces. Following the early field is the (random and denser) *reverberant field* proper (which we have already described). The quality of the reverberant field depends to a large extent on the nature of the materials off which the sound has been reflected. How much did they absorb and reflect (a rug compared to a glazed tile)? Did they scatter (diffuse) the sound or focus it?[48] From

43 This figure is not exact for all sounds; it varies with the nature of the sound, most directly with its frequency.

44 So if we walk to within about 10m or less of the same reflective wall the sense of an echo steadily disappears, the reflection 'gels in' with the original changing its colouration somewhat and possibly making it slightly louder.

45 Random in the sense there is no regular pattern – in fact any cave, however shaped, may now be modelled by computer and the reflection pattern predicted.

46 There is a transitional case in which the ear can get confused. This is wonderfully illustrated in some pedestrian underpasses which have been lined with reflective tiles. Here the sound of a shoe impact is reflected to and fro between the two parallel walls. These are often at such a distance that the reflection times fall around the critical discrimination time of about 50ms; a kind of ambiguous 'echo-reverb' is perceived. As it is often regular rather than random it can, at times, also appear to be pitched.

47 Even its absence tells us about the limited number of environments we might be in. Indeed humans find the lack of such cues disturbing – we hate being in a scientist's anechoic (reflection free) chamber; close your eyes and you feel you are completely isolated from the world – it is literally 'disorienting'.

48 The dome of the Albert Hall in London is an example of this. Over 150 years it has been the object of at least three major refurbishments aiming to diffuse the sound more randomly.

forest to bathroom we get a sense of where we are from the nature of 'early field' then reverberation.

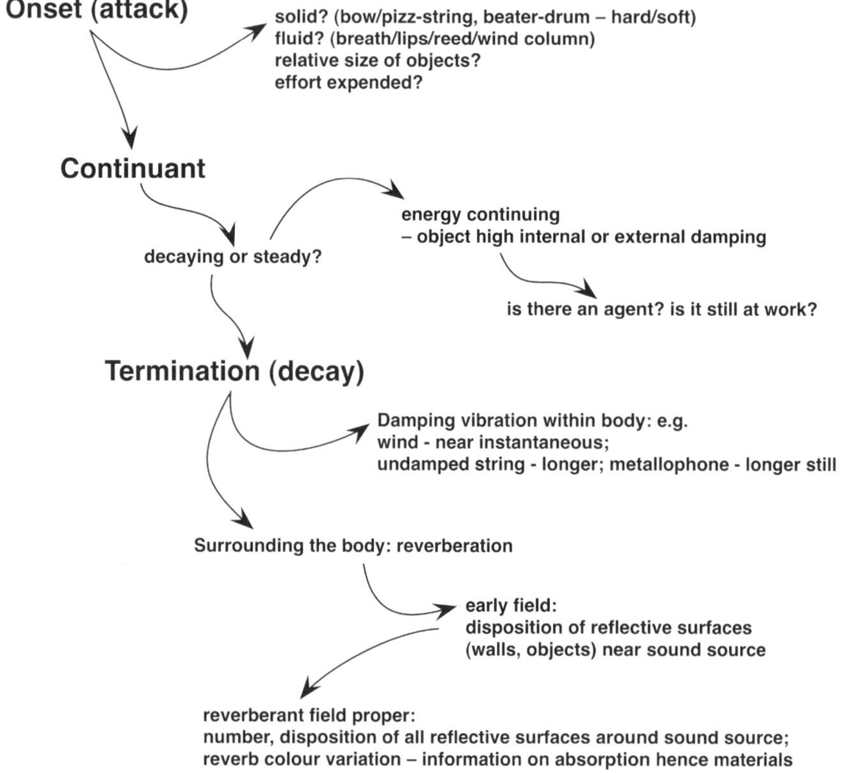

Figure 1.2: Acoustical information gathering

Space: The Direction of the Sound

The perception of sound direction has two sets of clues that overlap. The ability to create an 'auditory scene' relies, to a large extent, on the ability to discriminate sound by source location.[49] Secondly the radiation patterns of different sound sources tells us about their shape, form and how they are sounded. In traditional instruments, strings and woodwind are notoriously erratic in their sound radiation patterns across their range (Meyer, 1978). But we can tell if a mouth is facing us or facing away with great accuracy. This may make a great difference to our interpretation of attitude to us (or others). We can also sometimes detect the presence of other objects by *what they remove* from a scene. An additional body presence adds absorption and reflection, and under certain conditions we can detect where in the space and what size the

49 Discussion on 'looking at a space' and 'being immersed in a space' reappears in Chapter 6 (Loudspeakers).

'new object' is even when it emits no sound of its own making. It always reflects and absorbs and thus reconfigures the space itself to the senses of others.[50] Cues for distance combine an estimate of effort (greater effort usually produces a brighter spectrum) and loudness, combined with reverberation. We compare a trumpet playing quietly near us with one playing loudly some distance away. While both may have the same overall amplitude at our ear drum, we will understand the further trumpet as louder due to its spectrum (telling us greater effort is being expended) and there is also (usually) a higher proportion of reverberant to direct sound.

We will have to revisit this model for some aspects of the post-mechanical (electronic) universe we now inhabit. But in doing so we might bear in mind that Tim Ingold (2000) has challenged the accepted division of 'evolution' from 'history'. In this classical view the 'Darwinian ear' we have outlined above is part of evolution. Its more recent extension to matters of perception of electronically produced sound would then be seen as history (related to 'culture'). Ingold insists this is a product of a 'nature–culture' divide which is unsustainable and will forever leave us with an incomplete picture of the perception process. He argues that humans have always been in continuous evolution as organisms, developing skills within their changing environment. In this chapter we will move on from discussing clues to how we perceive the presence of *actions* and *agents* (and their environment) to clues as to how those agents might behave.

Psychological Presence: Will, Choice and Intention

Anticipating Moves: Games, Narratives, Performance

But identifying the sources and causes of sound may only be a small part of any response to sound. To survive we do not merely respond to the sound of (say) 'animal movement' and judge what it affords us. This depends on our immediate needs, it may be a threat to us or a source of food. But more subtly we may wish to *predict the next move*. We enter the world of *will*, *choice* and *intention*. We have every right and ability to describe our own thoughts and motivations but must gather every clue when we wish to know the will, choices and intentions of others. In the company of other creatures, body language gives us much additional visual information, but deprived of this and working with sound alone we will have even less to rely on and more work to do.

In different ways will, choice and intention are important constituents of two of music's key grand metaphors: *game* and *narrative*. In a game we might try to work out the intentions and choices of our opponents, and our choices in response; in a narrative we might try to establish the actors' identities (and even identify with them) and then follow their choices and decisions in weaving a 'lifeline' through the forking paths of the plot. But to these living dilemmas there is a mirror image set: *no choice, no will* and *no intention*. At first this description seems best to fit blind

50 It is also true that no human can be totally silent and we may be able to detect such sounds preferentially, perhaps not consciously knowing.

automata which indeed play an increasing part in the metaphoric arsenal of music. But it also fits Cage's 'imitation of nature in her manner of operation'.[51] So broadly this negative set will reveal just as wide a range of possibilities – from patterned to random. Organic, biological, physical and social systems metaphors play an important role in the new soundscapes of music. This need not be a dialectical pair (choice *versus* automata) but one in which the play of forces in the musical current moves between the two.[52] Such interactions are a powerful generator of musical ideas – as in any grand narrative: how do the actors in a Greek tragedy confront their 'inevitable' fate? In Chapter 2 we shall return to a radical reinterpretation of the 'non-human' (or at least non-sentient) side of this metaphor which attempts to deny the very separation ('choice/no-choice') I have suggested. Perhaps there is an attempt under way to heal a fundamental divide between 'nature' and 'culture' – I have termed this 'reanimation'. Aristotle's *final cause* forces its way back in to our attention: *why* has some person or other agent made the sounds the way they are? And (eventually) 'made the music the way it is'?[53]

In that musical structure and organization may be peculiar to a particular cultural group, the 'codes' of the music, the salient features held (more or less fuzzily) in common need to be learnt. Members of the community will learn these features sooner rather than later. As a visitor I may have difficulty sorting out what features are significant. The ethnomusicologists know this dilemma as concerning features which are *etic* (detectable and consistent) and those that are *emic* (significant in their own terms to members of the community encountered).[54]

Thus matters of will, choice and intention become indicators of an agent I am attending to, a discourse I am observing, perhaps even participating in and influencing. It is not therefore only the 'why' of the music I am attempting to unravel but clues as to what kind of feelings and expressions 'another agent' in the discourse embodies.[55] But in such encounters – especially in music – misunderstandings can lead to creative outcomes. It must not be assumed that knowledge is a *necessary* prerequisite for a meaningful experience of new music.[56]

In the ecological terms we introduced in the previous section, constructing another agent's possible strategies is intended to increase our possible choices and understanding of the situation (and hence our affordances). It is in effect an attempt to predict possible future events from ones already perceived. This is a skill exercised in both the playing of a game and following the structure of a narrative that might

51 At least at a human level; theists will have a different view at a higher level.

52 The distinction itself is open to question: I will leave it to philosophers to debate whether a computer algorithm may be said to display *will* or *intentionality*. This is, of course, a subset of the debate on machine intelligence.

53 It must be stressed that we do need to know the answer to this question to appreciate the music.

54 From the words 'phonetic' and 'phonemic' respectively.

55 We might see this as a difference between 'second person' discourse – I am addressing you and am being addressed by you – and 'third person' where I am only observing the discourse of others.

56 So-called 'intercultural music' through the ages has often been in part the product of emic/etic confusion and misunderstanding.

elsewhere increase our chances of survival. Children (and lion cubs) play games to learn and refine skills – and with a skill there is no boundary between physical and mental components. The games that acousmatic music plays re-engage some of the same faculties. The English word 'play' contains an ambiguity which illustrates precisely this dynamic relationship.[57] We play a game as well as an instrument or a recording. In this sense acousmatic music becomes more than a 'mere' play of shapes but less than a 'real' fight for survival, although developed listening is clearly a skill transferable to many other activities.

'Life as art' can appear to be an exclusively optimistic label. Cage, after all, thought of his approach as opening us up to 'divine influences' (and he nearly always refers in positive terms to the 'life we live'). He was known to all who met or saw him as a mild mannered, peace-loving and gentle person. But this could move very decisively to its opposite in many manifestations of the 'anti-art' movements of the twentieth century, from Futurist and Dada performances, to punk and shock performance art of the 1970s onwards. Descriptions of truly life-threatening events in aesthetic terms hover in this chasm. There is the direct evocation of the 1912 siege of Adrianopolis in Marinetti's novel (*parole in libertà*) *Zang Tumb Tuum* (Kirby and Kirby, 1986); Xenakis's description of allied wartime aerial bombardment as a strong influence on his multimedia idea of *polytope*, and Stockhausen's descriptions of similar activity over Cologne in the final stages of World War II as an influence on his sound world and theatre (Matossian, 1986, pp. 211–13).

The Analogue Studio as 'Performance'

Pierre Schaeffer has amusingly described his experiences operating the turntables in the pre-tape *musique concrète* studios of the late 1940s. He repeatedly refers to his desire for new instruments and the means to play them. At first describing a *piano à bruits*, he quickly envisages a better parallel in that of the organ. He thus imagines the first (disc-based) sampler:

> 23 April [1948] … Let there be an organ of which the stops each correspond to a disc player of which one would furnish the fitted turntable at will; let us suppose that the keyboard of this organ sets the pickups into action simultaneously or successively, instantly and for the duration that one wants … one obtains, *theoretically*, an enormous instrument capable not only of replacing all existing instruments, but of every conceivable instrument, musical or not, of which the notes do or do not correspond to the pitches given in the range (Schaeffer, 1952, pp. 15–16).

In this view the studio is a huge instrument ('l'instrument de musique *le plus général qui soit*' (p. 15)).[58] In effect one rehearses *actions* which produce the right *perceptions*. The finished work instantiates an idealized *performance* – only one which did not happen at one particular time. This would become a banal fact in both

57 The French words *jouer* and *jeu*, the German *spielen* and *Spiel* have the same connotations.

58 On June 4 he proceeds to predict computer applications, suggesting an 'enormous machine of a cybernetic type capable of millions of combinations' (p. 26).

the tape-based recording and *musique concrète* studios of a year or two later but that Schaeffer created it in a turntable-based studio remains a visionary moment.

In this early *musique concrète* studio Schaeffer had up to four turntables. These were replaced by tape machines from 1950 which changed the detail but not the principle of the physical relationship of operator and machine. A greater sea change occurred when the move to digital recording and storage reduced operational physical movement within the studio. It did not eliminate it, however. In an analogue studio the operation of tape machines and mixing desk faders required physical movement over a footprint up to the size of the studio itself. This has increasingly been reduced to a footprint the size of a qwerty keyboard and mouse mat, possibly retaining fader and other accessory input controls. Hence any residual idea of 'physical' performance is severely constrained.[59] The same is true when transposed to the concert platform. The body may 'jive' to the music with hands firmly anchored to (or at least hovering above) the *qwerty* keyboard and local accessories.[60] Thus our laptop artist who played solitaire to fool the audience during a 'live' performance was not truthful, yet this did not necessarily deprive the audience of a genuine pleasure in perceiving choices taken, pathways avoided, intentions fulfilled or unfulfilled which were already in the (pre-recorded) sound.

The distinction between studio composition and 'live' performance has developed a distinctly fuzzy feel. The best laptop performers – as all improvisers – claim a psychological buzz from public decision taking, including the possibility that they might (in their own estimation) 'get it wrong'. Improvisers have often talked of the *recovery* from moments of insecurity as key to good interaction. At another level DJs must always 'take from' the psychology of the audience, the 'feel' of the atmosphere to vary pace and tempo within the agenda of a controlled manipulation of the energy curve at the gig.[61] The participants might then judge that there are indeed intentional decisions being taken (on the basis of *choices*) and ascribe this to an agent.[62] The studio has thus moved out on stage.

In the traditional studio a composer's choice might take hours of listening to alternatives, finely tuned variants, including pathways well trodden, yet might still result in a work which is lively, surprising, fresh and unexpected to the listener. We must suspend our belief in the work's completeness until listening is over and although we may know it is fixed (and may have heard it before), the ritual of the performance still allows us to experience the 'game' of the narrative as it unfolds (as

59 My unscientific observations of (student) composers at work suggests they move 'to the music' much as a DJ does (significantly) – but their body movements no longer pertain to activating sound producing machinery. They have an empathetic resonance with sound much like dance.

60 Less physical but nearly as constraining to body movement is having the eyes glued to the screen.

61 Which has always had a sinister feel to those not in the scene.

62 Hillegonda Rietveld's book *This is Our House House – House Music, Cultural Spaces and Technologies* (Rietveld, 1998) starts with a story of her recovering from a 'mistake' in performance. The role of the DJ as entrepreneur and innovator permeates this text, but still needs its own definitive study.

in a movie).[63] The philosopher might tell us that there is no *logical* reason that all such compositional decisions could not have been made immediately, in real-time – essentially 'on stage'. But our belief as to how the work was created may, but need not, influence our appreciation of it – I say 'belief' rather than 'knowledge' because we may have erroneous information (as with our solitaire-playing laptop performer). It is perfectly possible to listen to a Beethoven sonata as if it were improvised[64] or to an Evan Parker improvisation as if it were strictly notated.

It may be difficult to describe any 'typical' studio working method but let us risk a generalization[65] to suggest that the cycle of *process-compare-combine* exists from small to large scale, usually a haphazard helter-skelter from one to the other. The laptop performer has chosen to move *some* of this activity to the live stage performance. The 'classic mix' approach makes *choices of combination* of largely 'pre-cooked' materials (some maybe not original); increasingly as real-time synthesis programmes become available an ever greater proportion of what used to be the studio's domain becomes available for 'live' working. There is, in principle, no limit to this development. The advent of 'live coding' – the 'on stage' creation and configuration of synthesis and processing modules – extends ideas of dexterity to a 'hand-eye-symbol-ear' cycle at all stages mediated by the technology (Collins et al., 2003).

Perhaps (rather like Jorge Luis Borges's fictional author Pierre Menard) we can imagine a world where a live laptop performer spontaneously recreates in real-time an 'acousmatic' classic.[66] The degree to which the composition choices made on stage *in practice* differ from those made in the less pressured atmosphere of the studio is one for future empirical investigation. This shift away from a 'studio practice in deferred time' to 'real-time on stage' composition relocates this genre closer to many non-western-art traditions. An important input is that of the 'atmosphere' of the performance space, as Evan Parker has remarked:

> My 'ideal music' is played by groups of musicians who choose one another's company and who improvise freely in relation to the precise emotional, acoustic, psychological and other less tangible atmospheric conditions in effect at the time the music is played (cited in Bailey, 1992, p. 81).

There is no logical or philosophical reason why an intelligent 'machine' could not have fulfilled this function and this cannot be ruled out. But Parker's ideal model

63 True for any recording of a piece, too. We suspend our belief that the recording is complete in 'reliving the moment' throughout the performance.

64 I deliberately avoid as an example the 'captured' improvisations of the fantasia tradition from Bach (and before) to Chopin (and after).

65 This remark is genre specific: it refers to a tradition which relies on a basically abstracted syntax (Emmerson, 1986b) – not one in which studio sessions are more slavish 'realizations' of *a priori* calculations.

66 That would actually be a combination of 'would typing monkeys eventually produce a work of Shakespeare?' with Borges's *Pierre Menard, Author of the Quixote* (in Borges, 1964). I already hear '1950s/60s electronic clichés' in recent real-time synthesis laptop performances.

stresses the interpersonal and interactive – issues we will return to. But first a short digression. How would we know if a person (taking intelligent decisions) had been replaced by a machine?

Are there Parallels to Turing's Criterion?

The British mathematician Alan Turing devised a simple behaviourist criterion for the evaluation of machine intelligence. If the responses of a machine were indistinguishable from those of an intelligent human then the former might be said to be displaying intelligence.[67] Only the observation of *responses* was pertinent to the question – it would not matter if the method of generating the responses was entirely different from that which humans use.

But this is an attempt to define criteria for assessing intelligent 'factual' behaviour ignoring questions of affective and emotional behaviour. Turing remains in a narrow 'problem solving' paradigm. Nonetheless there seem to be some parallels between Turing's 'judge' and our acousmatic listener. Unlike Turing's verbal 'question and answer' session as paradigm of behaviour (mediated via script such that 'tone of voice' is eliminated)[68] we have a more complex and ambiguous soundstream, but the questions are similar:

- What aspects of the sound flow have had conscious decisions taken about them?
- Has the sound been 'composed' (put together)?
- By what kind of agent?

But then there are the further questions of real-time. Even if I establish that the sound is constructed and organized by a given agent, there are two further overlapping questions:

- What aspects of the sound flow might lead me to believe that decisions and actions were being taken at the time of my hearing?
- If yes, is that agent actually present now?

These are exactly the types of questions arising from the transition we are discussing – from the 'live electronic music' (*prima prattica*) which extends the overtly human actions of the mechanical era ('humans playing instruments') to the radically different landscape of 'humans playing computers' and even 'computers playing computers' (a *seconda prattica*).

Does there have to be a thinking and feeling agent? If we cannot distinguish between a machine-generated and a human-generated soundstream then how do we respond? And does it matter? Below (in the next section) I will discuss Christopher

67 There is great subtlety in Turing's 'Imitation Game' which is simplified in this remark. See Turing (1950).

68 Recent explosions in the use of 'emoticons' in text messaging and email suggest it is omitted simply to be replaced by misunderstanding – we make our own interpretation of the tone of the sender's 'voice'.

Small's reframing of musical 'meaning' in terms of the relationships within the act of 'musicking'. It is quite possible we will feel very differently about machine-produced music *when we know this is the case*. When pulsars were first discovered there was a brief moment when astro-physicists in the discovery team (Jocelyn Bell and Anthony Hewish at Cambridge University) believed they had evidence of extra-terrestrial intelligence. The *periodic* nature of the pulsar radiation pattern was seen to be a possible constructed code rather than the product of a spinning neutron star.[69]

In Chapter 2 I intend to suggest another reading of the animate/inanimate division which this re-engagement with the entire sounding universe presents. But here I will conclude with a discussion on one final 'layer' of music making that our listening mind tries to find clues about. So far the 'agents' we have been referring to are relatively impersonal; they may be human – but will just any human do? What about the very real personality of the 'great performer' – the sense of presence? Since at least the classical era and the rise of the 'star' system,[70] Western music has thrived on the tension (even contradiction) between the work as transcendental, beyond individual interpretation, and the work as existing only in its moment of performance, through an interpreter whose personality is certainly not 'bracketed out'.

Personal and Social Presence: What you mean to me, Where I am and Who I am with

Relationships

Christopher Small places his attempts to decode musical 'meaning' firmly in the performative:

> I emphasize the importance of relationships because it is the relationships that it brings into existence in which the meaning of a musical performance lies. …
>
> 1. What are the relationships between those taking part and the physical setting?
> 2. What are the relationships among those taking part?
> 3. What are the relationships between the sounds that are being made? (Small, 1998, p. 193).[71]

This is not the place to examine all the many and various meanings of the word 'meaning'. The phrase 'what you mean to me' sums up the ambiguities neatly. On the one hand a kind of literal expression of the 'meaning of the utterance' (what *it* apparently conveys) yet on the other a notion imbued with the more personal,

69 Jocelyn Bell's own account is reprinted often, for example at: http://www.bigear.org/vol1no1/burnell.htm (consulted December 2005). See also the original report in Hewish et al. (1968).

70 Following the commercialization of music in the nineteenth century, these comments apply equally to 'classical' and vernacular/popular music developments.

71 For Christopher Small 'performance' as the fundamental act of 'musicking' can include any music producing activity (by implication this extends to playing back a CD).

at its most extreme: 'you are a wonderful performer, an idol whose every image and performance I and my friends hang upon'. Classical western musicology has ruthlessly separated the two and prioritized the former believing it to be somehow transcendental; more recent non-western and popular music study has understood more clearly that the given music (*a priori*),[72] performer, performance, audience, time and place cannot so easily be separated.

The fundamental questions asked in this chapter relate to how we might perceive these in the sounding flow. That is, what clues can we get to these more personal and social presences and where is the listener in these relationships? But there is something else suggested here. What I think of – how I relate to and value – *the entire* world of the music, its creation and performance, and the people within that, will be a fundamental part of its 'meaning' to me. Thus 'gleaning information from the sounding flow' must include the questions: where was the flow produced, who made it and where am I listening now? Who with? And how do I value these? All these factors will directly influence my response (the esthesis).

The answers to these questions have shifted radically in the acousmatic world. We might like to add one to the list: what are the relationships of those taking part to the sound production.[73] This was taken for granted in the mechanical world. Small discusses the relation of performer to instrument and audience to instrument in several traditions. He compares the pyramid of western art music with its concepts of 'virtuoso' down to 'amateur' (finally, creating an underclass who believe themselves 'unmusical' or even 'tone deaf'), with more open access musical societies in Africa and elsewhere (1998, pp. 211–2).

While at some levels creating much greater access to tools, technology has also had the effect of concentrating performance practice into small units, usually solo, occasionally duo, rarely more.[74] This follows from the concentration of sound producing power: a computer is not the equivalent of an instrument but of an orchestra (and an instantly flexible one at that). The composer becomes performer becomes conductor – as well as DJ and *shaman*. The concept of the laptop *ensemble* is rare.[75] Where it is attempted the concept of *instrument* (or at least ensemble *role*) is reinvented as a discipline and conscious restraint, rather than following inevitably from the physical situation. The orchestral ensemble (as a group of human agents) has evaporated. This may not be mourned by those who saw such an institution as a perfect reflection of (and metaphor for) a hierarchical and highly labour-differentiated society (typical of nineteenth century Europe). But apparently removed, too, is the possibility of larger communities of music making (along the more egalitarian lines of, say, a gamelan). One counter to this may come from the internet – the possibility

72 All performances have some *a priori* component: from the tradition behind the freest of improvisations to the over-notated western score.

73 Not to the sound produced (interpretation of the music) but to the methods and means of producing and projecting the sound in the space.

74 The intense beam of interest (and sometimes commercial interest) focuses more easily on individual performers. To what extent they have others join them in studio versions of tracks, or to prepare material for live shows is often not clear.

75 *Autechre*, *The Orb* (duos), the *Zapruda Trio*. I am referring to simultaneous performance in a physical space, not to the internet (or other network) performance (see below).

of an interacting set of 'equal' nodes contributing to the whole.[76] This will bring with it a new set of discussions on the consequences of the *dislocation* of simultaneous performance acts.

To make some sense of these changes let us use examples from the contrasting areas of classical acousmatic composition, the improvised experimental laptop tradition and examples of experimental 'electronica/IDM'. These are, I acknowledge, arbitrary labels. There are many more such genres, continually evolving and hybridizing. But they remain generalizations of some degree of identity and are not intended to be paradigmatic. There are exceptions to every one of them. The intention is to point out differences in the relationships that the music reflects and generates at the same time. For example the territory shared by these genres includes the *soundfile* – which is *one* trace of the work but not the sole one. It varies in meaning depending on its function and the relationships it engenders – which is not necessarily that intended by its maker.

Classical Acousmatic Composition

Most acousmatic works of the 'classical' tradition are usually 'closed' and 'formed' works. The vast majority are single composer creations. They are studio created yet only 'completed in performance' (that is they are not deemed to exist 'as art' stored on the shelf or hard disc unheard). The work claims to have a stable and continuing identity.

Performances are repeatable in core substance. Interpretation is limited to matters of forming and sculpting a pre-formed sound sequence 'into' a space (this is discussed in Chapter 6). The roles of composer and performer/interpreter may be separated. The role of the performer is the re-presentation of the composer's intentions; interpretation is limited within diffusion (as remarked). Venues for performance are designed (ideally) for full bandwidth and maximum dynamic range, with low noise floor. Seating is usually fixed, directional (often inherited concert halls); diffusion is often active and spatial.

Listeners are not an essential component of the performance; while required to complete the work their influence is small. Their listening is intended by the composer and performer to be total and exclusive. As it stands at the time of writing the idea of 'recording a performance' in this genre is musically meaningless as different interpretations are seen as venue specific. In the future the recreation of particular venues and variant interpretations of acousmatic works within them may become more meaningful.

Improvised/Experimental Laptop Performance

Most works from this genre are 'open' in content; there is a dynamic mix of elements: a work may consciously be 'formed' during a performance; or may retain a sense of 'flux' – that is the listener has heard a segment of an ongoing work without formal beginning or end. The material is created in a 'live performance' which may

---

76 See, for example, *Contemporary Music Review* 24(6) (2005) devoted to this theme.

include both real-time synthesis and studio-created elements. Performances are not repeatable in substance; there is no concept of interpretation. The work does not have a continuing and stable sonic identity though different versions of the 'same' piece may be performed. The roles of composer and performer may not be separated. The performance at a specific place and time 'becomes' the work. The role of any recording is ambiguous – most listeners treat it as strictly another object and not 'the original'. It may feed into future performances.

Venues for performance have variable form – they may be fixed or mobile: as 'hi-fi' as for acousmatic art music, but in other cases without large dynamic range, some have an 'active' social noise floor. Spatialized diffusion of sound is usually not considered as part of the presentation of the work. The listener is an important component of the performance, influencing pace and real-time choices of the performer/composer through a variety of feedback strategies. Their listening may be intended by the composer and performer to be total and exclusive but may also in practice be sampled and listener-constructed in form (depending on the venue and social environment).

'Electronica/IDM'

Most works from this group of genres are open in content but are from a range of materials with strong genre identity (elements of rhythmic underpinning for example). Such genres usually have a strong 'live performance' tradition even if, in fact, studio created materials, templates and set-ups confine the range of possibilities. Material (and whole 'works') may be used in subsequent performances, subsequent remixes by the same (or different) artists. The remix of a work is more than a reinterpretation, more a recomposition. Performances are not repeatable in substance; there is usually no concept of interpretation.[77] Performances contain a mix of recreation and new creation. The work may exist in an ongoing form as a CD track but then reappear in other guises in different subsequent mixes, remixes or versions. The roles of composer and performer may not be separated (unless remixed by a different composer). In venues for performance fixed seating is an exception, many have reduced dynamic range and high 'social' noise floor, diffusion is often omnidirectional and amniotic.

The listener is an essential component of the performance creating atmosphere and a group 'presence' which communicates strongly. However the degree to which this influences real-time choices of the performer/composer is complex and symbiotic. The two way exchange is often very strong. Their listening is likely to be sampled and listener-constructed in form (due to the venue and social environment) but may also be intensive and concentrated in personal listening spaces. The performance at a specific place and time 'becomes' a new work. The role of any live recording is ambiguous – it may be a 'document', a new work or a new source of material. In some senses some electronica albums are nearer the classical ethos with fixed studio-produced tracks – but which, unlike them, can have other functions, for example, remixed by the composer in future performance.

---

77 That is of an identifiable work – there may be recognition of substantial parts of issued recordings within the flux.

Genre/Subculture/Label

Thus genres and 'styles' cannot be defined independently of performance and listening practice – as it is in these practices that their existence *as works* comes into being. There is evidently a variety of functions for the recorded traces of the work. It will be a recurring argument in this book that the hybridization of musical types and genres may produce just as strong differentiation as has always been present in the musical universe. The evident reduction of barriers in the digital world does not always lead to a 'smearing' of function, aim and aesthetic. That the three areas used as examples above have a common technological basis for construction and dissemination, does not automatically mean that the relationships in the music-making all hybridize in a similar fashion. It may be that strongly differentiated musics *can* evolve from such similar technologies.

Performance, publication and dissemination are becoming ever closer in the digital environment. Nowhere is this clearer than in the changing role of the 'label'. One interesting thing about the term as used in contemporary English is its combination of two associated meanings. This started in its most general sense as some kind of attachment to an object, bearing its name, ownership, description or destination. The physical label attached to the centre of a phonograph disc giving manufacturer and music information took on the meaning of the production company itself and consequently its products. But this process can bounce into reverse and the term 'label' refer to a particular musical genre or even 'style'. Of course record labels have always supported a vast range of such styles – from wide multi-national to extremely specialist and local. Such specialist genre labels date back to the earliest days of classical, jazz and popular musics and the relationship of independent to major has ebbed and flowed (Chanan, 1995, especially Chapter 6).

Electroacoustic music was the first 'art music' to bypass the traditional publishing channels for whom recording was an important addition, bringing in income but not originally central to the enterprise. For this new music the recording was the major part of the 'artwork', standing free of paper representation. Labels such as the Canadian *Empreintes Digitales* declared their acousmatic products to be 'publications' (subsuming this older sense) and share royalties with their artists. Labels such as ECM and ReR emerged in the 1970s and 1980s, significantly covering genres of jazz and experimental music which also had little need of notated (and 'paper published') material. These were followed by the explosion in small independent labels and finally 'own labels' in the 1990s which became ever more sharply focussed on a small number of highly promoted artists. Thus labels such as Warp, Rephlex and Mego gave their artists a specific identity (genre) 'tag' – a 'Warp gig' would have a predictable 'flavour'. The label has increasingly become a subculture identifier. The difference with earlier decades is the integration of composition and performance, materials and objects, publication and dissemination. This is set to accelerate as the internet becomes increasingly the locus of performance in its own right and not merely a forum and marketplace for exchange.

Conclusion

It is not simply that the so-called 'natural world' or 'environment' has invaded the world of music. This separation is a misunderstanding that we shall return to in future chapters. There is an increasing mutual exchange as the synthetic and the human-made equally 'invades' what we once thought of as the natural. In trying to make sense of this rich sound environment we search for clues that help us to construct, not just dry objects and processes, but living decisions, choices, strategies and pathways. The acousmatic condition, in depriving us of what we have been told is the dominant sense perception of the late twentieth century media, has engaged and encouraged that most essential faculty, the imagination. But more importantly it has extended its domain in the arts of sound to areas previously believed (in the western tradition at least) to be 'outside' music. This will be examined further in Chapter 2.

CHAPTER TWO

The Reanimation of the World: Relocating the 'Live'

Introduction

> The second reason why I would be reluctant to restrict the taskscape to the realm of living things has to do with the very notion of animacy. I do not think we can regard this as a property that can be ascribed to objects in isolation, such that some (animate) have it and others (inanimate) do not. For life is not a principle that is separately installed inside individual organisms, and sets them in motion upon the stage of the inanimate. To the contrary … life is 'a name for *what is going on* in the generative field within which organic forms are located and "held in place"' … (Ingold, 2000, p. 200).

Tim Ingold has here boldly asserted a profound shift from object to relation in the way we describe 'what life is' (and by implication 'what live is'). The case needs evidence and we shall have to see if and how this shift helps us to untangle contemporary musical practice to try to make some sort of sense of it. I believe it may give us a possible clue as to how and why ideas of 'live electronic music' have shifted so radically in recent years. (The title of this chapter is an attempt to summarize this aim.) We also need some reexamination of history as it may also help to reposition certain developments which might now appear to be precursors of this shift.

At the core of this chapter is a discussion on the use of 'models and analogies' for the generation of musical material or structure. In this process apparently non-musical objects or systems generate data which is mapped (by analogy) on to some parameter of music. The explosion of interest in such procedures within the *avant-garde* of the 1950s was a conscious development but more recent applications suggest that these ideas have now been sublimated and absorbed into a vast range of sometimes explicit, sometimes less explicit performance and composition practices. We will examine the background and some classic works of that era. The final section attempts to fuse this with ideas of 'live presence' (discussed in Chapter 1). I will argue that much of contemporary practice reveals a process of 'reanimation' – a reengagement by musicians in the 'flux of the world's processes'.

Metaphorical Language: 'Science'

Twentieth century western art's engagement with the sciences and technology increasingly appropriated its language. In the 1920s and 1930s the new sciences of astronomy and atomic physics were moving headlong into popular imagery as well as into that of the arts. In a radio interview Varèse asked his listeners to:

> … visualize the changing projection of a geometrical figure on a plane, with both plane and figure moving in space, but each with its own arbitrary and varying speeds of translation and rotation … By allowing both the figure and the plane to have motions of their own, one is enabled to paint a highly complex and seemingly unpredictable picture with the projection (Varèse cited in Bernard, 1987, p. 7).

> Conceiving musical form as a *resultant* – the result of a process – I was struck by what seemed to me an analogy between the formation of my compositions and the phenomenon of crystallization … "… Crystal form is the consequence of the interaction of attractive and repulsive forces and the ordered packing of the atom". This I believe suggests, better than any explanation I could give, the way my works are formed … Possible musical forms are as limitless as the exterior forms of crystals (Varèse cited in Bernard, 1987, p. 17).

Cosmology had of course always had a strong relationship with ethics and philosophy (whether literally or metaphorically). In 1882 Friedrich Nietzsche wrote his famous 'description' of a universe which was losing its central authority. In 'The Gay Science' he talks of a madman (a kind of biblical prophet figure) who runs through the market place shouting:

> What were we doing when we unchained this earth from its sun? Whither is it moving now? Whither are we moving? Away from all suns? Are we not plunging continually? Backward, sideward, forward, in all directions? Is there still any up or down? Are we not straying as through an infinite nothing? Do we not feel the breath of empty space? ... God is dead. God remains dead. And we have killed him (Nietzsche, 1974, p. 181).

Schoenberg's transformation of this sentiment into musical terms in his essay 'Composition with Twelve Tones' was written nearly 60 years later in 1941, and seems not only to describe a serial universe, but to look beyond that to a much larger soundscape:[1]

> ... the unity of musical space demands an absolute and unitary perception. In this space ... there is no absolute down, no right or left, forward or backward. Every musical configuration, every movement of tones has to be comprehended primarily as a mutual relation of sounds, of oscillatory vibrations, appearing at different places and times. (Schoenberg, 1975, p. 223).

Pierre Boulez makes the metaphor even more explicit. He draws a parallel between the Newtonian and tonal music paradigms which had dominated the past and the revolutionary Einsteinian and serial music paradigms of the present and (he assumed) the future. Writing in the late 1950s Boulez declared:

---

1 As well as to the reality of manned space travel exactly twenty years later. Schoenberg might very well have identified directly with Nietzsche's 'madman/prophet' although he says he is referring to 'Swedenbourg's heaven (described in Balzac's *Seraphita*)'.

> Classic tonal thought is based on a universe defined by gravity and attraction; serial thought on a universe in continuous expansion (Boulez, 1991, p. 236).

What was an ethical and moral question for Nietzsche has become a matter of musical inevitability for Boulez – but his remark can also be interpreted as embracing a world well beyond the confines of serialism.

By the 1950s, especially within the orbit of German-inspired *elektronische Musik*, technical scientific language was understandably used for the synthesis of sounds but also appropriated and extended (with many misunderstandings and 'extremely loose' definitions) to broader musical concerns. Terms such as *parameter*, *formant*, *phase*, *spectrum*, and the like were applied to instrumental music (or at least to its theory and analysis). The apparent desire for a depersonalized, rational and objective discourse in much of the European *avant-garde* of the 1950s found its perfect expression through the language of science and technology.

The *Avant-garde* after 1945 and the Erasure of History: Automata and 'Extra-musical' Generative Procedures

With the discrediting of both the German romantic and French neo-classical traditions, the past literally lay in ruins. Perhaps personal expression itself had become associated with such a heritage. At least initially, impersonality was the order of the day. A claim to 'objectivity', a negation of history and hence part of the self, was the aim. The idea that 'systems other than the composer' might generate aspects of the music came to the foreground of *avant garde* ideas after 1945. We will examine examples of some of these ideas and their applications.

Degree Zero (Boulez and Cage)

At the time of their meeting in Paris in 1949 and the vigorous exchange of views and music, Pierre Boulez, Pierre Schaeffer and John Cage all claimed to establish this 'degree zero' for music in the West.[2] John Cage literally distanced himself from the idea of *any* tradition (central or local) whatever the group defining it:

> These two tendencies [the oriental and the occidental] met in America, producing a movement into the air, not bound to the past, traditions, or whatever. Once in Amsterdam, a Dutch musician said to me, "It must be very difficult for you in America to write music, for you are so far away from the centers of tradition". I had to say, "It must be very difficult for you in Europe to write music, for you are so close to the centers of tradition" (Cage, 1968a, p. 73).

There appears at first to be an important parallel with Boulez's claim made in respect of *Structures Ia*, written in 1952, his first (and only really strict) total serial work:

---

2 See Chapter 1 for a discussion of Pierre Schaeffer's position.

> For me it was an experiment in what one might call Cartesian doubt: to bring everything into question again, make a clean sweep of one's heritage and start all over again from scratch, to see how it might be possible to reconstitute a way of writing that begins with something which eliminates personal invention (Boulez, 1975, p. 56).

But the context of the Cartesian method of a reduction to a first principle (in Descartes' case *Cogito*) from which the next step and hence all else flows (*ergo sum*) places this in a tradition of renewal rather than outright rejection.[3] Each *reductio*, for both Cage and Boulez, showed its origins: the occidental reliance on the individual as the means out of the *impasse*, the oriental on a collective non-personal 'wisdom', most specifically the *I Ching*.[4] Cage stresses the similarity of their chart techniques but their divergence of motivation; writing at a time before their correspondence had been published (see Nattiez, 1993) he refers to material:

> … which would have shown agreement between us at the beginning, and then divergence exactly on this point of total control and renunciation of control. We were using the same techniques, which were charts. He had turned the series into a chart arrangement, and I had turned to charts first as magic squares and then later in relation to the mechanism of the *I Ching* for chance operations (Kostelanetz, 1970, pp. 17–18).

After such a momentary conjunction, each accelerated apart; Boulez increasingly to rediscover the personal *will* through the reinvention of technique, Cage to extend the *will-less* to indeterminacy of score and performance.[5]

These are two examples of 'tough' automata, relatively unrefined numerical systems (however generated). But there emerged a far wider range of non-personal, extra-musical ideas which progressively opened up the phenomena of the world (and beyond) to become inputs to the generation of musical materials. The extent to which these were *automatic* or *deterministic* varied; the composer's choices and influence on the result ranged over all possibilities.

Systems before Numerals

A full history of mimesis, metaphor and music is outside the scope of this book. Both mimetic and metaphorical relationships to things outside of the immediate music field have been with us for many centuries. Most obvious are such as the imitation of birdsong and sounds of war in the madrigals of Clement Jannequin, the symbolic representations in the music of Bach, or the programmatic stream in nineteenth century 'tone poems' (of, for example, Berlioz, Liszt and Strauss). Then there are

---

3 And for exactly the same purpose as Descartes himself who wrote of his profound rejection of earlier philosophies which he felt bound to attempt to renew.

4 This can be exaggerated: Cage did not discover his chance procedures, or the *I Ching*, by chance. There are many paradoxes within Cage's position which maintain an occidental view.

5 What distinguishes Pierre Schaeffer strongly is his rejection of both kinds of non-personal, 'systemic' choices. Neither Cage nor Boulez were to revisit the *musique concrète* studios after their initial visits and works (in 1949 and 1952 respectively).

also explicit references in the western music canon in well known works such as Beethoven's *Pastorale* symphony and Debussy's *La Mer*.

In the twentieth century a shift begins to a more literal reference to (even imitation of) such extra-musical phenomena. Italian Futurism suggests this rather than delivers it. The *intonarumori* make noise which resembles only limited aspects of the cityscapes celebrated in the Futurist manifestos. But in Russia the short-lived constructivist and Futurist movements produced music such as Arseni Avraamov's *Symphony of Factory Sirens*, performed in Baku in 1922 and Alexander Mosolov's *Iron Foundry*, an excerpt from his ballet *Steel* (1927) (Gordon, 1992; Avraamov, 1992). Such experiments consciously retained a concrete relationship of extra-musical to musical translation, in line with their political aims and objectives. Following 1945 in western Europe there was felt to be a need for a more coherent *method* to integrate these new forces more fully into the generation of musical materials (or structures).

Numerals were useful as they could so easily be translated into musical notation, but on their own they remained dry and abstract. Composers looked for more imaginative approaches. Even if not explicitly stated, the search was on for unifying and rational principles for the formation and structuring of 'art music'. Perhaps it could be found in the 'new sciences' of the atomic age and the space age. Both extremes of the scientific spectrum are beyond human timescale, appear eternal, to have no history.[6] Music made from such resources has in various ways claimed a sort of objectivity or at least a rationality. Interestingly both atomic and cosmic scales produce 'particular' (point) images which fitted immediately the 'pointillist' musical aesthetic which had emerged, post-Webern, from Darmstadt from the late 1940s. This was to be made explicit in an explosion of such developments in the *avant garde* of the 1950s. To examine this we need to make a substantial digression into the world of science and how one particular aspect of scientific method was appropriated wholesale by composers. We will examine the *theory of models*.

Models

In everyday speech we might explain something to someone by drawing parallels between two things, one they know, one they do not. The known is a 'model'. Scientists often use *models* to explain theories. Explanation involves the relating of unknown (or only partly known) configurations of knowledge into better known ones in a process which has no limit. In science, two theories are *isomorphic* if true statements in one theory may be derived from true statements in the other by a one-to-one substitution of terms. The behaviour of a simple pendulum and the output of an electrical dynamo may both be reduced to a single theory described in a simple equation (known as *simple harmonic motion*). When this is the case the pendulum is a *model* of the electrical signal and *vice versa*. Here the process or theorizing has been completed.

6 Notwithstanding the emergence of the *big bang* theory at this time (and the prediction of *Cosmic Background Radiation*).

Now, models have a useful role to play in research. When scientists investigate a previously unknown phenomenon, they may create a hypothetical model – that is a *known* system which they *assume* to be isomorphic with what they are investigating (the unknown). The model may suggest new research to be done to establish evidence for this correspondence. If no correspondence is found the model is useless and must be discarded. But if the correspondence is strengthened the theory of the model progressively becomes (with correct substitution of terms) the theory of the phenomenon being investigated. Models of economic activity, weather patterns, population growth, astronomy, atomic structure and a host of other phenomena have come and gone in the period since the rise of science with the Renaissance. All have functioned both to explain and to further research.

We can imagine a civilization in which, unlike ours, electrical sciences evolved earlier than mechanical sciences. They might thus use as a model the 'well known' (by them) electrical oscillation to further their explorations of the 'newly discovered' pendulum. The reciprocity of the two is to be stressed: the electrical oscillation can be used to 'explain' the pendulum as much as the familiar *vice versa*, depending only on which is the more understood to start with. To give two examples of well known models (literally): Watson and Crick's model of a DNA molecule (1953) was constructed from metal plates and clamps made exactly to scale in three dimensions. It presented something too small to be seen, at a vastly magnified scale; we feel immediately we can grasp something of its structure and disposition. The double helix was an elegant solution to how the constituent proteins balanced attraction and repulsion and, to a trained eye, possibilities of interaction and processes of replication are also represented (Watson, 1970: especially Chapter 27 and photo 15).

Thus models help us to understand the world by presenting the unknown in terms of the known – a known entity which appears to behave in the same way as the unknown. After a while we feel we 'know' both areas well. But a model is more than a representation, it is usually built in such a way that it has a dynamic function both explaining what we know, but also suggesting future tests and experiments.[7]

Let us finally look more clearly at the *correspondence* of these two phenomena – one known the other under investigation. The simplest word to use to describe this relationship is *analogy*, and it is this that will open up our discussion into music.[8]

Analogies

Now we must relate our model to what we are observing. Each metal plate for Watson and Crick represented a chemical constituent of DNA. The behaviour of a pendulum may parallel that of an acoustic wave (their mathematical descriptions

7 Karl Popper argues that a theory can never be proved *right*; we can build up more and more evidence in its favour but we can never be sure it is the *truth*; however, it can very simply be proved *wrong* (Popper, 2002b).

8 The distinctions made in this chapter follow Hugh Mellor (1968), although he distinguishes *model* (the entity) from *analogue* (a set of true statements about the model). While this distinction can be made for the musical examples to be discussed, it would make the descriptions unnecessarily complicated.

have exactly the same form). This relationship is the *analogy* – it links (or maps) relevant parameters of the model to what we have observed. Models have been used in all spheres of investigation as *visualizations of theory*. That is one method of explaining the unknown in terms of the known.

In acoustics, sound is difficult to explain as it cannot be seen and we have constructed models from the start. For example, for wave motion and behaviour, demonstrating propagation, reflection, refraction and diffraction we might use a water 'ripple tank'. Every audio computer programme is strictly displaying a model of a sound wave on screen. We take them for granted; the analogy is 'obvious' – time is mapped to space (horizontal), amplitude to space (vertical).

Symmetry Thesis

Our next excursion into scientific philosophy concerns an idealized and positivist theory of explanation known sometimes as the *symmetry thesis*. In this view explanation and prediction are symmetrical, one looking to the past, the other to the future:

> The perfect explanation of an observed phenomenon is one which would have allowed its precise prediction. (Hempel and Oppenheim, 1960, p. 22).

For example, the ideal explanation of the behaviour of a pendulum, allows us to predict the behaviour of all future pendulums. While this may be true for pure mathematics and physics it is evidently a lot more unrealistic for the social sciences and humanities. Although increasingly discredited – even within physics itself with the uncertainties of quantum mechanics – this ideal does lie behind many popular prejudices about the relationship of the various branches of scientific enquiry.[9] Karl Popper has even argued that such 'historicism' is a fundamental error when applied to the social sciences:

> … I mean by "historicism" an approach to the social sciences which assumes that *historical prediction* is their principle aim, and which assumes that this aim is attainable by discovering the "rhythm" or the "patterns", the "laws" or the "trends" that underlie the evolution of history (Popper, 2002a, p. 3).

We should bear in mind such an admonition when models are applied to music production – *behaviour* cannot so easily be predicted.

Into Music

Musicians essentially began driving model theory into reverse. For the scientist the 'unknown to be explained' is already there – something being observed which we want to understand. For the musician the entire edifice of the 'model and analogy'

9 There remain hard line 'reductionists' who argue that eventually all knowledge may be reduced to statements in physical science and hence ideally to this thesis.

structure is turned on its head and used to *create something new*. It becomes a *generative procedure*. The model may (but need not) help us to understand this *new music*.

Composers have not been consistent in their applications of models to the composition of music. For some, models have been a source of *sound material* (the form of the resulting work having nothing to do with the original model), for others, models have been a source of *form* (within which the material has been composed according to some other musical generative process). This division of form from content shall be a recurrent theme in our discussion of new music.

The Composer's Choices

Up to four areas of choice are available to the composer in the use of models in composition. The first two establish the model itself and its behaviour:

- First the composer chooses: *the particular model to be used.*

  Let us take as a simple example the *pendulum.*

  Its motion depends, however, on the choice of: initial variables in the model. In this case the period of swing depends on the gravitational constant (pendulums are slower on the moon – we cannot control this as it is effectively a constant on the earth's surface) and its length.

We might build a more sophisticated model which includes frictional damping and observe the pendulum swing decaying over time. Some models, however, do not need these initial variables and can spew out data for us as soon as they are chosen.

In the process of analogy two further choices are demanded to generate musical material:

- The composer must choose: *Which musical parameter corresponds to each variable in the model?*

  The *swing* of our pendulum might correspond to *rising and falling pitch*, or *movement in space*, or *changing density*; but in addition the composer must set:

  The parameter scale of this relationship. By how much does the chosen parameter of the music vary? – for pitch (say) is one swing a semitone or three octaves?

The analogy process is none other than the process of *mapping* found in many investigative mathematical and scientific procedures and now a commonplace in computer applications in music (Roads, 1996a).

Let us look at each of these choices in turn using more developed examples. Two groups of model types may be distinguished, those based on aspects of human behaviour and those based on observations of non-human behaviours respectively. The former include aspects of language, social behaviour and social structure, while the latter includes a vast array of types from the atomic to the astronomic, including mathematical algorithms, geometry and logic; architecture may be included here as it is reducible to aspects of geometry and number. Architecture is solid geometry, geometry is spatialized number (or dimension).

Models Based on Language and Linguistics

While music and language have been close and interactive throughout musical history, technology allows the use of language to become literal and manipulateable musical material. Linguists divide language traditionally into two levels. First the *syntactic* level, the rules of combination of words to form sentences. Secondly, the *phonological* (or *phonemic*) level, which concerns sounds and their permissible combinations into words within a given language. The two together combine to create 'meaning' the study of which is referred to as *semantics*. We may add two further areas to this classical grammar: what are called *paralinguistic* attributes, gestural and emphatic stresses and contours which profoundly effect meaning,[10] as well as a social dimension: monologue, dialogue, solo/chorus exchanges, and so forth.

Composers have never been entirely holistic in their use of models in composition. One model may be used to generate material, another (or none at all) to organize it. This is especially true with language models; few composers have used *all* the aspects of language outlined above in the same composition (as in real language taken as a whole). It is at the *phonemic* level that Stockhausen has drawn his model from language to generate the electronic materials for *Gesang der Jünglinge*. Stockhausen describes this work as 'Electronic Music to Daniel 3, 57–66' (Apocrypha), recording as material sung sections of the text using a boy soprano and combining this with electronically produced sound. Stockhausen follows the well-established relationship of periodic and aperiodic waves to vowels and consonants respectively.[11] But the relationship is not a literal one. The aim was not to perform 'speech synthesis' directly. While the basic analysis of speech was understood, the synthesis devices available at the time could perform neither the necessary formant synthesis for vowels nor complex noise synthesis for consonants. Nonetheless the *model* of the sung voice was actually present in the piece and directly informed the approach to the electronic sounds used. Stockhausen aimed to create a continuity of sung and synthetic elements so that the two areas might be subject to the same *musical* organization. This means he has attempted to create an *analogous* system of electronic timbres to the phonemes of speech. Recorded voice was a *phonemic model* for the electronic material (Stockhausen, 1958, 1964b).

Stockhausen was working on *Gesang der Jünglinge* in the studios of *West Deutscher Rundfunk* until shortly before the première in May 1956. In December of that same year György Ligeti arrived in Vienna as a refugee from Hungary, moved to Cologne early in 1957 where he stayed with Stockhausen for some weeks and began work on a series of short electronic pieces at the studio. His work *Artikulation* was created in the first four months of 1958 and shows the strong influence of *Gesang*

10 As we see in some of the works of Berio these may even be *abstracted* from a specific language and used as an independent resource.

11 He had studied acoustics with Dr. Werner Meyer-Eppler at the University of Bonn at various times between 1954 and 1956.

in a similar preoccupation with language models. In this case there is no specific text upon which to base the analogy; There is no semantic or syntactic language model. Instead the relationship exists on the other three levels. A *phonemic* model is used to define the electronic sound types. But although in Rainer Wehinger's published score (Wehinger, 1970, pp. 17–19) we see the work built up through what are termed 'words' and 'sentences', these terms are loosely used and such middle level structures are not generated from any specific language model.[12] However it is very clear that the *gestural* and *narrative* aspects of language have been fully engaged to create the final contours and combinations. We clearly hear 'monologues' and 'dialogues', for example see Wehinger (1970, pp. 29–30, Figures 13–15), which are in turn reinforced by being placed on separate channels in the final 4-channel (surround) distribution of the individual streams of sound.

The phonemic parallels are more strict than those of Stockhausen's *Gesang*.[13] Ligeti's synthesis methods result in 42 basic material types – though Wehinger is forced to reduce these to 16 in the score transcription (p. 37). The frequency with which the various sound types occur is determined by a complex relation which was probably not derived from a statistical analysis of real speech utterances. This is one reason why the sound world of *Artikulation* fails to develop the vowel/consonant antithesis of real language phonetics. It is finally the gesture shape and spatial interplay narrative that lends the work its language-like qualities.

It is, however, in the works of Luciano Berio that other levels of language model may most clearly be seen at work. In *Thema (Omaggio a Joyce)* (1958) (Berio, 1998), Berio uses as basic material a reading by Cathy Berberian of a section of Chapter 11 ('Sirens') of James Joyce's *Ulysses*[14]. Joyce makes extensive use of onomatopoeia and alliteration, and devises sequences of words with distinctively musical contour. Indeed Joyce used music as a model for his specific text, which in turn is a model for the Berio work. Berio himself has given us the following diagram which elucidates clearly the analogy between some of the phonemic combinations and musical articulations (from Berio, 1958):[15]

Imperthnthn	trill
Chips, picking chips	staccato
Warbling. Ah, lure!	appoggiatura
Deaf bald Pat brought pad knife took up	martellato
A sail! A vail awave upon the waves	glissando, portamento

12 Ligeti in fact used serial ordering, chance procedures and purely aural judgement at these montage levels in a 'two steps forward, one step back' pattern (Wehinger, 1970, pp. 11, 17–19).

13 Ligeti's electronic materials are created from a clearer one-to-one relation of vowel to harmonic spectrum, consonant to impulse (noise). The restriction to electronic sound alone makes the world of *Artikulation* more restricted than that of *Gesang der Jünglinge* to which it stands as a humorous miniature.

14 Shorter extracts in French and Italian are also used as material.

15 In fact the version of the text Berio (1958) cited is a short extract in English on Berio (1968?), the (undated) LP sleeve. For this version of the text Berio has added *portamento* after *glissando*. I have corrected 'bold' (misprinted on the sleeve) to 'bald'.

Joyce's writing technique makes an unravelling of the phonemic, syntactic and semantic virtually impossible; they become interdependent, relating to the overall narrative of the *Ulysses* story (a day in the life of Leopold Bloom). Berio, in 'retranslating' back into the musical domain, refers to 'a reorganization and transformation of the phonetic and semantic elements of Joyce's text (Berio, 1958):

> A polyphonic intent characterizes the entire chapter ... Here the narrative technique was in fact suggested to Joyce by a well known procedure of polyphonic music: the Fuga per Canonem ... it is possible, however, by developing Joyce's polyphonic intention to reinterpret musically a reading of the text (Berio, 1958).[16]

The speech material is often transformed beyond recognition using classical studio techniques, and while the original material is clearly *related* to the original speech, it crosses the boundary into more general *musical* textures and gestures. This is what clearly marks it apart from text sound art or concrete poetry. In the same composer's *Visage* (1961 on Berio 1967) quite another aspect of language is used as a model for the material. The work combines untransformed voice with electronic sounds. The two remain unintegrated and largely in stark opposition, the female character is a prisoner in a nightmare world of sounds which confront the humanity of her vocal utterances. Berio has written that *Visage* is:

> ... based on the sound symbolism of vocal gestures and inflections with their accompanying 'shadow of meanings' and their associative tendencies ... The vocal events from inarticulated or articulated 'speech' ... to patterns of inflections modelled on specific languages ... (Berio, 1967).[17]

The gestures and contours of language are abstracted and become material for Berio to create a narrative line linked to the film for which the work was intended.

Models of Social Relationship and Behaviour

Social *behaviour* implies a process in time, the dynamic interaction of elements, while social *relationship* may be a static snapshot of a state of affairs (possibly from within a behaviour sequence) and is thus independent of narrative time. This is the deepest and longest established of music's many models. Writings from ethnomusicology and the anthropology of music concerned with the origins of musical practice refer to the 'deep' articulation (even integration) of the social and musical. This is another such use of models as a conscious application of something that might already be built into the musical discourse at a deeper level. The consciously conversational model of some improvisation ensembles rekindles a very deep vein of musical expression which may (some argue) have predated language itself. Calls, responses,

---

16 Joyce uses a type of 'monophonic polyphony', in which differentiation of registers and materials gives an appearance of polyphony, and which we find also in Bach's solo instrumental works and in Berio's own *Sequenza I* for solo flute.

17 He has elsewhere described these models as including Hebrew, Neapolitan, Armenian, English and French (Emmerson, 1976a, p. 28).

solos, chorus may not strictly be metaphorical at all. They might instantiate prehistoric group sound exchanges, expressing a wide range of feelings from anxiety and fear through to exaltation and celebration. In his classic book *Wellsprings of Music* (1962) Curt Sachs argues against such simplistic and unprovable assertions. Yet they recur. In 1973 John Blacking boldly asserted:

> Ethnomusicology's claim to be a new method of analyzing music and music history must rest on an assumption not yet generally accepted, namely, that because music is humanly organized sound, there ought to be a relationship between patterns of human organization and the patterns of sound produced as a result of human interaction (Blacking, 1973, p. 26).

Bruno Nettl's *The Study of Ethnomusicology* (1983) is one of the best to examine the examiners. The cycles within ethnomusicology itself[18] are fascinatingly revealed as spirals: the search for universals in music alternates with periods of stressing difference and diversity, and a stress on the degree to which music is modelled on cultural behaviour also oscillates. Whether provably correct or merely held as romantic beliefs such ideas are clearly an influence on improvisers in practice.

However the *conscious* appropriation of such models to make (western art) music is a characteristic of the later twentieth century. The form-scheme of Stockhausen's *Momente*, for example, is based around three groups of 'moments' which may be played according to the rotations of a tree-like system not unlike an inverted hanging mobile.[19] Three letters designate the primary characteristics of the music 'K' for *Klang* (sound colour), 'D' for *Dauer* (duration), 'M' for *Melodie* (melody); these are combined in various ways to generate hybrid moments combining the characteristics to varying degrees. But it contains, too, a personal model in that Doris (Andreae) (his first wife) and Mary (Bauermeister) (his second) may 'rotate' around the always central Karlheinz (Stockhausen). The four small D-moments could also be seen as his four children by Doris (Smalley, 1974b, p. 295).

Used in music making such proto-models recapture and re-establish such links rather than invent them anew. Any tight improvisation group quickly drops their more explicitly stated aspects. In fact they often adopt strategies for undermining the more obvious of the language and communication relationships. For example Derek Bailey's discussion of the work of the ensemble *The Music Improvisation Company* quotes Evan Parker as commenting on the role of fellow member Hugh Davies:

> His work with the group also hastened the development of the several 'layers' approach to improvising, extending the basic dialogue form of the music which has been called ping-pong (Bailey, 1992, p. 94).

Layering is bound to undermine any simple communication model. Polyphony undermines *exchange* (which is more correctly *antiphony*).

Stockhausen's 'Texts for Intuitive Music' are poetic texts and scenario descriptions which range from metaphor to explicit modelling of social processes and behaviour.

---

18 Indeed whether such a separate field should even exist.

19 Itself a model, mapping mobility in space onto order in time. We shall discuss this further in Chapter 5.

Of the first set, *Aus den sieben Tagen* ('From the Seven Days') (1968), the texts *Richtige Dauern* ('Right durations') and *Treffpunkt* ('Meeting point') refer loosely to other performers while *Setz die Segel zur Sonne* ('Set sail for the sun') and *Kommunion* ('Communion') demand an awareness of other's actions for goals of harmony or communion between the performers (Stockhausen, 1970). In the second set (*Für Kommende Zeiten* ('For Times to Come') (1968–70)), the group of texts *Kommunikation* ('Communication'), *Interval* ('Interval'), *Ausserhalb* ('Outside'), *Innerhalb* ('Inside'), *Anhalt* ('Halt'), and *Schwingung* ('Vibration') represent not merely a model of social behaviour, but an ethical ideal for living (Stockhausen, 1976). Here we cross over from social behaviour as a *model for music* to idealized social behaviour *as music*.

Models Drawn from Observations of the Non-human World

Architecture and geometry: Xenakis's Metastasis

Architecture is reducible to the geometry of the printed page and we can consider them together. Iannis Xenakis worked with the architect Le Corbusier between 1948 and 1959.[20] He has, himself, often drawn parallels between the two occupations. The model for his work *Metastasis* (1953–54) is a plan, based on parabolic and hyperbolic 'ruled surfaces' (generated from straight lines) (Xenakis, 1992, p. 3; Matossian, 1986, p. 115). Interestingly, although *Metastasis* was completed in 1954, the idea was used again in Xenakis's design for the Philips Pavilion at the Brussels World Fair of 1958 (Xenakis, 1992, pp. 6–7 and 10–11; Matossian, 1986, pp. 114–117) – the physical construction of the model thus postdating its use in musical production. The *initial variable* in the model is concealed in the composer's sketches. All the shapes drawn are examples of *conic sections*, which have a specific mathematical description. The composer chose those necessary to generate the surfaces we see; each individual line has specific values for the general equation. For example a parabola is generated from the equation $y=a.x^2$; Xenakis has not indicated the particular values of the constant 'a' that might have been used to generated the surfaces we observe, but they could in principle be measured from the published evidence.[21] From the original sketches the composer chose the traditional mapping of graphic information into music: vertical corresponding to pitch, horizontal to time. We can observe on his sketches his subsequent decision on parameter scale:[22] for pitch: 3cm = 12 semitones; for time: 5cm = ♩ = 50MM (= the bar length in the transcribed score).

20 For a fuller discussion of this long and complex relationship see Matossian (1986).

21 This is not to assume he did generate the lines from an equation; he might have drawn them freehand, but this does not invalidate the principle.

22 By way of comparison, observe the obviously different scale and mapping factors used to create the Philips Pavilion from similar surfaces and ruled lines.

Behaviour of gas molecules: Xenakis's Pithoprakta

Brownian motion is a term used to describe the movement of microscopic particles in a fluid due to the kinetic energy present at any temperature above absolute zero. Any particle effectively executes a *random walk*, that is, it moves in a straight line until deflected by a collision with another particle. The distance between collisions will vary (as will the time between collisions) over a range whose statistical occurrence conforms to a *normal distribution*,[23] defined overall by the temperature and density of the fluid.

Brownian motion is essentially a *four*-dimensional phenomenon (three space and one time) and the flat two-dimensional, outside time, representation of the printed page is inevitably limited (Xenakis, 1992, p. 18–21; Matossian, 1986, p. 98). So one must be clear exactly what simplifications the composer has made. In the case of *Pithoprakta*, Xenakis has set the initial variables of the model as the 'temperature'. For some reason which he has not explained, he has set the 'collisions' to be, to a large extent, at regular intervals (or distances). On the graph one can see the many simultaneities at each 5cm – this corresponds to one bar of transcribed music. These 5cm bars are only ever subdivided into 3, 4 or 5 regular subdivisions (= 'collisions'),[24] a situation which is impossible in reality and fails to use his 'stochastic' approach in this instance.[25] He has reduced the model to each instrument being the equivalent of a person walking at constant footstep rate (from a choice of three) with equal probability of taking a step forward or backward (with varying step size within limits). Only the trace of this one-dimensional movement with time appears to get anywhere.[26]

Once again the composer has chosen to map traditionally. In this case the time dimension of the model becomes musical time (though with an arbitrary scale) and spatial displacement (averaged from the real three dimensional movement) onto the single dimension of pitch. The pitch scale unit is arbitrarily set at the standard semitone – the left margin of the original graph is marked in whole tones which are simply subdivided.

We have shown how a model may directly generate musical material in a simple process of choice, mapping and scaling. In these two preliminary examples from Xenakis, the influence of the most traditional aspects of Western notation is in evidence: the tendency automatically to equate vertical with pitch and horizontal with time. But we have also seen the inevitable simplifications that are made to enable such an adaptation to instrumental practice.

---

23 This defines an average (and most likely) value; the likelihood of other values reduces steadily the further away from this average. It has a classic 'bell shape' form.

24 Observing the graph one can see only 1cm, 1.25cm and 1.7cm line segments corresponding to these subdivisions.

25 See bars 52–59 of the score (partly reproduced in Xenakis, 1992, p. 17; fully in Matossian, 1986, pp. 96–97).

26 Imagine the person's feet being the pen of a pen-recorder as paper is drawn at constant rate beneath them at right angles to the direction of walk. The footprints would be the collision points joined together with straight lines!

Points: from Stars to Atoms

Astronomic observation provides some of the most striking models in this era. Star analogies lie deeper in the mythology of contemporary music, especially that known as *pointillist*, than the use merely of star maps. Stockhausen referred to Messiaen's *Mode de valeurs et d'intensités* as 'fantastic music of the stars' (Wörner, 1973, p. 80–81). The point star and the point sound were firmly related in the imagination. Star maps pose an interesting case. Although there is some local order in galactic configurations – spiral shapes and the like are products of gravitational fields on a vast scale – what we see is essentially the result of the 'big bang' (and still expanding). This appears essentially random, yet nonetheless we attempt to impose order on the apparent chaos, for example in the naming of constellations.[27]

John Cage has used star maps directly in several works.[28] In *Atlas Eclipticalis* (1961) pages from the star chart atlas of that name are subjected to tracing and fragmentation procedures to produce each of the 86 identically structured parts (Pritchett, 1993, p. 124–25). While the *Etudes Australes* for piano (1974–75) (Cage, 1975) involve a more direct combination of the star charts from the *Atlas Australis* with 'all the possible chord formations that could be played by a single hand on the piano' (Pritchett, 1993, p. 198). In these works the Zen ideas of *unimpededness* and *interpenetration* are illustrated perfectly. Zen reduces all apparent chance occurrences to events influenced by all other material in the cosmos. While philosophers and mathematicians increasingly engage with ideas of deterministic yet apparently chaotic universes, the exact nature of the 'big bang' in principle decided the disposition of the star maps we now see. In Stockhausen's *Sternklang* (1971) some material is derived from star constellations transcribed into graphic 'note' form. This so-called 'insert material' is integrated into the main 'model' material (Stockhausen's term), itself based on zodiac ideas (Maconie, 1990, pp. 210–213; see also the score, Stockhausen (1977)). To decide pitch, two of the 'star-pitches' are anchored to the prevailing harmonic chord[29] and the others added freely around them. Rhythm is given by horizontal displacement, and loudness of notes from the relative sizes of the stars.[30]

We may see, too, a connection to that other extreme of scientific observation: the point generated in X-ray crystallography by the particular displacement of a molecular structure.[31] The intersection of the various planes and angles of a crystal

27 The mystic dimension implied in the extension of astronomy to astrology (and signs of the Zodiac) suggests that same belief in a 'hidden order' implied in the very use of models in composition in the first place.

28 Cage's earliest piece to use star charts was *Music for Carillon No.4* (1961). The later *Etudes Boreales* (1978) used star charts to determine where on the piano the performer is to play (Pritchett, 1993, pp. 211 and 199).

29 *Sternklang* is based on an extension of ideas originally created for the earlier *Stimmung*; here each ensemble's material is articulated on a chord based on the second to ninth harmonics of a fundamental.

30 Simplified to five star size degrees of loudness.

31 A famous example (much republished) would be that of crystalline DNA (Watson, 1970, photo 8).

lattice produce a single point on the photographic image in a way strangely similar to how the cross-multiplication of serial matrices used in the production of Boulez's *Structures Ia* or Stockhausen's *Kreuzspiel* produces a single event. Stockhausen has consistently drawn parallels between the atomic world and that of sound synthesis and composition:[32]

> Who sees atoms? And yet everyone knows that all material appearance depends on their structure (Stockhausen, 1963, p. 50 (original written in 1953)).

> The discovery of the DNA code, for example, focuses on how you can create different species of beings by starting from the very smallest particles and their components. That's why we are all part of the spirit of the atomic age. In music we do exactly the same (Cott, 1974, p. 37).

While initially this analogy would have been with *sine tones*, it is perhaps not as robust as that between the atom and sound *grain*. The grain combines a frequency and time relation in exactly the same way as the wave-particle duality of the electron.[33] The theory developed by Denis Gabor in 1947 was taken up by Xenakis and developed in Chapters 2 and 3 of his *Formalized Music* (1992, originally written over the period 1955–65) which includes a description of the techniques behind his electronic work *Analogique B* (1958–59). In this work the tape part is constructed from a vast number of sine wave grains but its realization was severely limited in the analogue world, splicing such short segments of tape. Granular applications have been developed in the computer age as a major source of synthesis as well as the basis for one type of time-stretch processing. Many of the noise streams which can be developed from such granular processes have strong associations to real world sound streams formed by fluid flow (wind or water for example). This has been particularly developed and advocated by Barry Truax (see Truax, 1994) and used very notably in his work *Pacific* (1990) (Truax, 1991).

Stockhausen's *Kontakte* (1958–60) is also the product of a granular approach. The opening of the 'realisation score' (*Realisationspartitur*) (Stockhausen, 1968) is a diary of this painstaking exploration, using the simplest of analogue equipment. The quantum leap in richness of texture compared to previous works[34] is directly a result of the richness of the new 'sound atom' – the impulse – compared with the sine wave. A sequence of impulses (a 'rhythm') is looped and speeded up into complex (sometimes pitched) sounds with rich timbre, as well as spatially distributed into fantastic 'flood sounds' (*Flutklänge*). This – the composer's own – description is significant as the surround soundscape of the work has an 'environmental' feel unheard

32 Richard Toop also explicitly draws this parallel (on Stockhausen's behalf) in Toop, 1979 (p. 383).

33 This is literal: the 'Heisenberg uncertainty principle' has a precise equivalent for the sound grain: the greater its definition in time, the less exact its spectral distribution (and vice versa).

34 There are some moments in *Gesang der Jünglinge* which approach the flood sound density of *Kontakte* by using remarkably similar though less extensively developed techniques.

before or since in Stockhausen's acousmatic work.[35] In a famous passage at 17'05" ('Structure X', p. 19–20 of the score) a pitched sound slows down progressively to reveal its origins as a series of impulses which themselves reveal pitch. The strong relationship to the sound production of the internal combustion engine of a motor bike is frequently remarked upon by first-time listeners.

Need the Listener 'Hear' Models?

Composers' views vary as to whether the models they use need to be perceived by a listener. Does Xenakis want you to perceive 'gas molecules moving'? Maybe not, but he does believe it represents a deeper archetype of 'statistical' phenomena which permeate many aspects of our universe.[36] Do Cage or Stockhausen intend you to 'hear stars' or at least 'star maps' – not really, although they represent an image of isolated points in patterns which 'translate' very neatly into musical patterns and reflect deeper-lying ideas they hope to articulate. For Cage they create yet another mechanism for the removal of human intention and memory, and also perfectly mirror the Zen idea of 'interpenetration'. In Stockhausen's case the transition from astronomical to astrological has become clear in many of his works of the 1970s[37] and he intends a conscious knowledge of relevant traits to be brought to bear on the music and communicated to the listener. Humans have searched for relationships in star patterns (the constellations – Orion, the Plough, and so forth) and have dreamt of 'the music of the spheres' for many centuries.[38] The difference between the approaches of these two composers illustrates a key divergence in the use of models itself: for Stockhausen the 'intelligence' is 'out there' coming to us; for Cage there are no patterns or intentions to be decoded beyond those we bring to bear as individual listeners.

But perhaps both Ligeti and Berio *do* want you to hear direct parallels with linguistic and literary processes in their language-model pieces. The voice and language in general retain a privileged place in human perception. Through both 'noisy' and band-limited transmission (even deliberate sound transformation) we recognize and attempt to decode 'meaning' in a linguistic signal. Such language signals retain a strong degree of robustness. There was an over-optimism in these works of the 1950s that speech element synthesis[39] was attainable and that steady-

---

35 In the version of the work for live instruments and tape, the instrumental part for piano and percussion – that is, percussion – completes the essentially impulsive continuum. The impulse is the 'contact' between the instrumental and electronic soundworlds.

36 Leigh Landy has argued that the listener can learn to follow the 'seemingly impenetrable' organization of a work such as Xenakis's *Nomos α* if properly explained and contextualized (Landy, 1991, Section XVId).

37 Most especially a group centred on *Tierkreis* (*Zodiac*) (1974–75) including the massive *Sirius* (1975–77).

38 Although descending into a bizarre (conservative) anti-modernism, James (1995) is a useful discussion.

39 Speech element (vowels, consonants) – not speech proper; it was recognized that the synthesis of the complex interactions of elements upon stringing sounds together to form real

state imitation of vowel models (and simple noise band and impulse imitations of some consonants) would be recognized as 'linguistic'.

Yet all composers do seem to imply that the use of models does translate 'something transcendental' from the extra-musical to the musical – that there are 'ideas in common' that permeate through all our experiences of the world (and universe) whether traditionally musical or not. There has been a vast variety of model uses to create music – some overt and obvious, some completely secret.[40] There are also those of which the composer has little or no awareness, sublimated and taken for granted, possibly major articulators of the *Zeitgeist*. It is this that will lead us to the idea of *reanimation*.

Sublimation

The sublimation of such models into much composition and performance practice (using technology) happened progressively in the decades following this initial outburst in the 1950s. The publication of the Midi standard in 1983 defined well-tempered pitch, velocity (and 'channel') in simple numerical terms. Coinciding with a new generation of personal computers, the ability to generate note data algorithmically led to an explosion of programmes which could generate musical process according to rules. The degree to which these were user-defined varied greatly; some followed rules based on minimalism, others on stochastic approaches.[41] When fractals and chaos theory became popularized following the publication of Benoît Mandelbrot's classic work *The Fractal Geometry of Nature* (1982), these, too, were incorporated into algorithmic packages. Early examples[42] include *City of Congruence*, a movement from Michael McNabb's *Invisible Cities* (1987) (McNabb, 1989), in which all the melodic material is composed from fractal algorithms and Gary Lee Nelson's *Fractal Mountains* (1988) (Nelson, 1992), in which pitch, duration and velocity are generated from fractal functions.

At the same time these and other mathematical abstractions were finding increasing application in real world systems analysis in general. Urban industrial (usually electronic) systems could be described as *noisy* and *chaotic* as well as, for example, organic growth metaphors and neural networks being applied to environmental and ecological systems analysis. Thus almost without realizing it, an already latent tendency to appropriate such systems into music, brought such model thinking closer and easier to apply. The flux of the soundscape was found after all to be more subtle than the 'random' tag previously given (at least) to urban phenomena. Its patterns were revealed as subtle and complex, quite capable of mathematical description. From weather maps, through traffic patterns, radio and telephone

words was unrealistic at this time in the analogue studio.

40 From pre-electronic history comes the debate over Debussy's use (conscious or not) of fibonacci number relationships (Howat, 1983).

41 *Intelligent Music* (Joel Chadabe and David Zicarelli) produced *M* and *Jam Factory* in 1986.

42 Since the 1980s there has been an explosion of interest with (currently) many websites devoted to fractal music and its generation.

networks, the internet, human movement, animal migration, electrical activity, global warming maps – the world is emerging as a complex interaction of algorithms which attempt both to describe and (occasionally) to predict. While much has been made of the progressive integration of communication technologies in this period, there has been a similar and less remarked trend to integrate and relate the *language of systems descriptions*. This in turn has allowed a kind of multidisciplinary cross-over into the arts in general and music (and the sonic arts) in particular.

As we have observed musicians have for quite some time used the environment as a source for music generation. But when we look at more recent developments and the evolution of genres, the environment finds its way increasingly into music not only via recording and reproduction of *sounds* as such but through simulation of the characteristics of the systems' *behaviours* and their complexities (and occasionally simplicity). I am arguing, firstly, that a kind of *underground vernacular* is emerging. Secondly that the process is one of *exchange* and that a hidden consequence is that the 'live' is also being thrown back from human agency into the (so-called) 'inanimate' world. This is the process of *reanimation*.

Reanimation

Models are thus the doorway to the use of any observable phenomenon as a generator of music. But this gives the impression that the flow is all one way and that we (the animate composers and listeners) are possibly in danger of being overrun by the 'environment'. In fact such a sound environment might result from any mix of inanimate (for example, the product of seismic activity), animate but non-human (activities of plants and animals) or human-produced but alienated (urban and industrial systems, for example). But the process has also a reverse component. Tim Ingold's assertion quoted at the head of this chapter might be applied to this process. This suggests that in using many of these inputs to musical discourse we are forming *two way* relationships. We seem to be appropriating and plundering without giving in return even a sensitive acknowledgement but, in fact, we have at least a chance of *reanimating* these objects and systems which we thought to be 'outside of music'. They become animate through this *relationship with us* – '… life is "a name for *what is going on* in the generative field"' (Ingold, 2000, p. 200).

Thus the composer becomes a kind of *shaman*, drawing forth and revealing rather than setting down and representing. This might allow us to reinterpret several earlier twentieth century developments in a new light. I would suggest that metaphorical language has occasionally been taken too poetically and that the original writers' intentions may be somewhat more literal. These examples have in common the idea of the universe *as musical instrument*. I want to relate these signposts to contemporary developments. Henry David Thoreau wrote in his book *Walden* which inspired a range of thinkers from Tolstoy and Mahatma Ghandi to John Cage and Murray Schafer:

> Sometimes, on Sundays, I heard the bells, the Lincoln, Acton, Bedford, or Concord bell, when the wind was favorable, a faint, sweet, and, as it were, natural melody, worth importing into the wilderness. At a sufficient distance over the woods this sound acquires

a certain vibratory hum, as if the pine needles in the horizon were the strings of a harp which it swept. All sound heard at the greatest possible distance produces one and the same effect, a vibration of the universal lyre, just as the intervening atmosphere makes a distant ridge of the earth interesting to our eyes by the azure tint it imparts to it (Thoreau, 1986, p. 168 from *Walden* (*'Sounds'*)).

Futurism – the City Lives and Breathes

The Futurist manifestos are full of references to landscape, cityscape and soundscape as living and breathing organisms[43] – in the first case teeming with such organisms, in perpetual movement and interaction:

> ... we will sing of the vibrant nightly fervour of arsenals and shipyards blazing with violent electric moons; greedy railway stations that devour smoke-plumed serpents; factories hung on clouds by the crooked lines of their smoke; bridges that stride the rivers like giant gymnasts, flashing in the sun with a glitter of knives; adventurous steamers that sniff the horizon; deep-chested locomotives whose wheels paw the tracks like the hooves of enormous steel horses bridled by tubing; and the sleek flight of planes whose propellers chatter in the wind like banners and seem to cheer like an enthusiastic crowd (F.T. Marinetti: *The Founding and Manifesto of Futurism 1909* (Apollonio, 1973, p. 22)).

But also (in an early example of eliminating the unhelpful 'nature-culture' – 'rural-urban' – divide in landscape thinking), as a single living entity with a holistic soundscape adding to many better known examples of noise textures:

> To convince ourselves of the amazing variety of noises, it is enough to think of the rumble of thunder, the whistle of the wind, the roar of the waterfall, the gurgling of a brook, the rustling of leaves, the clatter of a trotting horse ..., and of the generous, solemn white breathing of a nocturnal city ... (Luigi Russolo: *The Art of Noises* (1913) (Apollonio, 1973, p. 85)).

We can interpret the likes of Mosolov and Avraamov's experiments (described above) – even the Futurist's *intonarumori* themselves – as a crude first stage at harnessing the sounds of this 'new instrument' under mechanical human control – literally, not metaphorically. Now recording technology (and systems modelling) has allowed a very real extension into its innermost working – the 'chaos' of a building's control systems can literally run a sound installation, the soundscape of the Futurist's breathing city can become its material.

Music as the 'Materialization of Intelligence' (Xenakis)

The ideas of Iannis Xenakis might appear to be alien to such an argument. His strongly rationalist position, suggesting a quasi-logical relationship of science and mathematics to music, retains a strongly objective and apparently depersonalized

---

43 Ingold suggests strongly that this kind of description is more accurate than saying 'as if they were living and breathing' – this form of words reinforces the metaphoric and 'conditional' aspects of such a description.

argument. He has described three modes of operation for art. *Inference* and *experiment* relate directly to scientific method, while *revelation* is immediate and unmediated.[44] He famously referred to music as 'materialized intelligence':

> But what is the essence of these [musical] materials? This essence is man's intelligence, in some way solidified. Intelligence which searches, questions, infers, reveals, foresees – on all levels. Music and the arts in general seem to be a necessary solidification, materialization of this intelligence (Xenakis, 1985, p. 1).

While not born of a religious 'spirituality' or life-force, this view of intelligence still suggests a kind of animation. Xenakis is arguing that the musical materials derived from the logics he finds in stochastic systems, gas molecule behaviour, Boolean relationships, set theory, games theory and the behaviour of other world systems[45] are instances (materializations), that is *more than mere metaphorical examples* of 'human intelligence'. Following his famous description of a political demonstration,[46] and its temporal and spatial sonic evolution, he adds: 'The statistical laws of these events, separated from their political or moral context, are the same as those of the cicadas or the rain' (Xenakis, 1992, p. 9). In a very real sense Xenakis has created a world which can act as a virtually unlimited source of musical material, not differentiating between animate and inanimate in the process. The world has thus become a vast musical instrument which can be heard through *sonification* – the instantiation of its processes in sound through their use as models. While Xenakis's view is anti-expressionist in a personal sense (the music does not express his or any other emotions), it is nonetheless a direct realization of the world and its processes and one which thereby 'reveals' an aspect of that world as a result:

> It ['art, and above all, music'] must aim through fixations which are landmarks to draw towards a total exaltation in which the individual mingles, losing his consciousness in a truth immediate, rare, enormous and perfect. … This is why art can lead to realms that religion still occupies for some people (Xenakis, 1992, p. 1).

This is an example of *ekstasis* – not so much a suspension as an enlargement of consciousness for the transcendental moment. This has many variants both religious, cultural, intellectual and philosophical. Xenakis is clearly painting the artist into the role of the priest or shaman (to which we shall return), significantly describing a loss of self into a 'truth' rather than into any collective spirit.

---

44 Which he declares is 'its superiority over the sciences' (1985, p. 4).

45 I avoid the term 'natural' systems.

46 Confirmed as an anti-Nazi demonstration in Athens such as that in which Xenakis took part in March 1942 (Matossian, 1986, pp. 21 and 58).

Flux and Flow: From AM and Short-Wave Radio[47] to the Internet

A radio receiver not only decodes human-intended communications but can sonify all available radio waves. These include the most primeval: the residue of the big bang itself is available,[48] as are many examples of global ionosphere and weather activity. Within the station signal system itself there are carrier and modulation tones and other 'inter-station' noise and tuning phenomena. The radio has been a source of sound materials most notably since John Cage's *Imaginary Landscape IV* (1951)[49] in which tuning and amplitude instructions are the result of chance operations.

Stockhausen claims deliberately to have avoided two of Cage's seminal sound sources, the prepared piano and the radio, until he received a tape of a version of his *Plus-Minus* (1963) realized by Frederick Rzewski and Cornelius Cardew in 1964 (Stockhausen, 1971, pp. 42–43). Cardew had used a 'transistor radio' as an ancillary instrument. Writing in 1965, Stockhausen remarks:

> The result is of a highly poetic quality, reached as a result of the way *Plus-Minus* is constructed: when such a result is obtained, detailed considerations of sound and material become unimportant. I now find myself listening more adventurously, *discovering* a music summoned forth from me: feeling myself an instrument in the service of a profound and intangible power, experienceable only in music, in the poetry of sounds (Stockhausen, 1971, p. 43).

Stockhausen's works explicitly to include short-wave materials cover the fixed electroacoustic work[50] *Hymnen* (1966–67), followed by his live electronic works *Kurzwellen* (1968), *Spiral* (1968), *Pole für 2* and *Expo für 3* (1969–70).[51]

The composition of *Hymnen* followed a decade of international travel culminating in his first visit to Japan in 1966[52] where he produced *Telemusik* in the studios of NHK (Japanese Radio), a piece which foreshadows *Hymnen* in many ways. Here the soundworld is dominated by multiple applications of ring modulation. Many of

---

47 In the discussion that follows Cage and Cardew refer simply to 'radios' (which would have been AM in this case and would probably have included short-wave band reception); while from his first work to use such a resource (*Hymnen*) Stockhausen refers to 'short-wave receivers' (*Kurzwellenemfänger*).

48 Cosmic Microwave Background (CMB) radiation was predicted in the 1940s and confirmed in 1964 (by Penzias and Wilson). While actually at super-audio frequencies it has been sonified by various means.

49 Cage had performed a 'composition with a radio' earlier at the famous 'happening' at Black Mountain College in 1952 (Goldberg, 1988, p. 126).

50 There is also a version for tape and instruments, as well as *Third Region with orchestra*.

51 A 'special' version of *Kurzwellen* for the Beethoven bicentenary in 1970 (*Kurzwellen mit Beethoven*) and a brief short-wave 'insert' in *Mantra* (two pianos and electronics) (1970) conclude the list.

52 On this trip Stockhausen met Daisetz Suzuki, who had given lectures on Zen at Columbia University in 1948 which Cage had attended and which had influenced him profoundly.

these processes produce sounds which resemble those from the short-wave radio[53] (for example when slightly mistuned from a station). The 'radio space' of *Telemusik* is one shared by many musics of the world, yet it both surrounds us and remains 'at a distance'. In *Hymnen* the third *Region* (section) is dedicated, significantly, to John Cage. Throughout *Hymnen* there are short-wave sounds (some simulated through studio processing) including searches 'across the dials' from which emerge the national anthems of the title.

But as *Hymnen* develops, a much more extensive canvas suggests a second more powerful image, that of an 'envelope' of radio waves around the earth which the composer and performers 'tune into'.[54] The work is not about travel to far away places so much as perceiving them and their 'signals' *from afar*. Of course movement and travel are suggested but they create a powerful *imaginary* journey. In a presentation on *Hymnen* at the Barbican Centre, London in October 2001,[55] Stockhausen talked of his childhood memories of the fast changing alliances (specifically mentioning Russia) which led up to World War Two. Then we must remember that the post-war cold war period was one in which radio was a front line weapon. Substituting for real exchange, which was limited and strictly controlled, radio was one of the major signifiers of cultural identity, art and propaganda. At another level it was also (in the short-wave band) a means of long distance communication between ships (using morse code).[56] Such signals took on the connotative meaning of separateness, isolation, great distance and remoteness – yet a distance we could perceive and transcend as listeners. There are two contrasting views of Stockhausen's use of radio sound. As 'basic material' the sounds produced are rich and complex, a 'simple' way of producing interesting electronic sound events. However, in the live works especially, these are more than 'sound objects' (in Pierre Schaeffer's sense), and relate strongly to the traditional idea of motif or cell. In the live scores, performers must 'search' the tuning dial and choose interesting events according to more or less defined criteria.[57] The events must be easily identifiable and strongly characterized with features capable of transformation and elaboration.

---

53 The modulation processes of these two domains have a common ancestry in the pre-studio broadcast and test equipment of the radio engineer.

54 As well as being one of the *vox populi* descriptions of the 1960s hippy, the tuning metaphor is found in non-short-wave works of Stockhausen such as *Stimmung* – tuning as in pitch tuning – he was well aware of the word-play in English.

55 Given on 13 October 2001 before a performance of *Hymnen*. Recorded by the BBC and available on the BBC 'listen again' service at: www.bbc.co.uk/radio3/world/ram/wstockhausen1.ram (still available as this book goes to print). *Hymnen* is also discussed in Chapters 3 and 4.

56 The author recently performed again a short-wave radio work originally performed in the 1970s. He was struck by the total absence of morse-code (replaced presumably by satellite linked communication) which has removed this last reference completely.

57 The act of moving the tuning knob is a 'performance action' and can itself help perform an event – for example, giving rhythmic articulation to a band of noise by sweeping back and forth across it.

Cornelius Cardew also introduced the transistor radio (as musical instrument) to Keith Rowe[58] of the improvisation group AMM when he (Cardew) joined it in 1966 (a year after its foundation). Rowe's innovative (always live) use of this resource shifts seemlessly from the *objet trouvé* philosophy that allowed whole passages of music and speech to be 'found' as one of the 'laminated layers' in *AMMMusic 1966* (AMM, 1989) to the refined and sensuous textures of *Fine* (2001) (AMM, 2001). There were never 'rehearsals' or any possibility of pre-knowledge of any recognizable content: the radio is both source of raw sound material and a source of excitation for the electric guitar (see Nyman, 1999, p. 129), yet totally integrated and never dominating.

The transition from the analogue world of AM radio (including short-wave) to the digital ubiquity of the internet seems in one sense logical and inevitable. Radio space still exists but many of its former functions have been replaced and it will eventually die a slow death following the mainstream analogue media 'turn off' planned for around the end of the first decade of the twenty-first century.[59] But internet art (at least in its audio forms) seems more concerned with *presence* – and the complete absence of perspective and distance.[60] The nature and contents of the information may give no indication as to its origins; cyberspace is in this sense 'nowhere' and 'everywhere'. Thus perspective has no immediate meaning as there is no distance.

Sublimating Models: Mimesis, Sonification, Metaphor

We have been juggling three terms: mimesis, sonification and metaphor. All three make use of the ideas of models and mapping, as we have introduced them above. The ideas overlap and interact – but not equally. *Metaphor* means a *displacement* of some kind. It has come to be used in the arts to also mean the *translation* of something from one sense (or art form) to another. Generally if the degree of displacement is reduced, then the idea of metaphor itself is undermined. If we examine twentieth century music (especially that enabled by technology) we see two streams emerging – one away from, one towards, metaphor.

Much programme music (old and new) is not strongly metaphorical in its representation of 'world events'. It moves towards the *mimetic* – a direct imitation (Emmerson, 1986b). Mimetic distance is steadily reduced and finally replaced by an accurate presentation of the 'original'. From Respighi's pre-recorded nightingale (in *Pines of Rome* (1924)) via Messiaen's birdsong transcriptions to the 'pure' soundscape artists,[61] the metaphor is progressively eroded. Christiane ten Hoopen (1994) has discussed the distinction we can make between representation and re-presentation:

---

58 For Rowe's description of his introduction to the short-wave radio and his philosophy of use see the interview by Dan Warburton (Warburton, 2001).

59 Though small networks and amateur radio may continue for many years.

60 It is a lo-fi soundscape in Murray Schafer's terms. Differentiation is negligible.

61 These may be metaphors for something else but not for the soundscapes which they re-present.

> This allows us to make a distinction between sounds which are meant to *resemble* ("... it sounds like ...") and sounds which *are* ("... that is the sound of ...") (ten Hoopen, 1994, p. 69 – '...' as in original).[62]

This strand of development moves clearly from the former to the latter. Of course this drive for 'accuracy' rests on many assumptions; there can be no single, agreed perspective for such a 'reality'. Furthermore, if acousmatically presented, recreation of the soundfield will, most likely, not correspond with the original as experienced *in situ*. Even when a visual image is present this may be the case. Sound design in film shows this to good effect – to recreate a sense of real space, many sound objects are exaggerated in perceptual presence and perspectives correspondingly distorted (Chion, 1994, especially Chapter 5).

The second tendency seems, at first sight, to be similar, but we can easily be misled. It has also been emerging at the same time and also aided by technological mediation. This is one in which the world (indeed the universe) is a source of systems information which may, but need not, originally have been accompanied by sound production. Its translation into a form of sound we want is the process of *sonification*. This, of course, involves the model and mapping choices we have discussed above. This enables an ever greater *metaphorical* sonic recreation of the world's phenomena.

For example, *Pithoprakta* is a *sonification* of gas molecule movement. We can, in fact, hear this movement in the form of microphone noise – air molecules randomly impacting on the diaphragm – which is inevitable at any temperature above absolute zero.[63] But Xenakis is sonifying the molecular trajectories which are, of course, soundless. All sonification of events that cannot in their original form be heard, or which are heard in a substantially different form, are metaphorical transcriptions.[64]

This is a profound model which lies at the heart of a wide range of music from algorithmic composition, to electronica, laptop improvisation, installation and internet music. Thus much of this activity is a re-externalization in sound of the processes and systems of the contemporary world. Sometimes the model has been literally built in (as in some algorithmic internet art). The system presents itself in sound consciously (even self-consciously). But in many cases the model has become internalized and sublimated, hardly conscious in its application even to the composer. Both of these streams 'aspire to the condition of the world'. I have already cited John Blacking's description of music as patterns of 'humanly organized sound' (Blacking, 1973). He might have had difficulty describing some of the work we are examining as *humanly* organized, although it has certainly been organized *by humans*. I am arguing that this is precisely the field where *animation* and *reanimation* comes to have meaning.

---

62 She concedes that the latter can be fragile and rests on a consensus of recognition of the source.

63 At which molecular movement would cease.

64 This is true even for sound events outside the audible range. We cannot strictly say 'this is what the ionosphere sounds like'. Too many such sonifications are presented without the translation to the sound we hear being made explicit (in an accompanying note).

Conclusion

In Chapter 1 we examined the increasing interpenetration of sound worlds and the erosion of labels such as 'abstract', 'imaginary', 'environmental' and 'synthetic'. In this chapter I have attempted to put some 'flesh on the bones' of the operation, to show how composers have increasingly extended their interests in 'non-musical' materials through the increasing use of *models and analogies*. Of course, in many ways this is but a return to some very primeval models of music as *revelation* of the world. I have suggested further that this process may be seen as *reanimation* – the opposite of the widely-held view that humans may one day disappear into a kind of machine-dominated cyber-reality. Reanimation of both sounding and non-sounding worlds through such 'models and mapping' and the consequent 'playing' of the soundscape as instrument have been presented as reaffirmations of life and 'live indicators' in music. It has emerged, however, that these reanimations are sometimes closer, sometimes more distant from human activity perceived as such. This is further discussed in Chapters 3 and 4.

CHAPTER THREE

The Human Body in Electroacoustic Music: Sublimated or Celebrated?

Introduction

> In opposition to all who would derive the arts from a single vital principle, I wish to keep before me those two artistic deities of the Greeks, Apollo and Dionysos. They represent to me, most vividly and concretely, two radically dissimilar realms of art. Apollo embodies the transcendent genius of the *principium individuationis*; through him alone is it possible to achieve redemption in illusion. The mystical jubilation of Dionysos, on the other hand, breaks the spell of individuation and opens a path to the maternal womb of being (Nietzsche, 1956, p. 97).

Nietzsche's division sets the individual and the group, if not at odds, then at least perceived as 'radically dissimilar'.[1] His discussion suggests they are, however, always present in some kind of spiritual struggle within art. But I wish to reread this in the light of contemporary developments: the Dionysian cannot deny human presence (it is its essence). But recorded music – especially acousmatic music – has removed the need for literal human presence in its making.

In chapters 1 and 2 'the environment' as a source of musical material both literally and metaphorically was a major focus. Living (usually human) presence was also discussed: what clues we might glean to come to know it in a musical performance (whether 'live' or studio produced). But this was a relatively dispassionate presence. In this chapter I want to look at how the *human personality* is actually 'celebrated or sublimated'[2] in a group of electroacoustic works. Beyond knowing (or believing) that I am in the presence of a human agent, what are they feeling? What are they trying to tell me? How am I involved or am I just a dispassionate observer (listener)? And what are the relationships of participating individuals or groups?[3] A real human presence in this sense must focus on a more personal (even intimate) set of cues and

---

1 While initially suggesting that all music was at root *Dionysian* and that the plastic arts and lyric poetry were *Apollonian*, his discussion ranges over all areas of interaction between the two principles across the arts in general.

2 This chapter originates from Emmerson (1999) and (2001a), and a preliminary paper given at a research study forum at City University, London ('Unpacking Pleasures in Musical Expression') in May 2002.

3 I am not covering gendered interpretations of these relationships of presence, or of the material types and metaphors made explicit for tonal music by Susan McClary (1991), but wish to draw attention to the urgent need for studies in this field. Hannah Bosma (publications on http://www.hannahbosma.nl) has made a substantial start.

clues. But rather like sound itself as it disperses in a sphere from its source, so human activity and 'personality' spreads out from the individual through immediate and local interaction, to larger groups and networks. Even at this stage in the twenty-first century we will not yet assume the complete dominance of technological mediation – at a primal level we still learn about such interactions in a direct physical way:

- *Heart beat*: we become conscious of this in ourselves at times of quiescence or stress, hear (or feel) it in others who are physically close;
- *Breath*: from the simple indication of an individual 'living and breathing' to an expressive indication of body state (from repose to 'ready for action');
- *Voice*: not disembodied in this case but expressing something personal: for example, a feeling, a desire, a personality;
- *Exchange*: conversation and interaction (one to one, one to many, many to many, many to one);
- *Touch and proximity*: the *sounds* of physical interactions (peaceful or hostile), the presence or absence of agents within the limits of personal space will vary with cultural and personal expectations;
- *Human movement*: a sense of both 'being and becoming' through a space or different spaces (this may be associated with narrative aspirations or the more intensive activity of dance).

Since the inception of *musique concrète* in 1948, human presence in general and human body sounds specifically have haunted the soundworld. This is not just through the obvious intrusion of the human voice into the discourse, but in reference to the body rhythms of limb, breath and heartbeat, and in the representation of personal and psychological spaces. In classical traditions we are not always at ease with these representations – anxiety and a certain tension are ever present. We rarely *celebrate* such a presence as distanced listeners (we do not *dance*) – although occasionally humour is allowed to break the tension – whereas in the more vernacular traditions, pleasure (and pain) are usually more directly articulated.

'Stockhausen vs the "Technocrats"' is the title of an article originally published in the *Wire* magazine in 1995. Dick Witts, while creating a programme for BBC Radio 3 sent a package to Karlheinz Stockhausen containing works by Aphex Twin (Richard James), Plastikman, Scanner (Robin Rimbaud) and Daniel Pemberton, asking him to comment. The artists were then shown the comments and given an opportunity to reply and the whole exchange was reported in this article. To most readers this must appear to be a hilarious document. Let us give just two quotations, firstly Stockhausen's advice:

> I wish those musicians would not allow themselves any repetitions, and would go faster in developing their ideas or their findings, because I don't appreciate at all this permanent repetitive language [...] I think it would be very helpful if he [Aphex Twin/Richard James] listens to my work[4] *Song of the Youth* ... Because he would then immediately stop with

4 *Gesang der Jünglinge* is consistently mistranslated; it should be *Song of the Youths* (there are three).

> all these post-African repetitions and he would look for changing tempi and changing rhythms … (Stockhausen et al., 2004, p. 382).

To which James replies (after listening to *Song of the Youth*[*s*]):

> Mental! I've heard that song before; I like it. I didn't agree with him. I thought he should listen to a couple of tracks of mine: "Didgeridoo", then he'd stop making abstract, random patterns you can't dance to. Do you reckon he can dance? You could dance to *Song of the Youth*, but it hasn't got a groove in it, there's no bass line (p. 383).

The relation between western 'art' musics and vernacular (or 'popular') musics in western society has a long and complex history; varying from engagement and synthesis to incomprehension and antagonism. Within this continuity there are periods of intensified exchange: in the 1920s, for example, it centred on jazz. Ravel, Stravinsky, Milhaud, Weill, Krenek, Shostakovich and many others (though not those usually associated with Schoenberg and his circle), absorbed elements of jazz 'style' (melody, harmony or instrumentation) into their western technique.[5] In the 1990s, however, the relationship with technology was a key focus, allied to an interest in repetition, looping and minimalism. There is a cautious consensus that this time around there was a profound difference. 'Art music' itself appeared to be increasingly isolated as a minority interest (not a new position to be sure, but increasingly emphasized). Within this, electroacoustic art music was joined and jostled by increasingly articulate genres of 'sound art' with entirely different origins.[6] These other genres had mostly been in existence for some considerable time but had been seen as part of an 'alternative culture' even 'underground'. In the postmodernist fragmentation and revaluation of genres, no one group could claim precedence as a 'mainstream'. As the network arrived in practice, it was quickly established that a more balanced exchange between different approaches to music (and sound art) making was possible. The most important new element was an attitude encouraged by the hybridization and integration inherent in the new digital media: *anything* could be incorporated into a musical syntax (Cutler, 2000; Waters, 2000). But I shall argue that some such exchanges are certainly not two way.

Stockhausen has published the correspondence from 1967 which gained permission to use his image on the sleeve of the Beatles' *Sergeant Pepper* album.[7] Increasingly an 'alternative' view of electroacoustic music history is appearing (in publications such as the *Wire* (UK)) which claims for all experimental music made with technology, a lineage including a mix of (typically) Varèse, Stockhausen, Xenakis, Cage, Pierre Schaeffer, Pierre Henry, Steve Reich and other '*avant-garde* pioneers' (Young, 2002; Cox and Warner, 2004). For individuals this is clearly true, and technologically true for them all. But while many experimental band members

---

5 And if 'jazz' is broadened to include other vernacular dance and music styles from Latin America, Europe and North America then the list is considerably longer.

6 Art School, Dada, sound poetry, hip-hop, many of the more experimental 'electro' styles (electronica, IDM). See Toop (1995 and 2004) for a ring-side view (or submarine journey) of this now vast arena (or ocean).

7 'Stockhausen and the Beatles' at http://www.stockhausen.org/beatles_khs.html.

turn out to have studied, or worked, with key 'classical' composers, there remains a divide, hard to bridge, between the two streams. This relationship is symbiotic. Reich, Henry, Parmegiani, Xenakis and others have been star guests (or at least their music has) at 'mixed' concerts with DJ-culture icons or have been remixed by electronica solo artists for CD.[8]

The borderline between reclaiming a history that has been unfairly appropriated by others and a process hinting at an almost defensive 'legitimation' is a fine one. The sentiments expressed in 'Stockhausen vs. the "Technocrats"' are refreshingly honest, direct and to the point. The admiration is clearly not only not mutual, it is hardly even one way. The question which arises for electronically created music may be posed as a balanced pair:

- Why exclude, even prohibit, regular, periodic, 'dance rhythms'?
- What are the consequences of their *inclusion*?

These questions are in themselves part of a larger discussion as to 'where' the human person is in much of the modernist 'art music' cannon – whether onlooker ('onhearer'), participant, distanced or immersed. This is simply a reframing of some of the endless list of dualities which has been used to describe this situation in the past: heart and brain, 'considered' and 'felt', Apollonian and Dyonisiac. Any synthesis in this dialectical struggle will be transient and illusory, as the flux of forces reconfigures and simple one-dimensional representations give away to multi-dimensional webs and networks.

The Roots of Music

This dualistic thinking tends to assume that music has its origin in the earliest experiences of our evolution, namely in the *body*[9] and in the *environment*.

The body

The body generates many rhythms and sensations with cyclic periodicities lying within the duration of short-term memory. The most important are breath, heart beat and the limb movements of physical work, dance and sex. These are a product of our biological evolution, our size and physical disposition in relation to the mass of the earth – hence its gravitational field – and would be different if we had evolved to be the size of a bat or an elephant or had the earth been a different mass.

8 For example: *Reich Remixed* by nine artists including Howie B, Coldcut and DJ Spooky (Reich et al., 1999); Pierre Henry is remixed by seventeen artists (including Fatboy Slim, Coldcut, William Orbit) on the album *Métamorphose* (Henry and Colombier, 1997); Parmegiani played the Cambersands Festival 2003 (curated by Autechre); Xenakis – *Persepolis Remixes* by nine artists including Merzbow and Otomo Yoshihide (Xenakis, 2002).

9 For this I am not assuming a mind/body duality – indeed in referring to the body, I refer to the 'total human animal' within which the mind is encapsulated.

The environment

The environment has a different timescale, both periodic and aperiodic and often beyond the limits of short-term memory. This often necessitates repeated listening (and observation) which encourages the consigning to long-term memory. This in turn stimulates contemplation and consideration of phenomena beyond our direct bodily control:[10] water (sea, rivers), wind, the seasons, landscape. This contemplation would include degrees of calculation and prediction, depending on the affordance of these phenomena to the observer. There also tends to be a degree of ritual observance associated with such *recurrence* (whether regular or not).

*

Body and environment are in perpetual interaction, of course, but sometimes uneasily. The relative values of contemplation and distance as against body action and involvement have varied from mutual support to outright hostility within the social fabric. There has always been an uneasy relationship of altar to maypole – often described in terms of a 'modern' religion with respect to its 'pagan' predecessors – alternating dramatically between destructive and punishing anger and wholesale appropriation, adaptation and absorption ('The day of the dead' in Mexico, for example). Early religious music of the European tradition articulated the contemplative (distanced) condition, banning nearly all aspects of body rhythm and expression for many centuries, aiming to create a sense of transcendental timelessness beyond that of the mere corporeal. Even breath was harnessed to the creation of long lines of chant, quite beyond the normal periodicities of regular breathing (especially if undertaking physical work). While the description of an activity such as singing plainchant as 'art' is quite recent, it embodies in prototype many of the values of what was to become musical art (in Europe) after the Renaissance: distance, contemplation and extended concentration.[11]

As the vernacular and secular European world invented 'art' as separate from religion, the emphasis shifted back from the timeless to the clear articulation of time (through meter and rhythm) – increasingly so from the period of the *Ars Nova*. This was finally crowned in the flowering of the Western Art Music tradition at the time of the Renaissance itself which increasingly threw the body and voice, dance and song, to the forefront of its discourse. But there is also a parallel flow. While we may not usually dance to the rhythms of the environment we have an apparently insatiable desire for mimesis of its sounds and their relations. From Jannequin's *Chant des Oyseaulx* through Beethoven's *Pastorale* Symphony to Debussy's *La Mer*, the relatively simple periodicities[12] of dance and song became progressively

10 A first version of ideas for this chapter (Emmerson, 2001a) wrongly gave the impression that the 'body' side somehow did not involve contemplation and consideration (and to an extent vice versa). Something I hope is better balanced here.

11 Although as Christopher Small (1998) has pointed out strictly silent concentrated listening at concerts only emerged as the norm in the nineteenth century.

12 In Western Europe but not many cultures in Africa, for example.

extended and distorted through the influence of these 'environmental' forces, finally being displaced altogether by the large gesture and the grand sweep of the elements – but always from a distance, in our memory and imagination.

In a letter to fellow composer Messager in September 1903 Debussy wrote:

> You perhaps do not know that I was destined for the fine life of a sailor and that it was only by chance that I was led away from it. But I still have a great passion for the sea. You will say that the ocean doesn't wash the hills of Burgundy and that what I am doing might be like painting a landscape in a studio. But I have endless memories, and, in my opinion, they are worth more than reality, which generally weighs down one's thoughts too heavily (Lockspeiser, 1978, p. 26).

But such memories were based on real experience. A friend of Debussy's reported in his memoirs an incident which probably happened in the early summer of 1889. During a holiday in Brittany he took a trip with a group of friends down the coast in a fishing boat in a terrifying storm. Debussy insisted on the trip against the captain's advice. After a while they were in serious danger. He is said to have remarked: 'Now here's a type of passionate feeling that I have not before experienced – Danger! It is not unpleasant. One is alive!' (Lockspeiser, 1978, p. 28).[13]

Many of the techniques of J.M.W. Turner (1775–1851) prefigured impressionism in painting. Debussy certainly knew Turner's work by 1891 and probably visited the National Gallery (where the best known were then housed) on his trips to London in 1902–3 at the time of writing *La Mer*. He later described Turner as 'the finest creator of mystery in art' (Lockspeiser, 1978, p. 22). His resonance with the artist was possibly based on shared experience. In 1842 Turner had undertaken a similar boat trip off the east coast of England. John Ruskin reports that the painter had commented:

> I did not paint it to be understood, but I wished to show what such a scene was like.[14] I got the sailors to lash me to the mast to observe it. I was lashed for four hours and I did not expect to escape but I felt bound to record it if I did. But no one had any business to like the picture (Tate Gallery, 1974, p. 140).

The result was his late masterpiece: *Snow Storm – Steam boat off a harbour's mouth making signals in shallow water, and going by the lead. The Author was in this storm on the night the Ariel left Harwich* (1842) (Tate Gallery, 1974, p. 127).

Debussy agreed with Turner that representation was not interpretation, and castigated Beethoven for over-literal representation in the *Pastorale* symphony:

> How much more profound an interpretation of the beauty of a landscape do we find in other passages in the great Master, because, instead of an exact imitation, there is an emotional interpretation of what is invisible in Nature. Can the mystery of a forest be

13 These comments by Debussy (and Turner, below) show strong parallels with remarks by Stockhausen and Xenakis on the (man-made) multi-media of military operations (especially from the air) during World War Two.

14 I interpret this sentence (adding emphasis) as in effect concluding '*felt* like' or 'was *like*'.

expressed by measuring the height of the trees? Is it not rather its fathomless depths that stir the imagination? (Debussy, 1962, p. 39).

Stravinsky's *The Rite of Spring* (1913) is an example of this confrontation at its most direct where the different rhythms of body and season meet in such a dramatic confrontation. The body dies at the end. This symbolic death was also in another sense very real: body and dance rhythms were never again to be central to the modernist aesthetic. *The Rite* left the world of western art music a dilemma. On the one hand there was the temporary response of neo-classicism with its appropriation of a wide variety of 'styles', including the dance rhythms of earlier centuries, jazz and popular musics.[15] On the other there was the continuation of romantic rhythmic rhetoric in the serial works of Schoenberg, which Boulez so detested.[16] Neither confronted this issue. The gauntlet was perhaps only picked up by Varèse and subsequently handed to Xenakis, the two progressively moving modernist musical language towards the environmental – of which science (since the Renaissance) has been the most ruthlessly 'objective', distanced and contemplative tool. After 1945 science and technology further expanded this environment to include the extremes of atomic and astronomic references (for example, Stockhausen's 'sound atoms' and 'constellations', both, interestingly, pointillist – these are discussed in Chapter 2).

The revolution of repetition

The recorded medium allows the literal re-presentation[17] of the sound of something – not just its mimicry through instrumental performance. Following the second world war, on separate continents John Cage and Pierre Schaeffer (with the assistance of others) gave the environment the apparently final and ultimate victory – the admission of all sound into the realm of potential music. Their meeting in 1949 in Paris remains a landmark moment as powerful as any of 1913. Their surprise at discovering the other had independently created the prepared piano and their shared delight in experiment with all sound and the power of recording to unleash its potential, gave way rapidly to disagreement on the role of the composer.

However the technology had hidden attributes that would never allow our binary divide to go away. Literal repetition of sound had been possible since the invention of recording, but constant repetition within short term memory time span had started as an accident. Schaeffer called it the *sillon fermé* (closed groove),[18] becoming shortly after the tape loop, in our own digital time set to the accuracy of a byte. Schaeffer (and later Steve Reich) observed how such regularly repeated sound rapidly loses its

15 Though not intended literally to be danced to by the listening public.

16 As expressed so clearly in his essay 'Schoenberg is Dead' (in Boulez, 1991).

17 Following ten Hoopen (1994) I distinguish *representation* which has a metaphorical implication – 'birds represent freedom' (Wishart) – and re-presentation, the 'presenting again' as (ideally) a repetition.

18 Schaeffer had limited control over 'loop' length with a nominally 78 rpm turntable; he had variable speed controls and could thus record at different speeds as well as playback transposed. The tape-loop based *phonogène* had a range of two octaves (Manning, 1993, p. 27).

source/cause recognition and becomes 'sound for its own sake' – even words when repeated tend to lose their meanings. Our listening focus changes and we become drawn inwards, immersed and perhaps even mesmerized. Thus (ironically) the ghost of body rhythms, moreover those linked to repetitious and mesmeric dance, and possibly immersion and loss of self into the group, come bounding back at the very moment the environment had apparently become completely available within the modernist tradition.

The revolt against the modernist mainstream which came to be known as 'minimalism' has the loop (at first tape but later played on instruments) as one of its major foundations. Steve Reich's first electronic work, a tape collage for the soundtrack of a movie *Plastic Haircut*, was made in early 1964 and constructed from loops of crowd noises (Potter, 2000, p. 162). Terry Riley experimented with shifting pattern tape loops, playing Reich the results (a work called *She Moves She*) at almost the exact time (late 1964) that Reich was discovering phasing techniques for what was to become *It's Gonna Rain* (Potter, 2000, pp. 117 and 165; also Reich, 2002, pp. 10 and 53–4). There are those for whom popular music and minimalism are both equally at odds with 'high art' ideals. Ironically, they argue that such exact repetition could be seen as *antagonistic* to the body – a *machine* rhythm, a prison rather than a liberation. Until relatively recently Stockhausen has overtly avoided metric music because of its connotations of militarism: a synchronized body rhythm had become a dangerous form of control:

> ... marching music is periodic, and it seems in most marching music as if there's nothing but that collective synchronisation, and this has a very dangerous aspect. For example, when I was a boy the radio in Germany was always playing typical brassy marching music from morning to midnight, and it really conditioned the people (Cott, 1974, p. 28).

Similarly, this was a perception exploited by Trevor Wishart in his classic work *Red Bird* (1973–77) (Wishart, 1992).[19] Rhythmic repetition is associated with 'factory' and 'machines'[20] which are here made from phonemes or 'body/animal' sounds:

> Each symbolic type is chosen because it either has a conventional symbolic interpretation (birds: flight, freedom, imagination; machine: factory, industrial society, mechanism) or such an interpretation can be easily established … (Wishart, 1996, p. 169).

The body is indeed ever present in *Red Bird* but imprisoned, even tortured.

But contrary to this view the loops (tape or instrumental) of minimalism restored the hope of ecstatic celebration – at least in the imagination if not directly on the dance floor.[21] If the loop had moved the focus unit back within short-term memory, the Midi revolution in the early 1980s opened the door directly to the return of body rhythm to the electroacoustic medium. While not confined to any group of

---

19 Discussed in Wishart, 1996, Chapter 8.

20 A similar view is taken in Charlie Chaplin's late silent movie classic *Modern Times* (1936) in its view of the factory as infernal dehumanizing machine.

21 Minimalism is cited as a major influence on some genres of Dance music and Reich has been sampled by The Orb (*Little Fluffy Clouds* (1991)) and in the DJ electronica album *Reich Remixed* (Reich et al., 1999).

composers this was clearly the case in the works of, for example, Alejandro Viñao (1990) and Javier Alvarez (1992) who insisted on retaining a central place for rhythm (sometimes based on Latin dance rhythms) within an electroacoustic milieu:

> Computer control of the electroacoustic environment makes it possible to formulate new pulse-based lines, polyphonies and resulting forms, reopening the chapter of pulse, rhythm and repetition which Europeans had 'declared' obsolete in the modernist 1950s … experimenting with new ideas derived from a multiplicity of sources (other cultures and the reformulation of Latin American rhythms) as well as those pulses and rhythms which can only be generated by computer … (Viñao, 1989, p. 42).

This 'instrumental' approach still maintained some distance from the source of its inspiration. As with the playfulness of (neo-classical) Stravinsky's rhythmic 'slips' and ambiguities, such pieces could never be an invitation *to actually get up and dance*. This approach nonetheless opened up once again a new engagement with a vernacular tradition. Steve Reich commented (in 1992): 'We are living at a time now when the worlds of concert music and popular music have resumed their dialogue' (Reich, 2002, p. 168). Some Schaefferian purists saw this as a betrayal. For them this was no 'return' at all, but its reverse – simply the extension of electroacoustic technology (not musical principles) into an instrumental discourse which had more easily maintained a relationship with the 'body' tradition (being in so many ways its extension). The advent of Midi, combined with the near contemporary sampler revolution, allowed and encouraged the free mapping of performance (body) gesture to sound. Instrument Midi controllers, drum machines and keyboards allowed and encouraged a new generation of 'technological' performance. The development of affordable technology for music production in the 1980s addressed ever more detailed levels of music information. Initially use of the small personal computer was limited to the manipulation and storage of 'events' (notes) in Midi format along with a limited amount of continuous (control) information. This handling of the simplest level of music score (step time) and performance captured information (real-time – simplified and excluding all but the most basic expressive functions) allowed rapid application in popular music which had always had its basis in the world of the body, of dance and of song.

But pertinent, too, is the fact that the music for 'chilling out' away from the dance floor was often called 'ambient' – a term and genre pioneered and developed by Brian Eno from the mid-1970s (Tamm, 1989, Chapter 10). This once again shifted the focus out to longer time scales. Eno's *Discreet Music* is one of the earliest ambient pieces. Dating from 1975, it is mostly automated: a synthesier with 'digital recall system' plays into an echo and tape delay system, 'two simple and mutually compatible melodic lines of different duration' (Eno, 1975). In this case the repetitions are clearly perceivable at a time scale of a few seconds.

> This[22] presented what was for me a new way of hearing music – as part of the ambience of the environment just as the colour of the light and the sound of the rain were parts of

22 The first sentence refers to an experience following an accident in which Eno found himself listening to a commercial recording at extremely low volume, barely audible.

> that ambience. It is for this reason that I suggest listening to the piece at comparatively low levels, even to the extent that it frequently falls below the threshold of audibility (Eno, 1975).

Later ambient works, developed through algorithmic generative programmes (such as SSEYO's Koan programme[23] to which Eno had been a consultant) can be created to ever longer time spans without exact repetition. Thus just as rhythm had once again 'invaded' electroacoustic 'art' music, so contemplation, distance and lack of short-term repetition had re-entered (so-called) popular streams.

From Events to Signals

Digital *signal* processing (as opposed to *event* processing) requires more intensive computing power. Whereas most software for signal processing had been developed in the 1970s, it remained the domain of powerful computers in large institutions throughout the most part of the 1980s. The information for (Midi) events had been severely simplified to the time-stamped ordering of 'notes'. For signals, the information is at an entirely different time scale, within the detailed and complex microsound. Much more had become possible than the recording, mixing and simple spectral manipulation available in the analogue studio. Thus affordable personal computers were not only able to address the Schaefferian tradition in the 1990s,[24] but were also able to extend and enrich it with practical and integrated applications of other disciplines. These include mathematics (chaos and fractals), acoustics (physical modelling), linguistics (generative grammars), psychology and psychoacoustics (timbral and spatial manipulations) and information science (including internet applications).[25]

Progressively throughout this period the dualities of modernism had given way to the pluralities of the postmodern: the continuous fragmentation, grouping and regrouping of ideas (Miller, 1993). Absolute boundaries between 'classical' and 'popular' forms become increasingly difficult to make out. The first stage of 'postmodernization' encouraged greater possibilities of interaction and exchange. The electroacoustic composer became increasingly open to many possible sources of influence and material beyond that assumed for the 'art' music tradition. This has included all recorded sound from the availability of 'world music' resources to the possible re-engagement with the body side of our divided universe (excluded by modernism) through Dance music. Dance itself exists in many fragmented streams (techno, house, drum and bass and so forth),[26] each in perpetual evolution, continually regrouping and interacting as befits an oral/aural music. It is possibly the

23 See www.sseyo.com (consulted December 2005).

24 Powerful signal processing programmes (including Cmusic, Andrew Bentley's *Groucho* and spectral transformation programmes by Trevor Wishart) were available for the Atari 1040, most notably through the Composers Desktop Project in the UK, from 1986.

25 Discussed as models for music in Chapter 2.

26 While there are a plethora of general articles and personal statements there is no definitive text to examine (let alone define terms for) this field. The most useful currently are

first popular music genre to be made with identical tools to an 'art' music relative. All of the hardware and much of the software can equally be used across the full range of genres. As important, its attendant DJ/club culture has articulated new listening modes, integrating sampling and mixing into the act of listening itself. The composer-performer-listener relation has shifted, allowed and encouraged by the technology. This might suggest that the scene had been set for a final *rapprochement* between body and environmental streams in music, even a healing of the mind/body duality through technological mediation. But as usual this has not been so simply attained, the emergence of *IDM*, 'experimental dance music' and *electronica* (and a host of other experimental sonic arts) has not brought an end to this distancing. These genres remain stubbornly separate from a mirror set of initiatives from within the 'art music' world. There are evidently persistent differences.

Ben Neill argues that rhythm, pulse and beat have been and remain fundamental in the development of music and that their exclusion from contemporary art music in the middle years of the twentieth century was an abberation initially set to rights by minimalism in the 1960s. Furthermore, following the technological revolution of the era, 'I saw then in the early 1990s that electronica was the new art music ...' (Neill, 2004, p. 389).

> Squarepusher's music and the work of others ... prove that it is possible for rhythmic electronic-music composers to work with the most abstract sound processes, experimental textures and techniques, as well as rhythmic materials that make reference to, but do not fit within, specific pre-existing dance music genres ... while popular electronic artists and audiences feel comfortable embracing the experimental sound production methods and ideas of art music, the crossover rarely goes the other way. High-art computer music that has not been directly influenced by minimalism and postmodernism remains elitist and disconnected from the larger cultural sphere, rendering it largely ineffectual as a twenty-first-century art form (Neill, 2004, p. 390).

This is accurate in its description of this mutual distancing but has the hint of a modernist 'only this way lies progress' line. 'High-art computer music [... is] disconnected from *the* larger cultural sphere' – (my italics) – is this sphere a single entity? And is 'being effectual as an art form' equated with a numerical 'popularity'? One of the saving graces of a postmodern view is that small group genres have a chance of staking a claim in a network of interacting nodes.

It is highly likely that 'high-art' composers will increasingly interact with post-dance electronic music, but possibly maintaining a critical distance and with very different aims and objectives. A minority interest is not necessarily an elite. But to come to terms with this accusation of elitism (undeniably true in literal historical terms) we must summarize a history in order to jettison its contemporary implications.

---

the entries for 'Electronica' and 'Intelligent Dance Music' in Wikipedia (http://en.wikipedia.org/wiki/Main_Page) – consulted April 2006.

From Involvement and Action to Distance and Contemplation

All music is functional. Whether to encourage productive movement (physical work), celebration, relaxation and entertainment (dance), or serious attention and contemplation, challenge and engagement, critique and reassessment, music has a role which must articulate or support that function. In turn that function can only be described in terms of the relationships supported within the social and economic structures of society.[27] Jared Diamond (1998, pp. 268–9) has delineated four stages of society's growth: band, tribe, chiefdom and state. The first two retain broadly subsistence economies with the second developing fixed dwellings and farming, and the latter two showing increasing differentiation of work function and authority. A subsistence society will tend to have musics that underpin and celebrate the work needed for that subsistence; only with surplus wealth and accumulation can there be room for specialist groups with their particular needs for music. In many societies developing along these lines the first such groups to emerge were the chiefs and elders, priests and shamans. As we observed above, in the short history of western music, plainchant (especially as it emerged in written form) is the first identifiable root for our western 'art' music.

First the church and then the state in the persons of princes and courts patronized their music.[28] As their own functions had grown further from the realms of repetitive physical work so their music reflected this shift to (so-called) aristocratic ideals, and their dance forms became ever more formal and remote from the 'vulgar vernacular'. Then with the rise of the industrial middle class in the late eighteenth century came the packaging of music (including classical music) into saleable commodity (Chanan, 1994). So art music increasingly became a kind of *commentary* (in metaphorical form) on the worlds of work and environment which I have claimed lie at their root. The sublimation of dance forms and a host of other signs and symbols from 'outside' music is a major characteristic of classical music (Agawu, 1991). This distancing which comes with such commentary is a kind of quotation:

- *Dance!* becomes "Dance";
- *Work!* becomes "Work"; and even
- *La Mer!* becomes "La Mer".

Lines of demarcation are blurred and can shift over time. John Dowland's galliards were probably composed to be danced to, whereas now they are 'concert music'. However with Mozart's minuets, some might make you want to get up and dance and may have been used as such, while others move a step away, on stage, 'out there'. Especially in the operas they become metaphors for 'those who dance'; in the finale to Act 1 of *Don Giovanni*, three dances are superimposed polymetrically to represent the characters' differentiated social status.

---

27 'I emphasize the importance of relationships because it is the relationships that it brings into existence in which the meaning of a musical performance lies' (Small, 1998, p. 193) as discussed in Chapter 1.

28 Whether originally described as 'art' is not at issue; it came to be so in the nineteenth and twentieth centuries.

In many cases the shift from action to quotation is conscious and deliberate. Art music has a long history of quoting from vernacular musics, since at least renaissance times (for example the many mass settings to use the melody of the fifteenth century popular song *L'homme armé*). In the late eighteenth and early nineteenth centuries, arrangements of folk music became a valuable commodity (Beethoven and Haydn both received such commissions). Then the wholesale appropriation of 'local music' into the mainstream repertoire of the so-called nationalist music traditions created an entirely new function for it as political and national focus. In 1904 Bela Bartok wrote to his sister:

> I have a new plan now, to collect the finest examples of Hungarian folksongs, and to raise them to the level of works of art with the best possible piano accompaniment. Such a collection would serve the purpose of acquainting the outside world with Hungarian folk music. Our own good Hungarians are much more satisfied with the usual gypsy slop (Griffiths, 1984, p. 17).

But this early approach (echoing the snobbery inherent in most nineteenth century appropriation of vernacular musics to 'higher status') gives way to a much more considered view in his later writing:[29]

> At the beginning of the twentieth century there was a turning point in the history of modern music. The excesses of the Romanticists began to be unbearable for many. There were composers who felt: 'this road does not lead us anywhere; there is no other solution but a complete break with the nineteenth century.' Invaluable help was given to this change (or let us rather call it rejuvenation) by a kind of peasant music unknown till then ... What is the best way for a composer to reap the full benefits of his studies in peasant music? It is to assimilate the idiom of peasant music so completely that he is able to forget all about it and use it as his musical mother tongue (Bartok, 1976, p. 340–1).

In the twentieth century the shift of jazz from a predominantly oral tradition to 'art' has shown parallel developments. The steady introduction of notation, 'theory', institutionalized pedagogy and copyright has contributed to a transformation of the oral tradition (Ake, 2002). This evolution has given us a fragmented spectrum of forms of jazz from those which retain their relation to dance and entertainment to those which demand concentration and contemplation, and probably repeated listening. The ghosts of these relationships, however, survive in our everyday tapping of feet or fingers to music, subconscious conducting of a band or orchestra, singing along to background music as it reinforces our body rhythms in shopping malls and train stations – and more overtly in self-absorbed 'air guitar' solos.

But the history of 'art' can also be seen as a history of exclusion from its production. At first through simple need: only those with authority and wealth commissioned and consumed art. Then in the era of the commodity, while mass consumption became possible, production remained in the hands of relatively few – the publishers, the promoters and the emerging 'star' system (Chanan, 1994). But in general we observe

29 Bartok was increasingly aware as his collecting became more widespread how inadequate the notation system of 'art' music was. His use of field recording was still followed by laborious transcription, often with innovative developments (for example, Bartok, 1976, p. 184).

the association of art necessarily with an elite, inherited, plutocratic or meritocratic. Thus forms of art became associated with social groups and their specific lifestyles, and not conceived as possessing qualities which could potentially be shared more widely. Our art music has evolved to be profoundly one of contemplation and distance from the bodily. Through a glass we darkly glimpse other places and spaces, other times and epochs. To say we lose ourselves in the music is to lose our corporeal sense. We put up with fixed and uncomfortable seats and the almost complete lack of communication with all but our nearest neighbours – the puritan ethic which imbues the ritual of the western art music concert (Small, 1998). But then again some claim *almost the same* attributes for (for example) some forms of dance music – the loss of self into the music and action; the ability (if you wish) to focus on minute details of sound quality and 'mix'. Some would even rate the venues as just as uncomfortable and discouraging of interpersonal communication.

To participate in any ritual we need to 'know the form', to have background information and experience to understand the procedures, the correct codes. But the 'double coding' believed to be a characteristic of post-modernist art by Charles Jencks (1986) relies, to a great extent, on a knowledge and understanding of *history* – generating a *self-referential* commentary within the tradition. This is as true for DJ/club culture as it is for the concert hall. It is as true for sample quotation in some hip-hop and dance music as for Berio's *Sinfonia* or the 'reworkings' of classics by Michael Nyman. But a contrary idea also plays a part: as many authors from Christopher Small to Tim Ingold have pointed out, art can *only* be of the here and now. We may call prehistoric rock painting 'art' but only because it functions as such to us; we have no definite idea what it 'meant' to its creators (Ingold, 2000, p. 130–1). Without such 'historical resonances', Purcell, Mozart, Berio – along with the many composers he quotes in *Sinfonia* – and Nyman become contemporaries. Our successors may progressively fail to decode the references, quotes and ironies – just as we increasingly fail to decode the symbolism in Bach, the 'jokes' in Haydn and the national anthems in Stockhausen's *Hymnen*.[30]

But something remains when this decoding fails: the works continue to 'signify', albeit progressively less what the composer intended from these references. Western musicology has tended to play up these *continuing* elements as evidence of a 'transcendental' aesthetic in art, usually abstract and denying anecdotal, extrinsically mimetic qualities.[31] Whether such a process will continue to apply to the postmodernism of quotation and irony when the references fail to communicate remains an open question:

> Therefore, to know whether art worthily fulfills its proper mission as initiator, whether the artist is truly of the *avant-garde*, one must know where Humanity is going, know what the destiny of the human race is ... (Gabriel-Désiré Laverdant (1845) quoted in Poggioli, 1968, p. 9).

30 See also the discussion in Chapters 2 and 4.

31 For example, programme music may be 'good' if the programme can be ignored and the more abstract 'musical construction' appreciated.

We no longer need to defend an '*avant-garde*', forging ahead into territory the rest of us will one day inhabit.[32] This was an intrinsically elitist argument whose historical baggage is now a burden. But the transition from elite to minority interest can be a difficult path. The 1950s *avant-garde* articulated the values of the modernist age and aesthetic. The key difference in our postmodern condition is that some may claim precedence within an assumed historical stream *but few will recognize such a claim*. Each of the coexisting interest groups in a noisy internet environment will claim its own criteria for value and quality. Giving up a claim to precedence is not the same as abandoning criteria for value. An example of this uneasy transition is reflected in changes in terminology. This can already seen in one English language description used about certain genres of electroacoustic music. In this field the term 'art' music is often replaced with 'academic' music. This tends to be that which the 'technocrats' (as described ironically above) use with reference to post-Stockhausen/Schaeffer 'concert hall music' approaches. This term is used to denote an over-reliance on theory, an inherent 'unpopularity' (even anti-popularity) and a perceived ivory tower separation from vernacular taste – in short 'elitism' reframed. But flowing against this view is a profound shift in the notions of 'popular' and 'minority interest'. In the world of the internet we are all in minority communities – yet conversely our constituencies of interest becomes potentially globalized.

The rest of this chapter will be devoted to examining a small group of works from the earliest in *musique concrète* to the most recent traditions which present us with an unavoidable sense of *corporeality*. This is felt not only in traces of the presence of a real human being and potentially personality, but also in music with a less distanced relationship to body rhythm and energy.

'*Solfège de l'Homme Sonore*'

A symphony in the pre-classical sense of *sinfonia* (a 'sounding together'), the *Symphonie pour un homme seul* of Pierre Schaeffer and Pierre Henry originally consisted of 22 movements at its première in March 1950. Later 'definitive versions' reduced this to 11 for broadcast in 1951 and for Maurice Béjart's ballet of 1955,[33] and 12 for the revised version, the stereo remix by Pierre Henry, of 1966.[34] The work was originally composed on turntables (1949–1950) – tape machines were introduced to the *musique concrète* studio only in 1951. Schaeffer (later) described the *Symphonie* as '... an opera for blind people, a performance without argument, a poem made of noises, bursts of text, spoken or musical (Schaeffer, 1973, p. 22). During what he called the period of gestation of the *Symphonie*, he sketched ideas for the sound material in his diary, imagining sounds, their sequences and combinations.

> The lone man should find his symphony within himself, not only in conceiving the music in abstract, but in being his own instrument. A lone man possesses considerably more than

32 For a discussion of the emergence of the 'avant-garde concept' see (Nochlin, 1968).

33 The sequence was re-ordered for the ballet and one movement reinstated, another dropped.

34 Used on *Pierre Schaeffer – l'œuvre musicale intégrale* (Schaeffer, 1990).

> the twelve notes of the pitched voice (*voix solfiée*). He cries, he whistles, he walks, he thumps his fist, he laughs, he groans. His heart beats, his breathing accelerates, he utters words, launches calls and other calls reply to him. Nothing echoes more a solitary cry than the clamour of crowds (Schaeffer, 1952, p. 55).

Schaeffer immediately started to construct scales 'from noise to musical sounds', dividing the material into sounds 'interior' and 'exterior to the man' (Schaeffer, 1952, p. 64).[35]

The first performances and broadcasts of *musique concrète* in Germany (including the *Symphonie*) were well received. According to Schaeffer (1952, p. 113) the *Symphonie* was 'welcomed with enthusiasm' at the Darmstadt *Ferienkurse für neue Musik* of 1951 and subsequently broadcast on the radio networks based in Hamburg, Cologne and Baden-Baden, while Munich devoted an hour and a half to a discussion on *musique concrète*.[36] During the *Ferienkurse* that year, Schaeffer joined Robert Beyer, Herbert Eimert and Werner Meyer-Eppler[37] in the historic seminar *Musik und Technik*. This was to lead to the foundation of the WDR studio in Cologne and the formalization of their philosophy of electronic sound synthesis and processing as the basis for composition.

Schaeffer and Henry's next major enterprize was an *opéra concrète*, *Orphée 53*, composed for the Donaueschingen Festival of 1953. Its performance created a scandal. Schaeffer's description of the event gives the impression that the audience was scandalized by a combination of neo-classical imagery, tonal reference in the instrumental music, but finally by the 27 minute long finale *Le Voile d'Orphée* (Pierre Henry's creation) with no accompanying action (Schaeffer, 1973, p. 23). This work – the only part of the music to have survived in performance[38] – is intensely expressionist. Sounds shift from truly acousmatic to 'representations' of Orpheus's lyre (harpsichord); the whole of the second half is based on the Orphic Hymn (invoking Zeus) declaimed in Greek with increasing passion and intensity. The earlier acousmatic 'veil sounds' give way to the 'lyre' which joins the struggle of the voice of Orpheus as he dies. It was this dramatic expressionist intensity (sustained over such an extensive time) that was anathema to the 'new music' festival aesthetic of the 1950s and led to the alienation of the Paris group:

---

35 Peter Manning's description (1993, pp. 24–26) is useful but he gives the wrong impression translating 'extérieur à l'homme' as 'non-human'. All the sounds are of human agency.

36 Although Elena Ungeheuer reports a performance of Schaeffer and Henry's *Toute la Lyre* (*Orphée 51*) at Darmstadt that year, four days after its Paris première, of which she reproduces a page of the programme (Ungeheuer, 1992, pp. 112–14).

37 Along with Theodor Adorno and Friedrich Trautwein among others. There had been a smaller such seminar the previous year at Darmstadt with papers from Beyer and Meyer-Eppler.

38 Henry created a shorter ballet version of *Orphée* in 1958 (issued on LP); both the original version, *Le voile d'Orphée I*, and a shorter version (part of the ballet), *Le voile d'Orphée II*, have been reissued on CD (Henry, 1991 and 1987, respectively).

> It is thus that we lost the battle of Donaueschingen[39] and that we were plunged for years into international reprobation, while there rose in the sky of Cologne, a dawn favourable to the hereditary and electronic enemy! (Schaeffer, 1973, p. 23).

Yet the philosophy of the *Groupe de Musique Concrète* moved in any case to less expressionist materials; human agonies and struggles so directly represented, as in the *Symphonie* or *Orphée*, were quickly abandoned. Pierre Schaeffer left the group in 1953, to return in 1957 when he helped reform the studio into the *Groupe de Recherches Musicales* launched in 1958. From that time the accent on 'research' was explicitly to exclude the anecdotal, expressive and personal qualities of sound. Something Luc Ferrari was to reject.

Tone of Voice

Luc Ferrari is well known for his relaunch of an interest in source recognition and the creation of soundscape narratives with his so-called *anecdotal music* (examined in Chapters 1 and 2). But less extensively discussed is his approach to intimacy – and even issues of privacy and possession. In an interview with Brigitte Robindoré he discusses a recording he made of a 'women encountered in a German market who plays with her voice while buying a kilogram of potatoes'; he goes on:

> How that women buys the potatoes is a mysterious and profoundly human thing and a profoundly sensual thing, too … Indeed, I preserve bits of intimacy, like stolen photographs … I bring it into my intimate world – my home studio – and I listen to her again. And here an extraordinary mystery is revealed … I am discovering this act in the studio as a blind person, as there are no more images … Speaking is so intimate. It comes from the deepest part of us: from both the head and the sexual organs, from the heart and from all that we can imagine. Speaking is a place where everything comes together (Robindoré, 1998, p. 15).

Music Promenade (1969 on Ferrari, 1995) is described as an 'anecdotal environment' originally for four independent tape tracks. Each is constructed from relatively long fragments of music (from military bands to 'memories' of his own instrumental music), television speech, singing, crowd sounds and many other human-produced sounds, as well as mechanical sounds such as those of the artist Jean Tinguely's constructions. Ferrari was one of the first composers to acknowledge and use the 'grain of the medium' – deliberate use of analogue distortion 'speaks' directly of (pre-digital) television soundtrack and AM radio recording which is their origin. But more interesting is what is distorted: we hear recurring loud and exaggerated laughter. In the concluding section he uses the voices of two young women from Hamburg (a clip from the soundtrack of his own short film *Les jeunes filles*).[40] The combination of anxiety in their speech, the pauses and intakes of breath, are exaggerated by some very subtle electroacoustic manipulation. The distant lo-fi recording is simply delay-

39 Which he had just referred to as 'une sorte de Waterloo'.

40 Hans-Jörg Pauli (publication undated, written 1969) sleeve note to LP (Ferrari, 1969?) from communication with the composer.

echoed in mono.[41] The alienation is palpable and unnerving. The work profoundly disturbs us in just the voyeuristic manner that Ferrari describes above. Is it right that we are listening in?

We examined in Chapter 2 the two electroacoustic works composed by Luciano Berio which foreground language and the voice. There the approach was structural (the language model as generator of materials). But here we must go further: this is not just any voice but that of Cathy Berberian. *Omaggio a Joyce* (1958 on Berio, 1968?) develops as material her reading of the eleventh chapter of Joyce's *Ulysses*. *Visage* (1961 on Berio, 1967) foregrounds her personality (as actor) directly representing emotional states through paralanguage, utterance, vocal (but non-verbal) gesture. Where *Omaggio* is a seemlessy integrated work where word becomes texture through technology, *Visage* is directly confrontational. The strong human presence stands before a synthetic sound canvas, crude and 'electronic' – while not seemingly derived from 'human sounds' as such, its sound world is visceral and contains short glimpses of language imitation. David Osmond-Smith (1991, pp. 63–4) reports that this 'performance' of the vocal part was assembled from recordings of improvised monologues using all kinds of vocalizations and inflections but without the use of actual words. Berio himself described her voice as 'almost a second *"studio di fonologia"* for me' (Dalmonte and Varga, 1985, p. 94).[42]

> … she performed vocal gestures – for instance, characteristic English and Hebrew intonations, the inflexions of television speech, of Neapolitan dialect, and so on … To start with I was thinking of *Visage* as a soundtrack for an imaginary drama (Dalmonte and Varga, 1985, p. 146).

The overall form of the work creates a narrative arch constructed from these paralinguistic states. The result was deemed 'obscene' by RAI-Milan (within which the studio was based) and banned from broadcast (Osmond-Smith, 1991, p. 64). The increasing intensity of the 'erotic curve' of the opening section, is released (apparently) in humour. But the laugh is nervous, and more complex and ambiguous emotions are developed as the piece progresses. The soloist is not only a prisoner in an increasingly oppressive sound world, but one in which sonic violence is evidently attempting to suppress her voice (literally).

The Composer Re-emerges from the Shadows

In Luc Ferrari's *Presque Rien no.2* (*Ainsi continue la nuit dans ma tête multiple*) (1977 on Ferrari, 1995) the intensely quiet voice of the composer (and very occasionally his female companion) comments on some of the sounds and feelings evoked. The very medium that excludes the visual domain allows the composer as presence to re-

41 Hearing your own speech delayed live causes stuttering.

42 Hannah Bosma has argued convincingly that her input constitutes co-authorship of both these works. Certainly in an electroacoustic tradition which values the creation of sonic material as part of the act of composition (and not prior to it), as well as in the world of co-authored improvisation this case would be taken seriously (Bosma, 2000).

emerge into their own piece *intermittently* – when silent the presence may be sensed but not confirmed. This often foregrounds the very technology that enables that to happen. Ferrari described the work after completing it as a:

> Description of a landscape of the night which the sound catcher tries to encompass with his mic.s, but the night surprises the 'hunter' and penetrates his head. It is then a double description: the interior landscape modifies the exterior night, adjusting it, it juxtaposes there its own reality (imagination of reality); or, one could say, psychoanalysis of its landscape of the night (Ferrari, 1980).

Even the smallest indication that there is 'an interpreter' (the composer) between us as listeners and the soundscape radically changes our relationship to it. The person behind the voice is a listener, too, but one captured in the frame. The first listeners were in the piece and encourage us (in whispers) to join them. When Ferrari describes the interpenetration of internal and external, we only have the external world of the loudspeakers. He is in effect suggesting the listening experience is our 'psychoanalysis' of what can only be an internalized experience (we were not there, we can only join them in our imagination – but that is powerful enough). The personal and landscape frames[43] are superimposed and interpenetrate: but in part 2 of the work a third frame interjects – an instrumental recording, distant and echoed, difficult to place 'out there' at all, almost an atmosphere rather than a place. Then in part 3 yet another frame interjects, a recorded electronic space quite dry, hence apparently abstract and separately focused from the other two 'outdoor' spaces (Ferrari, 1995).

In *Kits Beach Soundwalk* (1989 on Westerkamp, 1996) Hildegard Westerkamp both presents and represents herself along with the soundscape. However she is not strictly integrated with it (as in the Luc Ferrari), as her voice is separately recorded and distinct in studio (lack of) ambience.[44] Furthermore she 'plays with' the studio's technological possibilities to mimic, foreground, highlight and 'read' aspects of the 'natural' recording, not keeping the technological processes from us but presenting them as essential parts of the work. Hence the recording process is brought centre stage: she is present in front of us 'playing' the studio.

The composer makes regular appearances in the (113 minute) course of *Hymnen* where he is 'Stockhausen' (evidently the composer of the work) rather than 'a casino croupier' or a voice simply reading a list.[45] In *Region II: 2. Zentrum* (at 18'07" into the region), there is a moment where we hear the composer in conversation in the studio ('Otto Tomek sagte …'); that conversation is then played back and re-recorded *clearly in the studio* (capturing its ambience). Stockhausen is playing with layers of recorded time in such a way as to draw maximum attention to the recording process and the studio as artefact – as his assistant, David Johnson remarks 'We could go yet another dimension deeper'. But this exchange also reinforces the substance of the conversation. Stockhausen had included a quote from the Nazi marching song the

43 In Chapter 4 these are defined as 'local' and 'field' frames respectively.

44 There is a German language version of *Kits Beach Soundwalk* (Westerkamp, 1995).

45 Such as in Region I (9'31"-11'49"): 'Rouge, rouge […] "Winsor & Newton's Artists Watercolours"' (page 4 of the reading score).

Horst Wessel Lied on hearing which Otto Tomek[46] commented that it might arouse ill feeling. The composer responds: 'But I didn't mean it that way at all. It is only a memory.'[47] The very different recording quality for the 'memory' (a 'distant' lo-fi recording of the 1930s) was a 'window onto the past' in just the same way the artefact of the layers of recorded conversation remove us out of any abstraction and ground us rapidly in real time. The double perspective of the recording of a recording is perfectly mirrored in a 'window onto the historical past' within the flux of the work itself. The personal reflects the global – and Stockhausen was there in both cases; it is a very real memory.

Then there is the 'disembodied breath and voice' of *Region IV*. If we know the composer's voice then the breathing is clearly Stockhausen's with his characteristic vocal tract formant features.[48] This is reinforced through the two 'signatures' of this region – the spoken word 'Pluramon' – inserted twice into the breathing sequence (at 26'57" and 29'03 into the Region). Once the voice characteristic has been imprinted upon our perception the breathing clearly belongs to the same person. The composer has indicated he made some small edits but the breathing sequence contains long sections 'as recorded'.[49] The tendency for the listener to want to synchronize their own breathing with that in the work is very strong and empathetic.

Human presence in acousmatic music is often fundamentally frustrating even when joyous and celebratory rather than threatening or cruel. It represents a displaced 'other' – the other side of an impenetrable curtain. We hear (and hence observe) but we cannot communicate back. This will increase our unease – our frustration even. Thus sublimation and absence is often easier for us to handle, or perhaps we invoke humour to relieve the tension. We might be more comfortable with the abstract. We have eyelids to close, or mobile heads to look away to avoid discomforting moments in film, but no earlids to exclude sound. Fingers in, or hands on the ears are a poor self-conscious substitute. But the reminder of body involvement given us by dance references triggers an altogether different response. The human presence that is represented in the music is not individual but group inspired, celebratory and Dionysian.

Reengagement with the Dance (Electronica and IDM)[50]

Much has been written about a contemporary hybridization of possibilities, even genres of electroacoustic music (Waters, 2000), and how contemporary art music and

46 Head of the New Music Department at *West Deutscher Rundfunk* at the time.

47 The conversation is transcribed in detail in the programme booklet to Stockhausen Verlag CD 10. This even includes designating the 'time layers' described here.

48 This is strictly true also of the 'croupier' and 'red list' voices mentioned above, but they come across as 'anyone' voices whereas the sheer close presence of the breathing in *Region IV* ensures it is intimately dominant in the sound image.

49 Booklet to Stockhausen CD 10.

50 A definition of these terms is impossible. They refer to a cluster of practices, emerging from the late 1980s (though with many precursors) from a group of musicians and DJs – loosely centred on club culture – who refer to but stretch way beyond bounds the conventions

popular music have restarted their discourse (Reich, 2002). Nonetheless there remains a certain antagonism between 'art music' and 'experimental/club electroacoustics' as noted above. This is, of course, no barrier to the creative and eclectic musician from any background and bridges will appear in unexpected places. But common tools as flexible as today's may be applied to a wide variety of ends. I sense that there has been an assumption (deemed a 'fear' by some) that the removal of barriers might somehow lead to a 'greying out' of styles and approaches. From the 'art' side this has sometimes been perceived as a threat which might lead to 'dumbing down'. But such hybridization may mean the creation of new identities, not necessarily the loss of established ones – and in any case all genres were originally hybrids of previous strains. The approach in the discussion that follows is intended to make a first move to see if there are useful insights to be gained from attempting to establish more constructive exchange points in discussing the world of electronica and IDM.[51] By these terms is meant experimental electronic music forms which have emerged from a cross-cultural mix of (mostly) popular and (some) art-music influences.

Simply to apply the existing tools of the art-music tradition would fail to reveal significant elements of its meaning and experience.[52] Any musical phenomenon can be 'analysed'; the question is simply what kind of analysis is appropriate for the genre in hand and to what ends. This might include a 'leading in' to the musical relationships within the work, an explanation of how it arose historically and socially or a descriptive taxonomy with semiotic interpretation. An analytical tradition is also 'about' a kind of academic legitimation which often divides the practical music making community, as eventually academic discussion and practical pedagogy interact. Jazz has been transformed through this process; and other popular music making forms are following. With the establishment of such an infrastructure, it is not long before issues of authentic performance practice emerge. The cutting edge of each genre seems to gather in its wake a range of simultaneous 'authentic' histories. The same is true of electroacoustic music. As our current view sees the reduction of barriers between genres, so their histories begin increasingly to cross-reference. Thus the application of amplification and the invention of the guitar pickup (to be discussed further in Chapters 5 and 6) seem themselves to 'rewrite' other histories of recording and radio (which in turn contribute their own 'rewriting').

The analysis of electroacoustic music in its high art form is still in its adolescence but with the slow emergence of a language which is fundamentally post-Schaefferian (so far, at least when based on a listener and object-oriented approach). There is

---

of techno, dance genres and other electronically-produced popular musics. Some claim influence from the 'art scene' avant-gardes from Duchamp to Schaeffer and Stockhausen. Terms have become increasingly confused with the addition of the decription *laptronica* and the emergence of genres which drop rhythmic pulse and beat from their core repertoire (including such as *microsound* and *glitch*) (see Cascone, 2000 and 2003).

51 As opposed to discussing their *composition*; I am here concerned with how we listen to and talk about genres with substantially different aesthetic presumptions and artistic aims but with much in materials and evident technical tools in common.

52 There are elements of circularity in many analytical traditions: Schenkerian analysis arose from – and is best applied to – the classic-romantic sonata-form repertoire; applied to other classical genres it tells us less; applied to minimalism, nothing.

evidently an element of circularity here, especially when post-Schaefferian principles went into the creation of the work. This approach to analysis downplays contextual (and sociological) elements and is the heir of a tradition that sees the 'work' as somehow transcending all instances of its performance. For an art-form premissed on the *experience of sound* this is a paradox and presupposes an ideal listening environment broadly common across the range of works considered.[53] It brackets out the *real* context of the listening experience and how this influences the identity of the work.

It is evident in approaching the broader sweep of electronica that a vast new set of indicators is at work compared with the art tradition. There are influences on the one hand from a wide range of *avant-garde*, ambient and post-techno sound materials, on the other the production values for new listening, venue and dissemination habits emerging from the club, small venue, walkman and internet. Thus any attempt to encapsulate or explain the breadth of electronica will have to draw on both the sociological and phenomenological traditions of discussion which are discussed in Chapter 1. In choosing a group of works to examine, I included a number of the pieces sent to Stockhausen in 1995 for his comment (Stockhausen et al., 2004, p. 381): Aphex Twin (*Ventolin*, *Alberto Balsam*), Scanner (*Dimension*), Plastikman (*Sheet One*),[54] supplemented by an updated set by the same composers as well as some other well established electronica artists (Squarepusher and Autechre). While I was not assuming any commonality, continuity or coherence in style, there is in fact a lot in common: some material types as well as attitudes to spaces, their layering and manipulation.

But *where* we listen to the music is profoundly important to the definition of these new genres as is the *function* of the recorded trace of the work. The ideal environment (assumed for the art music tradition) simply cannot be defined. From personal stereo, home listening, to club remix the 'same' work may profoundly change. It is one of the clichés that listeners from the art music tradition too readily bracket together different tracks intended for very different performance situations. To complicate matters further, it is evident that these performance situations are not always easily separable. A piece mixed for personal listening may be profoundly influenced by the large scale venue experience of the composer and contain 'traces', distortions and artefacts more commonly found there. These 'worlds' where the music is heard leave traces in the music that the experienced listener knows (even if subconsciously).[55] I have therefore chosen not to examine any individual piece exhaustively, but to discuss the music under a series of short headings or 'pointers' all of which seem to speak of listening experiences common to a wide range of works. The observations make no claim to objectivity. I am, however, suggesting that – as critical listening is common to all the traditions discussed in this book – we might see the beginnings of a discourse based on a non-technical descriptive language of *what we hear*. I intend to avoid detailed reference to the Dance (and

53 See the discussion on loudspeaker performance in Chapter 6.

54 These are Aphex Twin (1995), Scanner (1995), Plastikman (1993) respectively.

55 These are thus emic differences not recognized as significant by outsiders.

other) music genres and sub-genres which are continuously referenced.[56] To use Kofi Agawu's terminology these references to other genres are *extrinsic* – they may at first sight appear to be intrinsic to the music but point outwards and refer to entire social cultures of their time (even when not intended by the composer). As with all the other music we have discussed those references will progressively dissolve over time in both individual and collective memory.

Listening Ambiguity

If the work exists only where the performance exists (and that may be in more than one form) then this is where critical listening should take place. But the performance space can be a home or personal system as well as a communal space. There is often much ambiguity as to where the 'performance' of individual works (as found on recorded media: vinyl or CD) is best sited. Some are painstaking studio creations, others use the studio as real-time tool – the recording paradoxically returning once more to documenting the performance activity. The relationship to re-mix and club culture varies from album to album, song to song. Some songs are more suitable for personal listening, others for remix, and many make no distinction.[57]

Artefacts/Disturbance/Distortion

Much twentieth century writing on western music placed noise not on a continuum of sound categorizations but as a separate characteristic outside of discussions of timbre and tone colour. Instrumental tone production had become increasingly uniform, standardized and 'clean'[58] over the course of the nineteenth century and noise was seen in acoustics texts as somehow an 'error' outside of the perfect model of the instrument. It was partitioned off within 'percussion' instruments, or considered as a specialist subset of 'attack' within the sound (see discussion in Chapter 1). Paradoxically, at the same time mainstream western classical music embraced a vast increase in the use of noisy percussion instruments from Mozart to Mahler and Webern. Finally the Futurists, Varèse and Cage (amongst others) began its rehabilitation. Jacques Attali has discussed its role as social indicator through sound and music production (Attali, 1985), other writers as a meaningful product of generation procedures and practices (Xenakis, 1992; Roads, 1996, Chapter 8).

---

56 I acknowledge that a definitive text on this subject would attempt to unite the historical, referential and phenomenological listening approaches. Here I concentrate on the latter.

57 For example, Aphex Twin's *Selected Ambient Works Volume II* (1994) is available in three formats: the Limited Edition UK (brown) vinyl, the regular vinyl edition and the Warp Records CD. See also Autechre's interview with Paul Tingen (2004) which raises some of these distinctions.

58 Other cultures have not had the obsession with purity of tone production. For example the sawari noises added to Japanese traditional instrument performance (biwa and shamisen) and the vibrating 'buzz' objects attached to the African sansa (mbira) which have the effect of obscuring pure tone.

As an almost exact mirror image of its increased presence in twentieth century western music practices, the recording and media technology took the *minimization* (and eventually elimination) of noise and distortion as an avowed aim. In the fourth quarter of the twentieth century recording quality improved to exceed the limits of human perception, theoretically having the capacity to become 'transparent' to the transmission of sound. That is where the first counter-revolution occurred. It is much easier to ascertain if a channel is 'faithful' in transmission if we recognize the sound transmitted and know what it should sound like. The presence of noise is a clear indication of a 'lack of fidelity'. This was traditionally considered an inadequacy to be 'improved'. Distortion, tape hiss, vinyl surface noise, low bit rates – all in their time were considered transitional to something 'better'. But they are also 'the grain of the system',[59] a signifier (a signature) of its idiosyncrasy and character, but also its 'time stamp' (its *timbre*). Such noise is identified with *the limits of systems* (both analogue and early digital). This factor is then turned on its head. A recognizable sound is overdriven, scratched or undersampled – clearly 'misrepresenting' the original in a way which gives the sound a characteristic *difference*: there are many examples in *I care because you do* (Aphex Twin, 1995). There may also be more than a hint of nostalgia. Aphex Twin (Richard James, born 1971) is of the generation to have worked through the final decade of transition (in the mainstream media) from analogue to digital formats and has 'remained true to vinyl' through the issue of tracks on this format before CD.[60]

In addition to such 'large scale' noise, there are more nuanced small noise artefacts. The 'cleanness' of samples (expected in slick pop music productions) is frequently subverted in small ways: small glitches; small distortion artefacts (on attacks) as well as deliberately 'cut short' reverb. While originally a product of lo-tech environments, home studios (including analogue and early digital gear), all of these noise artefacts can become a deliberate 'anti-hifi' nuance. These function both as an assertive 'memory of origins' in a less sophisticated environment and also a statement against the fake 'over-produced' perfection of the commercial world.[61]

Layering Spaces: Somewhere-Everywhere

In many Aphex Twin tracks there is an extraordinary distance – that amounts to a contradiction – between the techno rhythm layer and an ambient layer, for example in *drukqs* (Aphex Twin, 2001). The perspective sense of space is static for the duration of a song. The rhythmic drive is close with usually no reverberation, dense and overdriven, often distorted. It is often effectively centre mono, close, claustrophobic

59 See Barthes (1977) – *The grain of the voice* – also grain is one of Pierre Schaeffer's *three criteria of material* within his *morphological criteria* (Schaeffer, 1966; Chion, 1983).

60 I would distinguish this from the overtly nostalgic feel of some of the music in *drukqs* (Aphex Twin, 2001) which uses modal melodies, close-mic prepared piano, 'hints' of speech – all influenced by his professed use of 'lucid dreams' as inspiration (Young, 1995).

61 From the earliest fuzz guitar effects through punk and Lou Reed's *Metal Machine Music* overdrive distortion has been associated with the cacophony of hedonism and rebellion (Worby, 2000).

and 'boxed in'. There are only occasional streaks out to the stereo field. The ambient layer is far distant, sometimes seemingly unrelated in beat structure. It is strongly reverberated, having a wider image but with imprecise detail. This distant layer reaches towards us but never succeeds in arriving. There is always an 'impossible' or surreal relationship of the layers; they do not exist in the same space – and often not really in the same time. There is no transformation, and no mediation between these two worlds – a cohabitation without exchange.

The ambient layer itself is the foreground, of course, in those tracks described as such. In Aphex Twin's (1994) *Selected Ambient Works Volume II*, for example, the perspectives become correspondingly distorted. In those tracks featuring piano solo, spatial reverberation is replaced by piano resonance in absurdly close images; we are hovering inside the piano close to the strings – the audio equivalent of iMax cinema means the piano becomes an enveloping sensation. The ambient feel is no new age experience, no easy listening, even when isolated from the rhythmic pulse of the more techno-influenced pieces. The atmospheres range from strange and distanced, through alienated to disturbing. Ambiences 'naturally' drift: but instruments sometimes come adrift and simply move aimlessly across the otherwise static scene.

In many albums the central core of much of the rhythmic activity is focussed in a near-mono image. This is, of course, 'everywhere' when played back on a large sound system. Interestingly reverberation tends to have the same effect even for sources 'positioned' in a stereo mix; the original has a position, the reverb is only an uncorrelated mix of everything everywhere. Thus the ambient layer in many works is a different kind of 'everywhere' – amniotic and immersive.

Movement, Space and Virtuosity: Real and Imaginary

In the discussion in Chapter 4 the space frames of a 'real' environment from stage through arena to soundscape are considered as elements of the composer's toolbox. But in this music the frames themselves have a ghostly reference to a history in mechanical music. Each of the layers in many Aphex Twin, Squarepusher or Autechre tracks still indicate their origins in very 'classical' popular music models as developed through Dance genres. Not only the central and dominant position of the percussion space but in the 'impossible' acoustic spaces juxtaposed in the mix. The difference is that here these form the objects of *play*. In this music the spaces are much more elastic: what happens within the audible frame changes shape, size and layout at will. This influences how we hear the frame, what it represents becomes flexible and unreliable (in terms of real-world parallels).

We know the rhythm track is programmed as it has been for more than 20 years. But the perceiver's ear still associates extraordinary bpm rates, superhuman hit rates and impossible drum sound combinations as 'virtuoso'; the same energy generation and excitement follows. In Squarepusher's *Go Plastic* (Squarepusher, 2001) the virtuosity shifts to the surreal and extraordinary – the kit becomes plastic and elastic at once. Moving out from a mono centre image to wide stereo (and beyond) it grows and contracts like an organism, sometimes at bizarre speeds. The medium becomes the instrument.

Pitch: Modality – Melancholy

Post ecstatic, post exuberant ambient listening is very often melancholic. It is a recurrent historical trend in English-speaking countries especially that the expression of melancholy and nostalgia falls back on modality. Aphex Twin's simple repetitive melodic lines lie quietly but clearly in the ambient layer at some distance from the listener. In *drukqs* an almost 'folky' atmosphere comes across. There are occasional pentatonic references, too, in this album and in *Selected Ambient*. But whenever there is over-familiarity there is an antidote – an *estrangement*, most often a detuned (or retuned) pitch within the mode – something thrown in to surprise and possibly irritate within an otherwise banal melodic sequence.

Materials and Moment Forms

The archeology of the soundworlds of electronica would be a (much needed) book in itself.[62] There seem to be five generic streams, all with clear historical precedents: the rhythm stream, rhythmic bass line (usually synthetic), the sustained ambient layer (usually synthetic), real-world sounds (recognizable samples), melodic line (more or less pitched). These can all 'cross over' at the level of the 'event' – that is a beat or note which is clearly a product of sampler culture. Electronic sounds, too, may have real world references – for example to computer games sound effects (especially in their early years). Melodic lines may also be traced by any sound from sine-tones, samples, inharmonic sounds to noise band sounds. But to a surprising degree the streams established within any given work tend to remain intact – few have section divisions or dramatic changes of focus. Whether actual or not the idea of a work as a possible part of a remix or DJ set leads inevitably to a kind of 'moment form'. This is Stockhausen's term for sections of music which are 'not merely consequences of what came before or causes of what comes after' (Stockhausen, 1963, p. 250); they tend to 'start and stop' rather than 'begin and end'. For both Stockhausen (in the 1960s) and DJs of recent years the continuity of performance is formed from chaining such moments together.[63]

62 A good but basic list of sound equipment, techniques and sources used over the years is given in Rietveld (1998, Chapter 6).

63 In some moment-form works Stockhausen did suggest the possibility of choice even during the performance although he has over the years 'fixed' his preferred moment orders for such works (for example, *Stimmung*). Whether he detected such formal organization in the group of works he perused is not reported. Kim Cascone discusses this in Cascone (2000).

Conclusion – Postscript

Ben Neill's argument (quoted above) mirrors that between *musique concrète* and *elektronische Musik* in the 1950s. After Stockhausen's *Gesang der Jünglinge* (1956 on Stockhausen, 1991) was it 'all the same', as many textbooks suggest? There was greater exchange, perhaps, but the two strands of thought remain to this day in a sometimes uneasy combination (Emmerson, 1986b). And how, in turn, does *Gesang* relate to the music of the 'Technocrats'? Without the pulse they seem to demand, and its relation to dance, *Gesang* must come across as hopelessly Apollonian. The intensity of the experience of three youths walking in the 'burning fiery furnace' of the new music of the 1950s[64] is one of extreme discipline and control. The body is mortified and purified – and finally transcends the ordeal. Of course, not all electronica/IDM is Dionysian in its collective energy – much ambient music is restrained and contemplative. In times to come there may be increasing exchange between electronica and 'academic' electronic music strains but aims and ideas can remain different without mutual distrust. Their manifestations will hybridize and reconfigure but not all products of this process will maintain such a Dionysian intensity through the single attribute of *pulse*. Some may even reconcile the two streams of musical invention – the body and the environment – which have been the theme of this chapter.

64 Seppo Heikinheimo (1972) points out that in a passage *omitted from the English translation* (in *Die Reihe 6*), Stockhausen refers explicitly to '… an atheist, an idealist communist and a metaphysicist' which, looking at the original German context is unambiguously referring to Boulez, Nono and himself. Stockhausen goes on to declare that '… these three composers are personifications of three essential tendencies in present day intellectual life … only together do they make up the whole, the spirit of our age' (Heikenheimo, 1972, p. 80 translating Stockhausen, 1964a, p. 149).

CHAPTER FOUR

'Playing Space': Towards an Aesthetics of Live Electronics

Introduction and Background

The idea of any 'live' music is increasingly difficult to define, but there stubbornly remains much music which demands human presence and spontaneous creativity (physical and mental) in its production. To come to grips with this increasingly amorphous area we will discuss how our live musician (composer or performer) relates to, and articulates the *spaces of the performance* in terms of the *sound produced*. It turns out that this cannot be separated from spaces as articulated in acousmatic music in general. There is no one history. The first piece of 'mixed' music (that is music which combined traditional instruments with electronic sound) is sometimes given in text books as Bruno Maderna's *Musica su due dimensioni* (flute, cymbal and tape[1]) of 1952 (Maderna, 1967). But already in July 1951 Pierre Schaeffer and Pierre Henry's *Orphée 51*, for voices and tape had been premiered. Furthermore the term 'live electronic' has not only changed meaning in recent years, its history has been pushed not only further back but wider in scope. A retrospective 'race to be first' is absurd but does have the constructive side-effect of making us realize that we must not take any orthodox history for granted. John Cage's *Imaginary Landscape No.1* made use of variable speed test-tone discs in 1939. Earlier Dada and Futurist experiments are also better documented and acknowledged (Kahn and Whitehead, 1992; Kahn, 1999). In addition archive research now adds works such as Daphne Oram's unperformed *Still Point* for orchestra, recorded sound and live electronics dating from 1948–1950.[2]

This chapter looks at ways of approaching live electronic music across several genres. I do not seek a method which focuses on the phenomenological[3] nor (I hope) over-reliant on what composers argue 'is the case'. I want to suggest ways of approaching the field that will be helpful for both the composer and the listener and I hope to balance what composers *might do* with what listeners *might actually hear*.

1 Usually described simply as for 'flute and tape'.

2 Probably the first piece to use live treatments. Discovered by Hugh Davies and reported by him in his obituary of her for the Guardian (London) (24 January 2003) and more extensively discussed in a tribute article at http://www.sonicartsnetwork.org/Oram/oram.html – consulted November 2005.

3 Katharine Norman (2000a; 2004) has made bold and innovative attempts to combine description of sound works and examination of the processes of listening which inform our responses to sound. Her method of part layering, part parallel texts plays with the diachronic and synchronic possibilities for 'text' quite literally on the printed page.

Working Definition of 'Live' (for the Time Being)

We need a working definition, not to define boundaries for all time, but to set the limits of the stage we will occupy *for the time being.*
'Live' will here mean:

- The presence of a human performer:

who takes decisions and/or[4] *makes actions during a performance which change the real sounding nature of the music;*

- this embraces the historically accepted view of the 'live' as involving a human:

who produces sound mechanically; or who produces sounds on electronic substitutes for mechanical instruments using similar physical gestural input;

- but it also includes one:

who does not mechanically cause the sound, yet who may cause, form or influence it through electronically mediated interfaces under their immediate control.

There are (at least) two difficult borderline cases for electroacoustic music which reinforce the provisional nature of any definition. The diffusion/projection of studio-created acousmatic music on a multi-channel loudspeaker system is a 'live act' which brings the work into being. This does cover a continuum of activities from the spatial and dynamic distribution of an essentially predetermined soundfile to one in which real influence may be made through choice between options during the performance. I shall be discussing this further in Chapter 6 but not considering it here. Secondly we have machine-generated music without human input. In Chapter 2 an equivalent to Turing's test for intelligent machine behaviour was suggested for 'live presence' in the recorded (acousmatic) medium. Of course machine substitutes for human performance have been in development for many years in the whole field of interactive music.[5] This will also not be considered in this chapter.

The steady displacement of all parts of the acoustic performance world with electronic equivalents has not been a seemless linear process. The retention of *apparent* equivalence (in, for example, physical modelling software) has sometimes led to an uncertainty as to what would be the most suitable interface to *drive* the software if 'live' performance were an objective. In addition, earlier generations of electronic systems become themselves the objects of loss and rediscovery. Software is increasingly available to mimic accurately the sound of classic analogue

4 It might be assumed that most actions cannot be made without decisions but performance artist Stelarc has wired himself with electrical muscle stimulators which can be 'played' by someone else (or a machine). His website proclaims 'The body is obsolete' (http://www.stelarc.va.com.au – consulted November 2005).

5 George Lewis's *Voyager* has been a 20 year project aiming to establish an improvisation programme that jams with the author (Lewis, 2000).

synthesizers, for example, but this has usually neglected the tactile, 'feel' of the controls – not only those of the keyboard itself but of the ancillary knobs, sliders and (rare for analogue) information displays.[6] Hence, in an attempt to overcome this, some interfaces retain 'pre-electronic' performance practice (clearly mechanical in origin). The sound producing circuits may be analogue, digital or hybrid. This *tactile relationship* to sound production seems to function as a kind of 'paradise lost' and the community has a wide range of responses to this loss (many of which are discussed throughout this book). Let us review again the idea of 'dislocation'.

Dislocation and Causality (Real and Surmised)

We have already suggested (Emmerson, 1994a)[7] that there were three great 'acousmatic dislocations' established in the half century to 1910:

- *Time* (recording);
- *Space* (telecommunications (telephone, radio), recording);
- *Mechanical causality* (electronic synthesis, telecommunications, recording).

It sometimes appears in the literature that recent researches aim to 'roll back' these dislocations, to develop perfect tracking devices, establish 'perceptible and realistic' gesture-to-sound production mapping and thereby to recreate a controllable extended instrument. This approach seems to be at the basis of, for example, MIT's *hyperinstrument* developments since the 1980s.[8] More subtly we may opt for a more ambiguous relationship, mixing some directly perceivable cause-effect chains with (a) relationships of performer gesture to result which the performer may understand but the audience does not or (b) relationships of a more 'experimental' nature the outcomes of which may not be fully predictable.

But, as Denis Smalley (1992a) has argued for acousmatic music, in abandoning *any reference* to these 'links of causality' the composer of electroacoustic music involving live resources creates a confusion (even a contradiction)[9] and loses a possible tool for perspective and engagement between the forces at work and the audience. However, come what may, this loss *has* been embraced by a new generation of composers who reject this 'essentially mechanical' approach to what live music is. In the 1980s this transition was indicated at one level by dropping the word 'live' altogether and replacing it with 'real-time'. This was a direct result of the introduction of small portable personal computers that allowed real-time processing of Midi note

6 The mimicking of these awaits a new generation of interfaces (whether 'virtual reality' or 'real').

7 That paper went on to argue that a new generation of computer interaction software should be for strictly 'live' performance, restoring some of the 'cause-effect' chains which had been broken by recording and computer technology. The essentially conservative arguments of the paper have been substantially modified in this chapter.

8 Discussed in Chapter 5. See also Chadabe, 1997 (pp. 218–19) and: http://www.media.mit.edu/hyperins/index.html.

9 I am aware that this may be the composer's intention. This will be discussed below.

data information, the first Midi sequencers and programme-it-yourself compilers (LISP, BASIC, FORTH and the like). The Midi protocol (1983) defined music events very much in terms of the simplest of traditional interfaces, the keyboard. 'Note on/off, velocity, channel' was a fundamentally impoverished description of a performance gesture. It was nonetheless a breakthrough in being a universal cross-manufacturer standard. These developments resulted in a fundamental shift away from a human performer towards the computer as 'performance focus'. So this change of description was no Freudian slip, as many actions (and interactions) of people and machines on the concert platform in this era gave few cues (or even clues) to the listener as to whether there was any essentially 'live' (human-produced) activity. The problem was that this judgement was usually strongly guided and hardly objective. The concert listening conditions often included much non-musical information as to how the work was generated (programme notes, presence at a Computer Music Conference, and so on). If that could be 'bracketed out' then there was often little left to judge the effect of the performers on the sounding result. The PC performers of the 1980s were the precursors of the laptop performers of contemporary times. In Chapter 1 we examined the steady change in the meaning of 'live' as computers allowed all aspects of our 'being' (not just the physical) to be brought into 'play'. This chapter will look at a range of aesthetics of the 'live' from all these options – from the human gesture centre stage to the laptop performer who may give no *outward* indications of action.

The 'Local/Field' Distinction

A performance usually defines a space and the relationships within it (including listeners if any). I will start with a primary distinction in terminology; one which has its roots in this simple model of *the situation of the human agent in an environment*. It relates to the *body/environment* dichotomy discussed in Chapter 3 (and was first discussed in Emmerson, 1994b).

- *Local* controls and functions seek to extend (but not to break) the perceived relation of human performer action to sounding result.
- *Field* functions create a context, a landscape or an environment within which *local* activity may be found.

It is important to emphasize that the *field* as defined above *can contain other agencies*, in other words, it is not merely a 'reverberant field' in the crude sense but an area in which the entire panoply of both pre-composed and real-time electroacoustic music may be found. There may be other simulated 'performers', acousmatic and electronic materials, recognizable soundscapes as well as transformations of the live performers in such a way that 'local rootedness' is lost.

This definition aims to separate out the truly live element as clearly the 'local agency' in order to re-form more coherently the relationship with this open stage area, which may surround the audience and extend outside (see below). This does not preclude the possibility that these functions might interact and overlap – local can become field and *vice versa*. Nor does it preclude the possibility that

Prospero-like, the individual performer might *in practice* control all aspects of the piece from the largest to the smallest, both local and field.

The Composer/Listener Dichotomy: *Real* and *Imaginary* Relationships

Appearances can be deceptive. Performer-triggered real-time computations give no guarantee that the listener will *perceive* that a real human being has initiated or influenced a musical event. The *fact* that our local protagonist may trigger events, or processes, in the field is not our concern, only what *appears* to be true to the listener (Emmerson, 1994a). This distinction does, however, rest on perception. I have defined 'local' in a way which suggests the listener must perceive a causal relation between some performer action and a sounding result. However the composer as magician can create *imaginary* relationships, and cause and effect chains. In fact for the *composer* both local and field functions may have both *real* and *imaginary* causal components. *Real* relationships are indeed also 'real-time' and usually at time scales within short- to medium-term memory. Increasing time displacement between cause and effect will progressively undermine that relationship until it is no longer perceived.

The performer maintains an influence – a *real* cause – over the sounding result which the listener may follow:[10]

- through physical gesture directly effecting the overall sound which is processed (as in most early 'live electronic music');
- via an abstraction of some parameter sensed (analysed) from the sound (via an interface such as, for example Steim's *Sensorlab*);
- through transduction of some other physical gesture via a sensor (e.g. movement, proximity);
- through video tracking of a body movement.

Imaginary relationships, however, may have been prepared in advance (soundfiles, control sequences etc.) in such a way as to *imply* a causal link of sound to performer action in the *imagination* of the listener. An instrumental gesture appears to cause a sounding reaction in the electroacoustic part.[11] In the performance the listener only perceives the *net result* of the two and cannot (by definition) disentangle them. This is the composer's right – what *sounds* causal *is* effectively causal. The distinction of truly real and imaginary lies with the composer and performer, not the listener.

10 This list focuses on those actions a listener might have some chance of perceiving as causal – bio-interfaces, for example, are excluded – though we might in time learn to understand their action as causal.

11 I discuss this with respect to Denis Smalley's *Clarinet Threads* (Smalley, 1992b) in Emmerson (1998a).

Real and Imaginary Landscapes

I am interpreting the term *field* in a broader sense as any activity not localizable to the performer as source and which gives us a picture of what goes on around the instrument to establish a sense of wider location. Trevor Wishart has distinguished landscapes based on the four combinations of *real* and *unreal*, *objects* and *spaces* (Wishart, 1986). This discussion has two components: it includes both other sounds (often but not always pre-constructed in the studio – pseudo-agents created in advance) and also treatments (reverberation and other usually delay-related effects) which create a sense of 'being somewhere' (Wishart, 1996, pp. 146–7).[12] While these may both constitute elements of the field they will have to be controlled in very different ways. The possibilities are vast and can create effects ranging from the documentary (real soundscapes), through the surreal (conflicting but apparently real), to the entirely imaginary.[13] Here we are not concerned with the myriad types of electroacoustic sound objects and structures (of which typologies exist elsewhere) but with the *relation* of these to our live performer. These we must begin to describe. As a preliminary sketch we might create a list which reflects a simple description of the 'concerto' relationships of western music but worded to indicate deeper universals of musical interaction: supportive, accompanying, antagonistic, alienated, contrasting, responsorial, developmental, extended.

'Local/Field' and 'Control Intimacy'

If we do attempt to undo the 'acousmatic dislocations' referred to we have immediate need of the notion of *control intimacy* so well described by F. Richard Moore (1988). Moore was discussing the limitations of the Midi protocol to deal sufficiently fast and efficiently with parallel streams of control information which live performance transduction requires[14]. But the principle he describes is a wider one. In order to 'learn' a relationship and how to control it, the ability to articulate often *very small* changes in a parameter or group of parameters (*nuance*) demands a consistent and clearly perceivable 'cause-effect' relationship, in the 'right' proportion. An example from the mechanical music world would be subtle control of string or wind vibrato. A complex of small changes in finger position, pressure, velocity, and so forth, produce a correspondingly subtle yet quite perceptible change in the sound. Maintaining this sensitivity in the technologically mediated world demands sensitive and complex mappings of performer action to sound result.[15] Our local systems will

12 Wishart (1986; 1996) stresses the transformation of frame *content* where here I stress transformation of frame *disposition* – 'changes in perspective' would be an understatement!

13 See Field (2000) for an extension and elaboration of ideas of real and imaginary spaces.

14 Midi has remained surprisingly robust; attempts to 'replace' it with something faster and more efficient have not taken off – for example ZIPI (McMillen, 1994). There are signs that USB-based interfaces are replacing some midi controllers.

15 Violin and flute teachers do not, of course, deconstruct vibrato into parametric components; a performer learns to control the cluster of variables without necessarily detailed

need to articulate nuances of timbre and loudness (for example) currently distorted by insensitive amplification systems which do not allow the performer sufficient self-knowledge (accurate feedback) to allow 'intimacy of control' to be established. Simple subtleties of our mechanical world such as the directionality of the instrument are obliterated by current loudspeaker systems.

However I wish to go one stage further than Moore when he states that '*Control intimacy* determines the match between the variety of musically desirable sounds produced and the psycho-physiological capabilities of a practiced performer' (1988, p. 21). There are two possible outcomes for the listener depending on the nature of the 'musically desirable sounds'. Perceived as a direct result of a live performance gesture the sound's rightful place is in our local domain; but without this relation – I stress this is the listener's interpretation – it has more of a field function, as the result of the dislocation from performer as cause.

Reclaiming Local Control: Needs and Problems

I have argued above that appearances are everything: if in a musical discourse event A *appears* to cause event B *then it has done*. In practice, however, the performer in first generation live (and 'mixed') electronics was often severely disempowered. The electronics were pretty much in charge. It was common to hear the frustrations of the live performer, straight-jacketed by a tape part, unable to hear the overall effect of the electronics and clearly unable to influence many aspects of the performance.[16] Perhaps our ideal control position had moved to too great an extent towards the surrogate listener at the remote mixing desk. This must not blind us to the need to let the performer have additional control over all elements which we think important for the articulation of 'expressive' detail.

Some obvious points follow. First the need for performer awareness of timbral nuance, level sensitivity and inter-performer balance. Secondly greater performer control over mobility and directionality of original and modified source sounds. This 'local' control by the human instrumentalist demands locally focused sources of sound: in other words loudspeakers in the close vicinity of the source. There are two reasons for this, both of which are consequences of the central mixing console being remote from the performer. This might act firstly to restore the loss of a substantial degree of loudness control ('level intimacy') and secondly the perception of exactness of place of origin which has been lost in electroacoustic diffusion especially as performance spaces become larger. The virtual imaging of two (even high quality) loudspeakers at the periphery of an auditorium is insufficient. Any off-centre listener will lose the image[17] (if there was one to start with) and thus any real sense of a performer as source. We usually 'get away with it' because of the visual cues additionally available and sometimes a small amount of direct sound from the

knowledge of any individual one.

16 We might term this *control dislocation*.

17 Collapse of image into one loudspeaker is commonly a result of the *Haas* effect – the first signal to arrive at the ear tends to dictate the direction the sound appears to originate from.

instrument. Thus local and field loudspeakers should ideally not be the same type or be in the same place. One aspect of local performer amplification and projection remains unsolved. The balance of self with other performers is often carried out through the surrogacy of foldback – often inaccurate, distracting and interfering. Loudspeakers, like acoustic instruments, are directional and a similar set of skills to those developed by members of a string quartet but adapted to local electroacoustic projection needs to be developed.

Between the two poles of local and field lies the more subtle world of *play*. The inter*play* of these two spheres of operation. Of course a local event may trigger a field response or a field event may simply transform into a local one. Moore's 'control intimacy' refers to the self and its relation to sound production (control over the *phonology*, if you like); this suggests a more a local function. Of course the signals a performer puts out to the field environment need not have such an immediately perceptible causal link. Such signals may have cause-effect chains beyond short-term memory and therefore much more remote from the listener's likely perception (although the performer may still perceive them). Cause-effect chains beyond short-term memory can of course be learnt but probably only through repeated listening. We might consider giving the performer some say over what happens in projecting field information. This would complete our idealized control revolution returning considerably more power to the performer than current systems allow.[18]

Field Control and Sound Diffusion

This is the area of most conflict. From the originally French acousmatic tradition comes the art of *sound diffusion*. Originally this meant the active directing of a prerecorded signal to an array of loudspeakers (this is discussed further in Chapter 6). The fixity of any additional live performers (so-called 'mixed' music) has often been seen as a 'problem'. The instrument is rooted to a single location, visual aspects reinforce sound to locate the live source too firmly 'on the stage' while the electroacoustic sound can defy gravity and fly anywhere. One possible solution is to play *with* this dichotomy by considering the live element as fundamentally 'local' (in the terms discussed here). This is a limited view however. A truly innovative typology of live electroacoustic music will not play down this division, but add other dimensions to it developing new roles. Instrumental/vocal materials produced live may easily form part of both local and field functions when suitably processed.[19] Transformations and treatments may need to be controlled and diffused individually. Such developments might require additional performers or software but the possibility of restoring some control function to the performer should always be an option. In addition the simple two channel format of prerecorded material might give way to multichannel options

18 But this seems unlikely to happen. The laptop revolution has avoided or ignored these points; although once again centred on the performer-composer on stage, sound level and distribution is often not considered.

19 My own work *Sentences* (soprano and live electronics) (1991 on Emmerson, 2007) has two parallel streams of processing diffused on separate loudspeakers for local and field functions.

differentiated not by space (as in most 4, 8 and 5.1 channel formats) but by function. Material related to local functions might be differentiated from that for field use and independently diffused appropriately in the performance space.[20]

I have suggested several areas that control may be returned to the performer but the direct influence of the performer on sound diffusion is the most difficult. The very idea seems impossible – it is orthodoxy to assume that only a person at the optimum listening location can judge the acoustic balance. While observing that the actual location of mixing consoles in many venues (especially theatres) is not anything approaching the optimum, there is a case for arguing that future technology must adapt the concept of foldback to more subtly indicate the sound mix and level at the optimum location.[21] This would allow the performer to have (once again) some control, not only over their own local level and presence (as argued in the previous section), but over the overall field level and mix within the listening space.

Space Frames

I have elsewhere suggested the simple application of the idea of the *frame* (a defined area of interest) applied progressively from the largest to the smallest scale (Emmerson, 1998b). Our mechanical sound universe existed from the level of a *landscape* (bounded by the acoustic horizon) part of which we designated an *arena*, within which we found a *stage*, upon which we framed an *event* (Figure 4.1). For the sonic artist using contemporary technology the process may continue, bringing the microscopic levels of sound into closer focus within the event. Amplification opens this up in the acoustic world while digital technology, most notably via the theories of Fourier (spectra) and Gabor (grains),[22] allows us to go down to the smallest of particles and even beyond to the individual glitch and byte. At the other extreme technology allows 'super-frames' such as the radiophonic horizons of Cage's *Imaginary Landscape No.4* or Stockhausen's *Hymnen*. These are metaphors, in practice, as the sounds do not *as such* exist 'out there' in the ether, but then nor do they exist 'in' electronic circuits – both need sonifiers (transducers). Finally the internet as a site for music has taken over from the universal 'radio-frame' as the ultimate all-embracing terrestrial frame.[23] In the hands of artists these frames now become mobile, flexible and even overlapping – and may contradict real-world expectations. This goes beyond using fixed perspective in composition. Perspective itself can

20 In both cases, whether live processed or pre-recorded, different musical functions may use different physical spaces (positions) to articulate their presence, requiring increasingly flexible routing and distribution on diffusion systems (often built with fixed stereo in mind).

21 Or some other more general indication of 'out there'.

22 An uncertainty principle such as that declared by Werner Heisenberg for electrons exists between these two: the more precise the quantum of sound is defined in time, the less exact its spectrum definition.

23 UK sound artist Jem Finer's use of radio signals from outer space as an important part of his installation work (see http://cosmolog.org.uk/ consulted December 2005) transcends this frame further.

become a malleable object, changing with time, conflicting with expectation. Frames may now become objects of musical discourse.

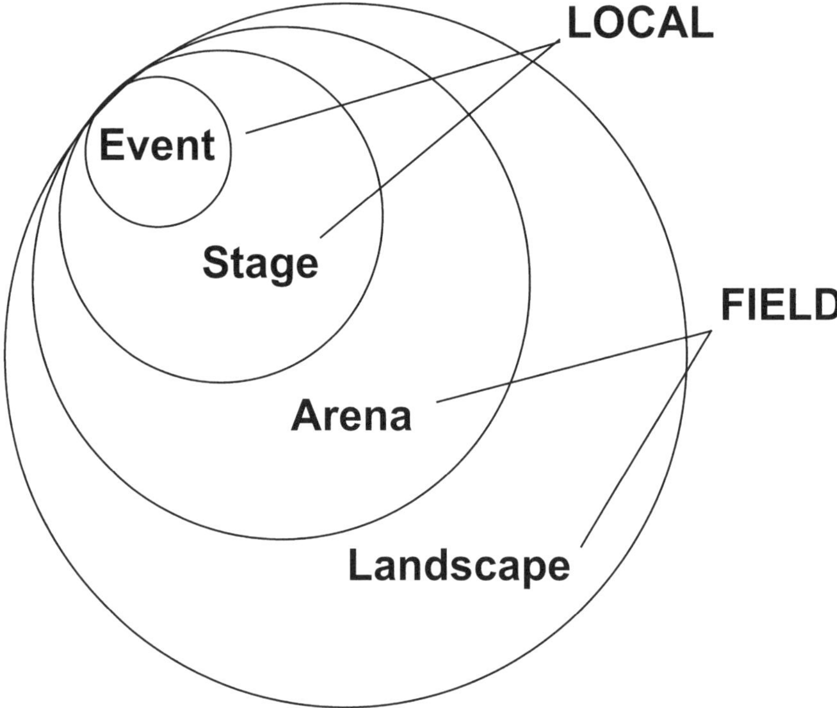

Figure 4.1: Local and Field space frames

Although derived from a discussion of live music, all frames may be present in a recording or in acousmatic composition. Recorded music does away with the arena and the stage as 'real' places where musical events take place and replaces them with the personal listening space. But, of course, as in all acousmatic conditions, simulation may be accepted as 'reality' by the listener, although there will inevitably be compromises when the playback situations are of a different scale with respect to the original. This may be intentional – a soundscape may be designed for living room listening – or just inevitable – Cage considered the recording of a performance event such as *Variations IV* strictly as a separate event, even a separate performance. Furthermore a recording may then be replayed within another such set of frames. It may be part of a real performance on a real stage or a simulated 'walkman space'. The experiments of twentieth century composers, most especially those from the American experimental tradition using acoustic resources, had already eroded the old frame boundaries. Charles Ives's *From the Steeples and the Mountains*, *Universe Symphony* and other sketch works anticipate the spatial experiments from the era after 1950; Henry Brant has used vertical dimensions as well as surround sound in his works (Harley, 1997). Electroacoustic means have extended the process and created total flexibility. Works by John Cage, Alvin Lucier and David Tudor have all explored such space-frame transformations (we shall return to these later).

Listener-Defined Stage

But then frames may be defined by the listener: there is nothing to stop me declaring part of a landscape to be a stage. Cage might allow us complete freedom to define our frames of listening although other composers might try to direct us. This may have two versions: for the first we remain stationary and our attention may be re-focused on different localities around us. This may be motivated just by our curiosity or maybe a sound has forced us to focus on it through some quality or strategy of *drawing attention to itself*. But secondly actually walking through (say) a Cage performance is a quite different experience from listening to it from a fixed perspective. We will constantly have to refocus on local detail – even though that may be projected to us from some distance away. Stockhausen has tried to imitate this real listener movement in the issued recording of his piece *Sternklang* (1971 on Stockhausen, 1992)[24]. This is to be performed by five separate live electronic ensembles positioned around a park outdoors, and a mobile percussionist. The commercial recording was made with the groups in isolated areas within the recording studio, the percussionist in a separate booth. The stereo version was mixed from the 16-track master to simulate changes of real location by the listener. Individual ensembles fade in and out following the 'sound runners' of the real performance who 'transport' musical materials between them. The result is a very 'imaginary' walk as all ambience and the acoustic effect of the real parkscape is omitted.

Frame Play: Interactions of 'Local' and 'Field'

Playing with the frames I have outlined is common currency in radiophonic drama. We might hear the innermost thoughts of a protagonist in an intimate close space, superimposed on immediate locality and then environment, all clearly differentiated. These are of course differentiations of perceivable physical quality, the characteristics of spatial awareness which we examined in Chapter 1. But more subtly we can also use frames in a less literal, more metaphorical manner. A stage has a privileged position in my focused view. 'Stage' suggests an area of clear perception from which we receive detailed, information-rich signals and to which we devote maximum attention. We hear detail best, and perceive direction most accurately, in a forward 120° arc. This is also complemented by its being the zone of accurate vision. But I can move my head such that other equivalent boundaried areas can have an equivalent role. All frame relationships are transposable using technological mediation: we may expand a micro-level event to become a landscape. Something that was originally a detailed aspect of a 'small' sound might be so magnified and stretched that its inner details appear *as if* they had field and landscape functions – which would need to be projected accordingly. The dense almost granular 'floodsounds' of Stockhausen's

24 Recorded in 1975.

Kontakte move across the entire arena of perception; yet they are clearly 'enlarged' versions of many of the smaller sound textures that interact with the live instruments. Conversely an entire soundscape may be reduced to the musical size of a micro-event at local level.[25]

We may also reverse frame 'roles' in live electronic music: the instrument on stage can simply 'disappear' into a continuous field of sound, relinquishing its role as instigator of locally focused interest. This can be true in mixed electroacoustic works in which the live instrumentalist produces essentially the same soundworld as that pre-recorded – in which case one might argue that the composer might just as well have pre-recorded the live element and mixed it in. However, the spectacle of the instrumentalist's struggle against the elements may be one real aim of the work, thereby producing an expressive and dramatic result.[26]

Works which 'play' with space frames have been discussed in all chapters in this book. There is a seemless continuum from live electronic works to acousmatic works which encapsulate live activity and manipulate space frames similarly. The two domains are closest, of course, when simply listening to recordings. We trust our judgement in listening to a *recording* of a live work; we use acoustic cues to place the performers in some kind of 'real' space simulated between our loudspeakers. In practice 'live' recordings are subject to all the editing skills that an acousmatic work also demands. Discussed elsewhere are John Cage's *Roaratorio* and Alvin Lucier's *I am sitting in a room* (Chapter 5), David Tudor's *Rainforest* series (Chapter 6) and Luc Ferrari's *Presque Rien No.2* (Chapter 3). The World Soundscape Project and some of the subsequent work of its members centres on *Landscape-Arena-Stage* frame translation. The sound landscape is projected into the listening space becoming the new environment within which the listener creates their own stage of focus. Sometimes Murray Schafer's idea of *soundmark* acts (like a landmark) to anchor that focus. Interestingly, soundscape listening engages one of Pierre Schaeffer's listening modes usually excluded from musical listening – the *information gathering* mode. The signals of the Vancouver soundscape give us a glimpse of the real cityscape and how it functions (World Soundscape Project, 1997).

Electroacoustic means also give composers the opportunity for a play of contradictory, paradoxical or conflicting frames (true to a degree in the Luc Ferrari example discussed in Chapter 3). Different stages, arenas or landscapes may be superimposed and transformed. In completely acousmatic music there is no grounding in real physical presence and the frames essentially float in an unpredictable listening landscape in which any one frame can seemlessly move into the foreground or retreat into the distance of our perception. Even in live

25 Examples might include David Tudor's *Rainforest* ideas (resonating objects from pre-recorded materials (some environmental) (Rogalsky, 2006)) or Christina Kubisch's installation *Oasis 2000: Music for a Concrete Jungle* (listener mixing of natural sounds on headphones (Hayward Gallery, 2000)). But this near opposite of Cage's 'amplifying small sounds' has not been much explored.

26 Examples of this would be Horacio Vaggione's *Tar* (bass clarinet and tape (1987)) (Vaggione, 1988) and Jonty Harrison's *EQ* (soprano saxophone and tape (1980)) (Harrison, 1996b).

electronics *local* is continuous to *field*: the borderline varies with musical context and remains completely fluid. For example, the field could be the 'inside' of an extended instrument reaching out from the live performer to envelop the audience through amplification and diffusion. My own work *Ophelia's Dream II* (singers and live electronics) (1978–9 on Emmerson, 1993) attempts to place the audience inside Ophelia's head. Four microphones surround her head at mouth level, each routed to one of four loudspeakers surrounding the audience. As she rotates we observe her from outside yet the sound surrounds us.[27]

Paradoxical space frames have always existed within recorded rock and popular music. Creative mixing designed to differentiate the traditional elements of vocals, drum kit, guitars, synthesizers and other instruments have always created separately identifiable space frames for each. This is consciously designed to encourage clear and differentiated auditory scenes to be established. Listened to dispassionately they are paradoxical because impossible to coexist in 'reality'. This feeds directly the paradoxical and surreal 'space frame play' so evident in much electronica/IDM (in tracks by Aphex Twin and Autechre particularly – see the discussion in the concluding section of Chapter 3).

Landscape, Space, the 'Live' and Narrative

The aesthetic aims of acousmatic and live electronic music can be increasingly interpenetrating. I have argued elsewhere (Emmerson, 1994a) that Denis Smalley's (1986; 1992a) ideas of *surrogacy* and *indicative field* – originally applied to acousmatic music – may and should be extended to include live instrumental gesture. I wish to extend that argument here to include framing and landscape functions in live electronic music. This articulates the surreal notion that the mechanical instruments of the western tradition can somehow 'return' to the landscape from which (in mythic history) they came. I wish to argue that live transformation (even of an apparently abstract kind) creates landscape functions which our Darwinian ear attempts to relate to real world experience. The auditory system searches to establish frames of reference when confronted with spaces, real or imaginary. Using electronics we may conjure up this increasingly wide set of alternatives. On the one hand the composer may attempt spatial re-presentation, that is the recreation of an appropriate 'real' space to support a narrative; this can approach a kind of onomatopoeia in which the idiosyncrasies of a real space may be mimicked. Then (alternatively) we have already discussed the increasingly 'remote surrogate' spaces that we can create in the studio or, more importantly, in real-time. But what kind of landscape might we be in and move through? We may move from direct imitation – the acoustics of a forest or mountain landscape – through increasingly vague evocations to more remote impressions of colour and texture.[28] In addition we can create imaginary landscapes – the 'mindscapes' of expressionism. These ideas may

27 Any highly spatialized multi-mic amplification of extended instrument technique may have this effect.

28 This range of options is exactly parallel to the 'mimetic' and 'aural' axis I described for the *materials* of electroacoustic music in the so-called 'language grid' (Emmerson, 1986a, p. 24).

overlap, sometimes reinforcing, sometimes contradicting each other within the same transformation. Sound artists have just the same possibilities of surrealist image, dreams and fantasies as any Dali or de Chirico. Such an axis, however, appears to require the overall hi-fi soundscape that Murray Schafer demands – one of high dynamic range and low masking noise. We shall return to a discussion of urban (lo-fi) influences on this soundscape below.

Space itself can 'tell a story'. A sense of space, of being and existing, now forms part of all the acousmatic arts of radio, recording and sound-art. And most radically, 'spaces' are appropriated and re-mixed in the dance/techno and plunderphonics world. Hence space and perspective are now truly materials with which we can compose (as 1950s idealists had always hoped, but without their obsession with numerical abstraction). But recording of a space also captures time, both time in general and 'a time' (a historical event). Exactly as with space there is a sequence of possibilities from literal to remote. From, for example, the 'events' of Paris in 1968, to crowds in general, to crowd-like behaviour, there is a continuum of 'temporal distance'.[29] The mark of a 'good' work in this sense is that the transition from being a *note mémoire* of a specific event to being heard as something more universal is made seemlessly. The composer's intentions may or may not influence this. Nothing can be guaranteed. Perhaps the intention was to create a 'mere' document, a recording of a place at a time. But some soundscapes (Vancouver, 1973, for example) in which there is only a re-presentation of the historical document may become increasingly both beautiful and instructive.

But composers should always be careful of assuming continuity of historical significance. Recorded spaces can carry great symbolic or iconic references which may fade or radically change with passing time. Listeners in 2008 may have no resonance with the 'events' of Paris in 1968[30] or the soundscape of the 1960s in general. Stockhausen's *Hymnen*, based on national anthems of the world, was completed in 1967. It creates a meta-space, a world space, through the image of a radio-space – but a substantial proportion of the anthems he used have now disappeared and been replaced; or have substantially different historical resonances – that of the USSR, for example. *Hymnen* has made a radical transition from being thoroughly contemporary ('reflecting the world now') to being 'of its time' (the Cold War).[31]

29 Thus Luigi Nono has worked at the literal end with direct reference to specific 'demos', Iannis Xenakis at the opposite end with a very remote surrogate (see Chapter 2).

30 Specific historical resonance is an aspect of the mimetic in electroacoustic music not fully explored in the literature. For example, many of Luigi Nono's electroacoustic works are intentionally laden with such specific time-stamped references (through text or site-recordings), for example: *A floresta è jovem e cheja de vida* (1966) (The Vietnam War) (Nono, 2000) and *Non Consumiamo Marx* (1969) (Paris/Venice demos 1968) (Nono, (1970s undated LP)).

31 See also discussion in Chapters 2 and 3.

New Spaces and Perspectives: the Flat and the Immersive

Local and field functions and relationships may be changing in a world where mechanical instrumental gesture has been absorbed into the computer. My description of the local consequences of the live performance act, linked to the mechanical as it was, may seem to be fast disappearing. But the 'local gesture' reappears in another guise. As we saw in Chapter 3 body gestures come back in their indicative form of *metre*. But this is no longer produced by the physical (metrical) action of a real performer, but chosen from a pre-recorded library or generated (though looping, for example). The diffusion/projection of this more recent 'live' sonic art is also of a different kind, rarely in the concert environments envisaged for an earlier live electronic music (described above). Two new kinds of listening spaces relying on technology for their sound systems emerged from the 1960s to the 1990s. Both are totally immersive, but one is large and public, the other small and private. First the spaces of leisure listening, increasingly with the participation of dance, group encouraging and inclusive; secondly the space of the 'personal stereo', individual and exclusive.

Club spaces have developed in a variety of ways depending on the dominant genre of the music played in them. In many cases the soundsystem is predominantly monaural (or at least non-spatialized) at source. All parts of the space have to receive a broadly similar mix of the sound. Any sense of place is generated within the real space of the performance and thus the 'space of the work' is only truly created in the act of performance and is not encoded in its recorded form. In some experimental music spaces a stereo system might be used but rarely in a manner which relies on spatial sound image. Stereo image creation using Blumlein theory recording (the standard) is impossible in such situations. Blumlein stereo can only be perceived from a stable vantage point outside the loudspeaker plane – the listener must 'look in'. Being inside an immersive PA system will destroy all but discrete 'in and from the speaker' information. The image is here totally immersive, designed to envelope, to create a total space into which intrusion of extraneous sound is impossible, not because it is excluded but because it is masked. The image is close, surrounding and omnidirectional, possessing a kind of amniotic reassurance.

Personal stereo space is flat. The exclusion of directional information formed by extremely subtle interference from the pinna (the fleshy outer ear appendages) leaves us with a close, relatively flat image. There is some possibility of limited depth information in such systems. But when the material for personal stereo space comes from a tradition of popular music mixing practice, within which dynamic range is severely reduced, then there is a tendency for the image to collapse into the plane of the head. This produces a similar kind of immersive result that was true in a club space although here the image is no longer outside, but within. Thus club and personal stereo spaces are not merely complementary they can become mutually reinforcing. Although a key difference is at the social level (our third discussion in Chapter 1): here they are opposites, club space being essentially a group space by definition, material held (roughly) in common across a large number of listeners at the same time.

This begins to address a fundamental divide in contemporary composition. In the acousmatic concert tradition the relentless use of 'remote surrogate' spaces and landscapes may have the same alienating effect that Denis Smalley (1986) originally argued would result from overuse of remote surrogate sound morphologies. This assumes that the spaces are encoded in the work. Much recent electronica and experimental IDM uses grossly simplified spatial frame distinctions – leaving the real frame of the performance to provide it. The personal stereo is a surrogate of the immersive PA space.[32]

'Live' and 'Mixed'

In English the term 'live electronic music' has often meant *both* music produced and performed through real-time electroacoustic activity of some kind *and* music which combined live performers and fixed electroacoustic sound ('tape').[33] In French the former is now known as using *traitements en temps réel*. But this has never superseded the phrase *musique mixte* which had earlier come to be used for any music combining live performers with music on tape (or better in French, *sur support*). But, unlike the English equivalent, the French usage of *temps réel* extends to studio processes.[34] Thus at the GRM in Paris the *Syter* (*Système temps réel*) was developed as a tool that processed sound in real-time in response to gestural and other control inputs. It was used in both studio and 'live' concert systems.[35]

The questions posed by mixing traditional instruments (or voices) and pre-recorded materials are considerable. The acousmatic world has no boundaries while that of the western instrument has developed with an increasing elimination of all but a narrow range of timbre variation, the promotion of stable and fixed pitch, fixed tuning and, perhaps most important, the virtual elimination (or at least minimization) of noise components. Instrument construction technology and performance practice tradition had been in close alliance in the late eighteenth and early nineteenth centuries to aim at this ideal. Each of these sound worlds interpenetrates the other leading to many approaches to composition. In some the instrument aspires to the acousmatic, in others the acousmatic adopts instrumental sounds and gestures, or perhaps the two cohabit but remain sonically separate.

---

32 And possibly vice versa in the iPod era.

33 There is much ambiguity about this. The (self-declared) 'live electronic' ensembles of the 1960s and 1970s tended to use this label freely to include both, though many composers made a clear distinction between describing their work as 'live electronic' or for 'instrument/voice and tape'.

34 Computer technology had been introduced at the GRM from 1975. The first system ran (in computer music's traditional terms) in *temps différé* (differed time), the second ran in *temps réel*. Both concerned the treatment of sound in the GRM sense (DSP), the precursor of GRMTools.

35 As in the INA/GRM (2004) *archives GRM* CD4 called '*le temps du temps réel*' which includes a wide variety of acousmatic, mixed and 'live' electronic works. Whereas CD3 ('*le son en nombre*') presents works composed using the system *en temps différé*.

Mixed Pieces: Extending the Acousmatic into the Instrumental

One tradition of instrumental amplification in mixed music concerns pieces in which the instrument 'aspires to the condition of the acousmatic'. The visual aspect is thus of no importance; any sense of causality with visible instrumental gesture is secondary. Indeed the more extended the instrumental sound world created by the composer and peformer, the greater the difficulty of surmising a real physical 'playing technique'.[36] The natural tendency to search tends therefore to result in the game play (by the listener) of 'how *was* that sound made?' – which should ideally be suspended within Pierre Schaeffer's notion of *écoute réduite*. This ideal is rarely reached; there are moments when the instrument disappears into the ongoing flux (whether perfectly balanced with its flow or masked by its density).[37] But there is a strong tendency for the instrument to reestablish its presence separated from the electroacoustic soundworld. This is sometimes through body gestures, such as hand action (for example, key clicks), breath contour, melodic fragment 'standing out'; but also clearly through the idiosyncrasies of amplification. The electroacoustic part has in all likelihood been created without room ambient information, whereas the amplified instrument (however closely miked) is bound to take something of its space and throw it back, making integration of the two very problematic (if that is the aim). There is a sense in which this approach articulates a struggle – the western instrument is designed to be recognized for its uniform timbre and pitch production but is asked to rediscover its more diverse primeval capacities. Boulez warned against such extended 'noise and artefact' techniques on standard instruments, declaring:

> … the peripheral effects and characteristics that the instrument-makers rejected … are taken over and used as central characteristics. … It is not by bringing the periphery into the centre that you solve the problem of instruments. (Boulez, 1975, p. 116).

The 'peripheral' sounds to which Boulez refers are those we do *not* associate with 'normal' production. But if they are beautiful, interesting and reproducible they may redefine themselves away from the periphery and into 'the centre'. Wind instrument key clicks and multiphonics have made a hesitant first step in this transition; but a vast array of non-pitched, noisy, artefactual sounds are an inevitable demand of a tradition which seeks to relate the instrument[38] to the wider acousmatic world.

In Jonty Harrison's *EQ* (soprano saxophone and tape) (1980) (Harrison, 1996a), the electroacoustic soundworld takes off from an initial close contact with the live extended percussive instrumental and vocal sounds, and steadily expands from these archetypes to a much expanded dramatic vista. In Denis Smalley's *Clarinet Threads* (clarinet and tape) (1985 on Smalley, 1992b) a range of sounds from controlled varieties of pitched contours and timbres, coloured breath gestures to percussive sounds are used to anchor, provoke and respond to the electroacoustic world. The

---

36 This is much more difficult with vocal performance. The voice is much more stubbornly anchored to its source in human perception – for good evolutionary reasons.

37 I have discussed this above with respect to space frames.

38 It is strangely another case of mimetic imitation – one way the instrument can relate to, and integrate with such an extensive soundworld.

piece plays with a wide variety of relationships of (musical) cause, effect and independence (see Emmerson, 1998a). A further extension of this is to present only the amplified instrument without any treatment or pre-recorded material. A wide range of 'extended' works exist for which amplification is necessary to capture and project nuance, 'small sounds', subtly modulated noises – some using multi-microphone techniques which spatialize the sound in performance.

The material of Trevor Wishart's *Anticredos* (amplified voices) (1980 on Wishart, 1992) is the nearest to an 'acousmatic voice' that I know – but in a way that is, paradoxically, profoundly vocal. It is the culmination of about four years of research:

> The approach adopted here is to regard the human voice/mouth as a flexible sound-generating device, like a sophisticated synthesiser, and investigate from first principles what it can do (Wishart, 1979, p. (2) (unpaginated)).[39]

The contrast with the embodied voice of the victim in *Red Bird* (1977) could not be greater although the sound transformations of the analogue studio are here replaced with virtuoso performance within the vocal flow. But *Anticredos* does not (and does not intend to) dislocate the material from its vocal origins; in re-engaging with a 'pan-linguistic' range of sounds (which at birth we all possessed), Wishart transcends any specific language and creates an extraordinary soundscape. Spatial movement is at the service of separating individual streams and their transformations. *Anticredos* reacts against the 'representational' element in Wishart's earlier work and even more extraordinarily, avoids any anecdotal aspects of the voice. In doing this, its very real message – that through transformation 'the piece arrives' [and by implication, we arrive] 'at sound worlds which were not contained in, nor predictable from, the starting materials' (1992, CD note) – is reinforced.

Direct amplification of a purely instrumental extended soundworld was the focus of a group of composers based in France in the 1970s. Vinko Globokar's aim was to 'articulate sound and its transformation without electroacoustic means' in works such as *Fluide* (1967), *Ausstrahlungen* (1969), *Atemstudie* (1970 on Globokar, 1970s LP, undated) and *Echanges*, *Res/As/Ins-spirer*, *Discours IV* (1973–74 on Globokar, 1978). He even declares in a note for the latter: 'I must emphasise that no electronic equipment is used in any of the three pieces to transform the sounds'. Works commissioned by the French flute player Pierre-Yves Artaud (especially those for bass flute) are also at times far from the 'central' soundworld of the instrument. For example, Paul Méfano's *Traits suspendu* (1980 on Méfano, 1981) and Michael Levinas's *Froissement d'ailes* (Levinas, 1978) clearly articulate principles of timbral morphology near to the electroacoustic soundworld of the French tradition.

39 *Book of Lost Voices* (Wishart, 1979) was a short-lived publication (written during the composition of *Anticredos*) that became Chapter 12 of *On Sonic Art* (Wishart, 1996 (original 1985)); introductory material was, however omitted.

Mixed Pieces: Extending the Instrumental into the Acousmatic

Conversely we have an approach which seeks to preserve instrumental writing in something close to the traditional historical. Whether using real-time processing or pre-recorded sound this approach is focussed on extending existing instrumental technique, even to create new instruments in so doing. Pierre Boulez's criticism of Schaeffer's aesthetics stems from his belief that the sound world of *noise* has too great a relation to 'everyday life' to be brought under complete compositional control:

> When noise is used without any kind of hierarchic plan, this also leads, even involuntarily, to the 'anecdotal', because of its reference to reality. Any sound which has too evident an affinity with the noises of everyday life … with its anecdotal connotations, becomes completely isolated from its context; it could never be integrated, since the hierarchy of composition demands materials supple enough to be bent to their own ends, and neutral enough for the appearance of their characteristics to be adapted to each new function which organizes them (Boulez, 1971, p. 22).

The role of technology for Boulez is clear: mechanical technology extended instruments in the nineteenth century, this role has passed to electronic technology in the twentieth (and twenty-first) centuries. But he started off by rejecting live electronics and seeing technology as a tool to develop new instruments according to newer 'contemporary' sound production principles which moved away from the homogeneity of the western instrument:[40]

> … so rather than trying to solve this fundamental problem by the use of electronic means, we might just as well tackle it head-on and find out what can be done when instruments are no longer homogeneous, and no longer dependent on tempered scales, but are indeed capable of using a large number of different scales, as and when desired (Boulez, 1975, pp. 116–17).

Here, though, *scale* can include scales of timbral change, chords, spatial movements, and so forth. Written at a time slightly before the foundation of IRCAM (in 1974), these objectives quickly transformed into the more realistic ones in which live electronics could produce the effective sounding results *without* the mechanical rebuilding of instruments.[41] Andrew Gerzso describes the transformation processes of *Répons* (1981–84 on Boulez, 1998) as:

---

40 A train of thought that dates back, at least, to his encounter with Cage's prepared piano in 1949 – though Schaeffer and Henry were conducting similar experiments preceding this encounter.

41 Few proposed redesigns of instruments have emerged from IRCAM in the subsequent 20 years, although research continues (see http://www.ircam.fr/recherche.html – '*Amélioration de la lutherie traditionelle*'), but physical modelling – mimicking the instrument's physical operation in software – has moved this stream of thinking towards *virtual instruments*. To date Boulez has not used these outcomes.

> modulation of one instrument by another; retardation and changes of phase to create complex rhythmic motifs; frequency shifting; control of the overall distribution of sound on the general speaker system (Gerzso, 1984, p. 27).

But the dilemma remains for Boulez: the technology extends what we already know, furnishing the composer with increased control over timbre and space, rather than extending the performer's instrument and its capabilities and possibilities in performance.

It is quite possible that mixed electroacoustic music (as it has been constituted to date) will disappear. The fixed nature of the electroacoustic part means that in many cases – unless the composer does not consider synchronization of live and tape important – the tape part is a dictatorial and perfect metronome (beating clock time). Especially where cause-effect relationships are to be 'created' through live-tape coordination such split second timing is essential. While some latitude could be built in through multiple cues, there is a feeling amongst many performers that the medium itself is inappropriate for the flexibility demanded by different acoustics, venues, audiences and other musical variables.[42]

Yet Javier Alvarez's *Papalotl* exploits this straightened relationship: the fixed electroacoustic part acts as an extension of the instrument but the instrument is also 'directed' by it. It was created from inside piano resonance recordings ('samples' for the Fairlight CMI)[43] and 'extends' the instrument, in the composer's words:

> … the piano provides the upper partials of the entire spectral composition of the work, while the tape part constantly touches upon fundamentals (Alvarez, 1989, p. 228).

> … the idea of creating a 'giant' instrument inside of which the performer and listener alike experience the resonance … of the strings' motion, becoming an ordinary piano of extraordinary power (Alvarez, 1989, pp. 229–230).

The rapid fire exchanges between instrument and electroacoustic part have the feeling of an energetic hocket (of the kind found in Andean double pipe playing) and generate an excitement which adds directly to the musical experience.[44] The complex cross-rhythms create very real coordination problems and the sense of tension is palpable in performance. The composer relates this to his rejection of '… conceptions [which] tend to reinforce a lattice based idea of temporal relations rather than dealing with motion in terms of shape, behaviour and physical response as in dance' (p.206). He summarizes: 'In *Papalotl*, it is the incessant shifting of the pulses which constitute the piece's most important structural identity' (p. 222).

---

42 Strictly speaking this is a separate question from *interaction*. The derrogation of *time* to an external and inflexible authority is a fundamental flaw in mixed music.

43 One of the first samplers: eight voice memories, each of just under 1s at full quality bandwidth.

44 See Alvarez (1989) for a full examination of *Papalotl*.

Contrast—Confrontation—Relation

A juxtaposition without mediation is still a relationship. There are, of course, compositions which confront the issue in a different way and juxtapose soundworlds without any attempt at any formal timbral integration. Katharine Norman has written mixed pieces which deliberately exploit this contrast. *Trying to translate* (for piano, tape and live electronics) (1991[45] on Norman, 2000b) superposes two very contrasting sound spaces: the electroacoustic part consists of a montage of different sounds and reminiscences. The composer has written:

> So often pieces for instrument and tape concentrate on finding points of contact between two worlds, making some kind of aural translation between acoustic and electronic sound. I decided to explore the polarity between the instrument and the tape, treating the issue as a feature rather than a problem ... Piano and tape inhabit the same world but differently (Norman, 1991).

The fact that the voice recordings allude to something specific – the translation between Gaelic and English and the loss of Gaelic traditional psalm singing in Scotland – is a celebration of the explicit difference between speech and music, explicit verbal 'meaning' and the more subtle 'translation' that music entails. Juxtaposition of these two worlds unmediated, suggests that possible mediation is negotiated by the listener alone. The contrast between speech and music layers might lead us to a confused switching of perceptual focus[46] between the two but such inconsistent ambiguity is part of the process of translation.

François-Bernard Mâche has suggested that the two worlds of animal sound communication[47] and musical gestures are profoundly related. The relationship for him lies at mimetic and gestural levels: sound structures and contours, rhythms and calls *reenter* his musical syntax through direct imitation. These he describes as *sound models* which have a universal applicability (Mâche, 1992). He argues that *they were always there at the origin and root of musical discourse* but they may be used to reinvigourate the empty rhetoric of late modernism. If we were crudely to describe the tape/instrument duo in terms of a 'culture/nature' divide then Mâche sets out to subvert the distinction. In *Korwar* (harpsichord and tape) (1972) (Mâche, 1990; 1994), the harpsichord 'imitates' the sounds of the Xhosa language, the rhythm of birds wings and a wide variety of animal sounds.

> *Korwar* is an attempt at a response to the nature-culture dilemma. The role of the harpsichord is neither to be opposed to the recorded sounds nor to comment on them, but most frequently, 'plated' onto them, to signify, itself, this instrument of charged heredity, the profound identity between musical gesture, animal cry and the palpitations of the elements (Mâche cited in ten Hoopen and Landy, 1992, p. 86).

---

45 Erroneously 1992 on the CD cover (Norman, 2000b).

46 Especially as the recorded voice part is for the most part mixed at a relatively low level in the available recording (Norman, 2000b) – we have to make an effort to focus on it to hear the words clearly.

47 He includes human language here – the Xhosa language (with its variety of consonantal clicks) is a central element of the tape for *Korwar*.

But as if to point up the relationship, Mâche *maintains the separation* of the two domains in the sound diffusion. He specifies clearly *local* loudspeakers for the harpsichord[48] while the tape is to be projected on a separate system (as the *field* within which the harpsichord 'plays'). Clearly separate yet clearly related. Whether Mâche intends all the animal sounds to be recognized specifically is unlikely – but an overall sense of origin is driven from those that are likely to be recognized as animal (grunts, bird calls and cries) into those that will clearly be unfamiliar to most listeners (underwater lifeform sounds, for example). Mâche creates ensembles of instrument and animal: duetting with wild boar, boar and later starling, for example. This environment is constructed carefully in a way which articulates a strong evolving form – a musical sensibility has 'orchestrated' the animal sounds; this is no soundscape.

Luigi Nono's *La Fabbrica Illuminata* (1964 on Nono, 1992) is also discussed in Chapter 3. Here it serves perfectly to illustrate the direct confrontation of live performer and pre-recorded electroacoustic material. I have suggested that *La Fabbrica* is a paradigm case of dialectical thinking in this field: the human pitted against the machine (Emmerson, 1986b). In fact the solo soprano is one of many 'live presences' in the piece – the others on tape tend to represent the 'group'; in this case those whom Nono considered the music served (the factory workers). The tape does not extend, complement or develop musical 'material'. Its material is the slogan, the sonic representation of industrial and dehumanized processes. In its concert performance the spectacle of the solo performer surrounded by four channels of pre-recorded sound which also surround the audience, is an essential entrapment within the theatre. Nono (like Brecht) challenges us for more than an aesthetic response. His position is political and ethical at the same time.

Representing 'Living Things': Frames in the Acousmatic

Chapters 1 and 3 focus on the *representation* and *perception* of 'live presence' in acousmatic music. In this chapter we have focussed on music including live performers and how this music might work with 'local' and 'field' space frames to overcome the differences and contradictions when the fixed instrument is brought into a relationship with the infinitely flexible acousmatic sound medium. Increasingly we realize that there is no fine line separating this discussion from acousmatic music itself. Much such music (without performer) also addresses the live in these terms and we should not exclude reference to it. The frames we have discussed for live music are based on real ones; there really is a performer, on a stage, in an arena, somewhere in a landscape. But of course any recording transforms this into *the imaginary*. So conversely we also listen to acousmatic sound and try to guess the frame within which it *might* be set. We do not just hear a crowd sound; its recorded acoustic tells us 'in a room' or 'on a street'. We attempt to reconstruct the frame (in the same way and from elements of the same information we examined in Chapter 1).

48 He specifies one microphone feeding one loudspeaker placed directly behind the harpsichord with an option to double this up still keeping the speakers close to the instrument.

Thus it turns out that this entire discussion can penetrate into the acousmatic domain, especially in those works where 'life activity' is represented,[49] landscapes of sound are discernible, and interaction of these elements part of the musical argument.

Michael McNabb's *Dreamsong* (1978 on McNabb, 1983), is clearly a set of scenes that morph seemlessly from one to the next:

> The sounds thus range from the easily recognizable to the totally new, or, more poetically, from the real world to the dreamworld of the imagination, with all that implies with regard to transitions, recurring elements, and the unexpected (McNabb, 1981, p. 36).

The frames transform from the opening crowd (the 'arena') which dramatically collapses onto the 'stage' voice which transforms to the detailed 'event' of the bell sound. But even when not so specific, the emergence and disappearance of the soprano throughout the piece combined with the relatively 'instrumental' nature of the electroacoustic soundworld creates the theatrical impression of *performance stage*, bowing out with Dylan Thomas's voice (1981, p. 51).

In Trevor Wishart's *Vox 5* (especially in the surround-sound four-channel version) the field and frame transformations are exceptionally clear. The work:

> … presents the image of a single supervoice located at front centre stage, whose utterances metamorphose into natural events – the sounds of crowds, bells, bees and other creatures, and less specific sound events – poetic images of the creation and destruction of the world contained within one all-enveloping vocal utterance (the 'Voice of Shiva') (Wishart, 1990).

The creatures and sounds appear and transform across and around the audience space, which represents quite literally the landscape frame, 'the world' which has become the stage in front of the 'super-human' mouth of Shiva (normally a 'local' object but here the literal origin of the 'field') (Wishart, 1988). These in turn coalesce into the final thunderstorm (and its slow retreat).

Robert Normandeau's *Mémoires vives* (1989 on Normandeau, 1990) 'throws' recognizable musical fragments into the distance – from the stage through the arena into an apparently endless space beyond. The space frames are seemlessly linked; the admonition not to overuse reverberation in acousmatic environments is subverted – the piece is 'about' such a vast reverberant space; but reverberation is a characteristic of reflective surfaces, not endless space. A cathedral or woodland is reverberant, but a moorland soundscape is near-anechoic. The knowledge that the music fragments are from a series of masses for the dead, thrown out to echo and reverberate to extinction in the distance, reinforces the poetic image of the losing of 'vivid memories' *within* not outside.

The Laptop Revolution: Abandoning Instruments, what is there to watch?

In Chapter 1 we discussed what clues we might glean to allow us to ascertain whether a live performance is actually taking place. Physical gesture need no longer *cause* the sound in any physical sense. At its most paradoxical the 'laptop

49 Including machines as 'human constructions'.

performer' may move little and think a lot: the clues of *will*, *choice* and *intention* will be inferred from the sounding flow or through apparent responses to the sounds of other performers. The conductor gestures and the music pours forth – just as the conjuror uses elaborately choreographed hand motions to 'bring forth' the image or transformation required. While the DJ does not produce the sound in a mechanical sense, their highly coordinated actions must synchronize, launch, cross-fade and mix a variety of sources. More difficult to grasp will be the possible responses to the audience, many such performers claiming a close and interactive relationship with their listeners. they must judge the collective response to space and pace and make decisions on this basis. One slip and the continuity of the ritual might be lost – although 'recovery' is a skill in itself as all the best performers take risks.

But how might this change of focus effect the results? For Kaffe Matthews the emphasis on 'decisions in the now' is what motivates the new relationship with the computer. Her work has shifted clearly from instrument (violin) with electronics, through live sampling to laptop performance. As this trajectory – uniquely in one individual – follows the trends we are discussing in this chapter, it is worth looking at in more detail.[50] Her initial attraction to electronics in general was through the immediacy of the live performance experience extending the range of possibilities towards sound quality and away from traditional 'notes';

> I began playing a violin with a MIDI trigger, so that I was able to play samples from the violin … Working with electronics, you can work with sounds that are outside the traditional paradigm of music. You're able to work with texture and density, color and shape – the size of the sound. Melodic and rhythmic concerns disappear (Huberman, 2004).

Her first two albums ('cd-Ann' and 'cd-Bea' (Matthews 1997; 1998) cover this work. Recordings of performances using Steim Studio's *LiSa* software, the gestural world of the violin is imprinted at many levels: the melodic material – notwithstanding the comment above, modal fragments and harmonic pitchfields recur – the single very physical down bow gesture, the pizzicato morphology, the held continuous string textures. But there followed a reaction against the more voyeuristic visual aspects of performance in order to emphasize the 'deep listening' experience:

> I wanted to come down off the stage. When I'd been playing violin, people had looked at me as if they were watching this performing monkey: Oh God, look at that girl with the violin and all that technology! All I wanted was for people to turn their eyes off and get down to some listening. "No, there's nothing to watch here!" (Huberman, 2004).

What then emerges is the machine not only as partner, but as improviser of unexpected and unimagined material:

> One of the big attractions about working with a computer was that the machine … would do things and make sounds I would never have imagined on my own, which were often

50 I am indebted to the interview of Kaffe Matthews by Anthony Huberman in *Bomb* magazine issue 89 (Fall 2004) for the following quotes, republished on Kaffe Matthews's website www.annetteworks.com (consulted September 2005).

> the most interesting things. And these were not sounds that I owned or that were a product of my toil, but simply material I could use, more like in a collaboration … It was about collaborating with this instrument that could produce stuff … I started putting the machine in situations where it was going to produce sounds that I wasn't thinking of (Huberman, 2004).

But in a studio the unexpected can be tamed and contained. To be live is to *have to* respond because there are people listening:

> Every movement of mine will do something very powerful to the music, and I decide what to accept and what not to. … *Really, I'm working with this very fragile human boundary between success and failure. One minute you're walking along and everything is breezy and beautiful and the next minute it's a bloody disaster* … it's about all of it happening in the now. I am using this moment. After all, that is all there is. So what happens when we make music out of it? (Huberman, 2004 – emphasis original).

But then full cycle to the visual. The violin may have gone but not the human presence, we are fascinated by what it is doing and will employ all the senses we have; for example, the noise-sample-centred 'cd-dd' (Matthews, 2000) and the much more 'electronic' 'cd-eb + flo' produced live from theremin and room feedback material (Matthews, 2003). We are observing a kind of 'live studio' composition where mistakes – perhaps there are no such thing, just consequences – cannot be 'corrected':

> It's funny because for a few years I'd been going, "Don't watch me, shut your eyes and listen. There's nothing to watch." But everybody does watch me. Well, a lot of people do. And I'm always saying that there's nothing to watch and gradually I've learned that there is. They watch my face. They watch me get surprised, fed up, angry and then excited. They stand over my shoulder and watch my computer screen. It all actually gives them a way into what's going on (Huberman, 2004).

Although it must be said that focus on expressive body language is nothing new, from agonized pianist to transported rock guitarist – not forgetting the soundless conductor's closed eyes and ecstatic look.

Polyphony – Density – Improvisation

The move from a solo performer with a single computer to a duo, trio or more confronts an issue which spans all genres of music – polyphony. Put in contemporary terms, this means more than one simultaneous coherent 'line' of musical thought. Polyphonies exist in most cultures: some highly coordinated, as in much gamelan music, Banda-Linda trumpet hockets, Bach fugues; others deliberately disengage the layers and allow the listener the freedom to form much more subjective relationships (or not) within the passing 'stream of consciousness', as in the American experimental tradition from Ives to Cage and beyond. The situation is made more complex in the contemporary computer environment. In principle the sound producing power of a solo performer has become polyphonic – capable of creating many layers of the musical stream. Thus the move to groups of performers in this field has been tentative and solo artists remain a majority.[51]

Evan Parker is credited with coining the term 'laminal' about the improvisatory techniques of the improvisation group AMM (usually a trio) whose work from the 1960s focused on the layering and evolution of textures rather than detailed exchange/solo/group interactions (Prévost, 1995, p. 143).[52] Participants and observers in this kind of improvisatory activity stress a kind of listening much closer to that of the acousmatic composer, focusing on matters of texture, balance, detail, grain, shape. To this they add a stress on interpersonal sound communication which is profoundly 'live' with a strongly ethical (even political) stance. 'From the very beginning AMM was a vehicle for continuous self-invention' (Prévost, 1995, p. 12). But the technology of those years (when used) did not easily allow the storage and replay of many layers *from each individual*. The performer rarely created a polyphonic texture: the individual was the agent and agency of a single stream.[53] But carrying the idea of *lamination* through to current developments might help explain the emphasis on solo artists; now an individual performer is in command of a potential polyphony – and neither performers nor listeners can easily decode 'a polyphony of polyphonies'.

There seem to be two contrasting strategies in response to this vastly increased power. The first has been poetically described by David Toop (2004, pp. 14–16). A kind of simultaneous 'happening' in which musicians are booked for a performance who maybe have never played together before – or certainly not regularly – and who are often very dissimilar in performance 'style'. How their 'voices' (single or polyphonic) finally 'mix' will be truly unpredictable. 'The way to enjoy this event, to build structure and meaning, was to find a location somewhere within the web, then feel the threads grow and mutate in all dimensions. This was true for the players, too' (Toop, 2004, p. 16). Strangely many such events counter completely the solo/duo dominated CD label environment described above. A sometimes large number of such soloists coalescing in a short sharp evening's electronic jam.[54]

Secondly, a contrasting case, is to form a stable group and openly to address matters of interactivity, density, polyphony and comprehensibility across rehearsals and performances. This latter example includes the Zapruda Trio from this improvisatory tradition. In *Live at Smallfish* (Zapruda Trio, 2000) the sound layers are clearly differentiated in texture, pace and tessitura. Space is also used to great effect in separating the strands. This is not the 'oceanic' experience that David

---

51 Labels such as Warp and Rephlex are dominated by solo artists.

52 See also Chapter 1 where I cite Parker's comment on the similar role of Hugh Davies in *The Music Improvisation Company*.

53 This tradition, although elaborated and extended through Lawrence Casserley's live electronic processing, is continued in the work of the Evan Parker Electro-Acoustic Ensemble (for example, Parker et al., 1999).

54 David Toop describes such an event with about seven participants, the majority otherwise well known soloists ranging from Eddie Prévost (AMM) to Tom Jenkinson (Squarepusher), which produced very uneven results (Toop, 2004, pp. 36–38).

Toop describes – omnidirectional and amniotic – but one in which individuals have become much more clearly differentiated.[55]

Postscript: the Unexpected is always upon us – Live Coding

The most unexpected interface for live sound control to have reemerged in recent years is the *lexical*; reading and writing. The increasing dominance of graphic interfaces for music software obscured the continuing presence of the command-line tradition, the code writer, the hacker. The code writing of *deferred time* computer programming may be assembled out of time order, debugged and optimized. The idea that writing code for sound production and processing might be a *performance* activity is at first consideration akin to a composer writing out a score during a performance in response to what has just been heard. In an article which combines a description of practice with a preliminary statement of aesthetic aims, Nick Collins, Alex McClean, Julian Rohrhuber and Adrian Ward (2003) ask rhetorically:

> Why not explore the interfacing of the language itself as a novel performance tool, in stark contrast to pretty but conventional user interfaces? We certainly contend that music-making is more compelling with elements of risk and reference to the performance environment, and that the human participant is essential to social musical activities. (Collins, McClean, Rohrhuber and Ward (2003), p. 322).

The sense of danger and risk is explicit in the activity, but they also suggest an extension of the idea to include *game* scenarios, whether collaborative or competitive.

Summary and Conclusion

There are many aesthetics of live electronic music. We can, in the first instance, view the differences historically: I suggest this is no simple evolution but a series of small revolutions centring around the very notion of 'live' activity in relation to new developments in technology. I would designate three paradigms to date. The first was enabled by the steady miniaturization of circuits following the adoption of the transistor and the subsequent development of voltage controlled synthesis and processing in the mid-1960s. Musically it has two focuses: signal processing of live instrument or voice and/or their combination with pre-recorded material (sometimes referred to as 'mixed' electronic music). The second paradigm centres on the revolution of the small personal computer and the invention of the Midi standard in the early 1980s. This enabled 'event processing' in so-called 'real-time' (via Midi), driving usually synthetic sounds with relatively little signal processing, any acoustic instrument or voice becoming progressively optional. The third was a consequence of a quantum leap in processing power for personal computers (and the emergence of the laptop) in the mid-1990s, to allow real-time signal processing as

55 David Toop's 'oceanic' metaphor is well used both in *Ocean of Sound* (Toop, 1995) and *Haunted Weather* (Toop, 2004) but in its overarching power I sense something drowning, too.

well as eventually absorbing most aspects of both studio and performance systems. This encouraged the combination of all the previous possibilities in an open mix of event, signal and pre-recorded sound processing but usually omitting any live production of acoustic sound. At each juncture the previous 'archaeological layer' has not peacefully given way to the next but has carried on, adapting and upgrading its technology, but not itself substantially changing aesthetic aims. The newer approaches are usually developed by new generation musicians who reject (or at least ignore) the previous aesthetic positions. Thus we have a mix of 'live' electronic practices cohabiting with occasional hybridization.

In parallel to developing notions of 'live' go changing ideas of 'space'.[56] I have suggested that in both live electronic and acousmatic music composers play with 'space frames', whether recorded from the 'real environment' or created artificially. With new technology these have an increasing flexibility and can join in the creation of new narrative strategies. I have suggested that – for those wishing to retain a link to the live acoustic music world – ideas of 'local' and 'field' help partition the spacescape and can help reestablish perceivable causal links of performance gesture and sound at the local level. In the field of 'mixed' music – instrument or voice combined with pre-prepared sound – the two worlds might so easily be in conflict: fixed against flying, infinitely malleable against refined and constrained – not to speak of the longer performance tradition of the instrument. Each has invaded the other with mixed success but striking individual examples. As at some time in each chapter of this book we are faced finally with the apparent paradox of a music described as 'live' but with no vestige of acoustic sound production. It might further be presented to us in spaces that are omnidirectional and immersive, that even allow us to 'form' the work ourselves by changing position and perspective, and sometimes by sampled listening. In this we create our own musical space in conjunction with the space of the performance. These spaces were always there, of course, but have now become more fully integrated into the 'total' experience.

Everything we have talked about in Chapters 1 and 2 and chapters 3 and 4 of this book rest on two 'mirror' technical tools: the microphone and the loudspeaker. They are the twin doorways connecting the electronic and acoustic sound worlds. They are a ubiquitous and integral part of the dislocated world we inhabit. Chapters 5 and 6 examine each in turn and their contribution to 'living' music.

---

56 See also Landy (1991, especially Section IX) for a discussion on listening and performance spaces.

CHAPTER FIVE

To Input the Live: Microphones and other Human Activity Transducers

Introduction

Getting world-produced activity into a suitable form for machine interpretation of some kind is a multi-dimensional matter.[1] Humans, for example, produce all kinds of signs of life, mechanical, electrical and electro-magnetic. All our existing senses plus some enhancements given to us by science (the ability to monitor brain activity, for example) may be brought to bear. The first such transducer of human activity to the electrical world was the morse code key, a simple 'on-off' switch which revolutionised text communication starting in the 1830s. The microphone was the second, translating changes in air pressure (constituting sound waves) into voltage (or current) variations – an 'analogue' of the original. Then there was the harnessing of keyboards (and other 'controllers' modelled on existing acoustic instruments) which developed slowly throughout the twentieth century. And since about 1980, the principle that *any* human activity might be used to control sounding devices has led to direct links to cybernetics, haptics, robotics and the vast range of human-computer interface research, including bio-physical (Roads, 1996a; Paradiso and O'Modhrain, 2003). The consequences of these last may only now be glimpsed, so this review will go from firmer to more speculative ground.

The Microphone

The microphone invented genres – crooning would not have been possible without it, and later rock 'n' roll. 'Close mic' techniques try to exclude the environment, the room, the space and lead directly to the projection of intimacy. But the sound changes, too, the bass frequencies are boosted; we move nearer and are enveloped (bass frequencies are less directional) – which might be reassuring or threatening. In Stockhausen's *Mikrophonie I* (1964) (Stockhausen, 1974; 1995) this is an active tool of sound processing and an incidental one of theatre. For Cage the intimacy of 'small sounds' (not normally heard beyond a few centimetres) could be shared and encouraged (microphone as 'microscope'). But the microphone is also spy ('bug') and ubiquitous mouthpiece (the mobile/cellphone), transforming the spaces

1 All of the interfaces and transducers discussed in this chapter may also be used to capture any 'world activity' and the boundary between this and *human* activity will not be clear – as discussed in Chapter 2. Nonetheless much research is devoted to *human* activity transducers and interfaces and our focus will remain there.

around us into potential performance. Once the junior partner of the loudspeaker, the microphone is catching up in the invasion of our personal and public spaces.

The microphone has never been a passive observer. It started life at the same moment as its mirror twin the loudspeaker in the earliest telephone of Alexander Graham Bell in 1876. The human voice was the first and most important sound source, making all the more shocking its disembodiment and dislocation. In the telephone the process was electric from the start while Thomas Edison's invention of a year later (1877), the phonograph, retained a reliance on purely mechanical recording and playback processes for many further years.[2] The reason was simple: the first electric microphone and loudspeaker were adequate only for that sound source most robust to distortion and noise, the spoken voice. The system had a frequency response barely adequate to allow the recognition of vowels. We recognize speech (even more so the person speaking) through greatly distorting transmission and reproduction systems. The brain is extraordinarily flexible at understanding context within language streams. The words 'sun' and 'fun' heard via a telephone receiver in isolation may be indistinguishable, yet in the majority of normal speech contexts we make relatively few mistakes decoding them. But for song (especially at the extremes in tessitura) this microphone was clearly inadequate until the complete range of pitch fundamentals (and the hope of hearing the first formant for vowel recognition) was available.

The point of the following taxonomy of microphones is not to concentrate on technological improvements or evolution. Each of these types of microphone adds its own contribution to the resulting sound. As electroacoustic music has evolved, however, the 'grain' of recordings (carrying historical and location information) has become an intrinsic part of their perceived quality. The ideal of a 'transparent' sound somehow independent of its history might be seen as both unattainable and even undesirable. We shall return to a discussion of these traces later in the chapter.

Air
- Carbon – telephone
- Dynamic – moving coil
- Capacitance – capacitor, electret

Contact
- Piezo – bridge/body (string) transducers
- Moving coil – cartridge (turntables)

Electro-magnetic
- Metal string (guitar) pickup

The principles of microphone design and construction were established quickly after Alexander Graham Bell's first successful telephone of 1876. The very first microphone in this set-up involved a diaphragm connected to a metal pin dipped

2 The first commercially available recording made with electric microphones was made in 1920 (Copeland, 1991, pp. 15–17), but realistically there was approaching 50 years between the invention of the phonograph and the first full electric recording and playback systems (1877-ca.1925).

into dilute acid in a metal container. The sound vibrated the diaphragm, varying the degree of submersion of the pin and the resistance of the pin-container circuit. Bell quickly replaced these with dry 'magneto-transmitters' for his first fully tested circuit, requiring the user to shout (and the receiver to listen very closely). Within a year he gave a public demonstration over an 29km connection (Solymar, 1999, p. 100). In fact in the immediate years that followed a rich variety of designs (including all the principles still in use today) were tested, finally settling on carbon granules as the variable resistor (Eargle, 2004, pp. 1–3). This design was optimized from the early 1890s and in dominant use in all audio till the electric era was launched in the 1920s, continuing in telephone technology to the present.

In the carbon microphone the diaphragm impinges on a 'button' container that is compressed or decompressed by its vibrations. This varies the resistance of the carbon granules and hence modulates a dc current which is passed through. Even in theory the transduction here is *non-linear*[3] (the higher the input the more distorted the sound) but interestingly a certain amount of distortion increases intelligibility, through a perceived increase in higher frequencies (Eargle, 2004, p. 4). Poorly transduced low frequencies tend to be 'filled in' by the perception system. This is the so-called 'missing fundamental' phenomenon in which low harmonic partials are reconstructed from higher ones.[4] This gives us the recognizable 'tinny' sound of the telephone, which is effectively acting as a band-pass filter in the hi-mid frequency region, luckily where speech recognition is at its most sensitive.

The advent and development of *wireless* (radio) telegraphy and later broadcasting were both revolutionary 'one to many' methods of dissemination as opposed to the 'one to one' of the first wire age. From the 1890s these also brought greater demands to bear on the electroacoustic chain. Microphones were used to modulate the radio signal directly. In the absence of electric amplifiers this severely limited their range. Following the invention of the valve by Lee de Forest in 1907 there was a major leap in possibilities as the first valve amplifiers were developed. The microphone-plus-amplifier chain was now powerful enough to drive both wire and wireless transmitters with more than local reception, most notably that developed at AT&T (later Bell) Labs in the USA. This allowed both the first US coast-to-coast telephone service as well as the first trans-atlantic voice broadcast in 1915[5] (Solymar, 1999, pp. 159–162). Following the first world war the advent of public radio networks was meteoric. While initially using carbon microphones, Western Electric and RCA in the United States, and Neumann in Europe developed a new generation of microphones based on *capacitance* and *moving coil* principles (Borwick, 1990, pp. 9–12).[6] While initially for radio broadcasting, the same technologies rapidly moved into recording,

---

3 The change in current is not exactly proportional to the change in resistance.

4 Common in any small (for example transistor radio) loudspeakers where we perceive low pitches even when they are not physically reproduced – although in telephones they are not even transmitted.

5 Marconi's first transatlantic broadcast had been of morse code – or at least a repeated modulated pulse. The date of 1901 has been contested but by 1903 there was a reliable link.

6 Also history documents on http://www.neumann.com (consulted December 2005).

quickly displacing mechanical-acoustic means throughout the recording chain from about 1925.[7]

The second kind of microphone to be seriously tested and used was based on principles of capacitance.[8] This is a measure of the ability to store charge on (slightly simplifying, for our purposes) two parallel plates. If a dc voltage is applied to the plates a charge results (following the equation Q (charge stored) = C (capacitance) x E (applied dc voltage)). The nearer the plates are to each other the greater the capacitance. If the microphone diaphragm is made into one of the plates by being coated with an extremely thin layer of conducting material, then its vibrations (following the sound pressure) will result in similar changes in capacitance over time. In fact if the charge (C) is constant, the change in capacitance causes a ripple in the voltage (the signal) between the plates which can easily be separated out.[9] While of higher quality, the signal is also at very low level and requires an immediate amplifier stage. A close relative of the capacitor is the *electret* microphone. Some (then) newly discovered materials (such as *polytetrafluoroethylene*) can hold charge permanently. Phantom power is not needed for the capsule (though many designs will still require it for associated amplification) and the circuit design can be simplified. This has been the principle used in recent miniature microphones for 'concealed' use (attached to clothing) and for instrument amplification (see below).

The same principle that drives most loudspeakers, that of the moving coil, was slightly later in being applied to microphone technology and only came into common use in the early 1930s. Sometimes known as a 'dynamic' microphone, a coil of wire is attached to the diaphragm. Suspended in a permanent magnetic field, movement of the coil generates a voltage across its ends, which is proportional to the velocity of movement. This relates to the *pressure* of the incoming wave; as this is not directional, this design produces in principle an *omnidirectional* characteristic. Equal amplitude waves from any direction cause an equivalent electrical output. In practice the case and body of the microphone act as an obstruction (increasingly for higher frequencies) to waves coming from behind the diaphragm. Thus even omnidirectional microphones become more directional at higher frequencies.

A variant of this approach is found in the *ribbon* microphone. Here the diaphragm itself is made to be conducting and replaces the coil in the magnetic field – the function of the two elements is combined. The ribbon is directly moved by the sound wave pressure and a voltage generated across its terminals. A common feature of this design is the suspension of the ribbon such that both sides could be open to incoming sound waves. This leads to a 'figure of eight' response – two equally sensitive zones 'head on' to each side of the microphone (though producing voltages

---

7 The development of 'talking films' (*The Jazz Singer* was released in 1927) completed what was clearly the most radical decade of development in electroacoustic audio technology following the end of World War One.

8 Edison had developed a prototype and established the principle of operation as early as 1879. The modern capacitor microphone dates essentially from 1917 with developments by E.C. Wente at Bell Labs for Western Electric (Eargle, 2004, pp. 4–5).

9 The applied dc voltage is known as 'phantom power' to the microphone.

of opposite sense, '+' or '-').[10] This is known as the *pressure gradient* principle – it is the *difference* in pressure between the two surfaces of the ribbon that causes the displacement. Introduced by RCA in the USA from 1931 it was this microphone that was made famous by 'crooners' such as Bing Crosby (see below). It was also popular in broadcasting and is commonly seen in many BBC photos of that era.

Directional microphones, for example those with a *cardioid* response, may be constructed by combining omnidirectional and figure-of-eight systems[11] or by a newer generation of designs which use a single diaphragm. This is open directly to sound at one side and restricted access to the rear side, where the sound waves must traverse an *acoustic labyrinth* with consequent delay. Properly timed this results in decreased sensitivity to sound from the rear direction and hence the required directionality (Eargle, 2004).

The term 'contact microphone' is sometimes misunderstood or at least misused. Most commonly the misconception is to apply the term to any miniature microphone used in close proximity to the sound source. True contact microphones are designed to transduce the *mechanical vibration* of the source directly to an electrical signal without the 'intervention' of the air as medium. Once again a moving conductor (usually a coil) in a magnetic field can fulfil this function. Here, however, the diaphragm is not needed. If attached to a vibrating source object the coil-conductor is moved directly and a varying voltage results. A classic moving coil contact transducer (not here called a 'microphone') is found in high quality turntable cartridges[12] in which vibrations of a needle are converted to a changing voltage.

Another transducer technique results from the *piezo-electric* phenomenon. Quartz and certain crystal salts of potassium, ammonium and lithium exhibit the phenomenon of developing a voltage from one side to the other when deformed.[13] In fact crystal (air) microphones were common for amateur use in the 1960s, but of low quality and sensitivity. However, correctly engineered this class of transducer has been used in many industrial contact applications, as well as in the design of underwater signal detection. Also small sound transducers for such as string instruments may be attached to body or bridge to pick up the sound.[14] In addition general purpose pressure sensitive detectors which use this technique are now common and may easily be applied in, for example, interactive installations.

The electro-magnetic pickup[15] is that commonly found on electric guitars and requires metal strings. The individual pickup consists of a permanent magnet with a copper winding. A moving metal object (the string) in the vicinity of the magnetic

10 Not to be confused with stereo – the two are added at the diaphragm by definition.

11 While more difficult to construct these have the advantage of remote control variation of the directional characteristic. But to behave equally sensitively over a useable range requires the natural resonance of the diaphragm to be damped. There is a trade off between linearity and sensitivity (Eargle, 2004).

12 Lower quality cartridges often used *piezo-electric* techniques (see below).

13 Of course this is a small deformation, within the elastic limit of the substance and well below fracture levels! This is also the principle behind 'crystal radio sets'.

14 Most notably those pioneered by Barcus-Berry (USA) from 1963.

15 This is strictly neither an air pressure nor a contact device; it is exactly as its name – an *electro-magnetic* transducer.

field changes its strength which in turn induces a voltage in the winding. An individual pickup is used on each string; as the quality of the sound varies along the length of the string several sets of pickups are sometimes installed. Unfortunately *any* stray electro-magnetic field (such as produced from the mains) is picked up and hum reduction techniques[16] have been developed. The Gibson Guitar Corporation introduced the first true electric guitar (the *ES150*) in 1936.

Finally there are miniature electret microphones that fit either close externally (for example in the mouthpiece (flute) or bell (saxophone)) or (more rarely) internally inside the mouthpiece itself. These are not strictly contact microphones although they are loosely described as such by some performers. True reed contact transducers (attached to the reed directly) have been devized using piezo-electric techniques.[17] It is difficult to say, however, exactly how this signal relates to the more complex waves within the main air column of the instrument which are much closer in form to what we normally hear.

Directionality, Proximity and Distance Effects

It will be clear that microphones do not behave quite like ears, still less like 'two ears in a head'. From some parts of the classical music recording industry to soundscape recordists there are continuing pressures towards recreating the 'original' soundfield at an 'ideal' point. The two principles of operation *pressure* and *pressure gradient* produce *omnidirectional* and *directional* (broadly 'figure of eight') responses. If we combine these two principles in a single microphone then a variety of directional sensitivity patterns can be constructed (Eargle, 2004, Chapter 5). In addition 'super-directional' microphones (used, for example, in film location recording, journalism, nature recording and spying) can be constructed using interference techniques, acoustic lenses and reflectors. But just like instruments which do not radiate all parts of their spectrum equally in all directions, so microphones have varying direction sensitivity over the audible frequency range (and beyond). As observed above high frequencies are masked by the body of the microphone; whatever its construction it becomes increasingly directional at high frequencies. As smaller microphones are constructed the effect is reduced but it could never be eliminated (unless a point microphone could be invented).

For pressure gradient (directional) microphones the displacement of the diaphragm is proportional to the difference in pressure from one side to the other: this consists of two components both of which depend on the *distance travelled* between the front and back of the diaphragm:

a) On the one hand the wave's pressure changes all the time (in the nature of sound) and the instantaneous value of pressure gradient across the diaphragm is simply given by the *phase difference* between front and back. For a fixed

---

16 Such as Gibson's *humbucker* pickup (designed by Seth Lover in 1955) which uses a double pickup engineered to produce phase cancellation of the noise common to the two.

17 The Barcus-Berry piezo device described in Rehfeldt (1977, p. 78) for the clarinet has been discontinued and replaced with an electret (air) version.

path difference between the front and back of the diaphragm higher frequencies will exhibit higher pressure differences.

b) On the other hand there is a pressure decrease across the diaphragm due to the falling off in energy as the wave travels away from its source. This is given by the inverse square law of energy dissipation which is not dependent on frequency.

The resulting output is the net addition of the two components and gives (interacting with the mass of the diaphragm) a boost to the bass end. At greater distances the inverse square 'fall off' within the microphone is relatively smaller and the bass boost negligible. As the source distance is reduced this component becomes increasingly dominant and bass lifts around +20db may easily be obtained (Eargle, 2004, p. 65). When used in live performance this directly resulted in the 'crooning' sound, mimicking the closer mouth-ear relationship of intimacy and confidentiality, reassuring both in song ('White Christmas') and in the 'late night, relaxed and intimate' style of continuity announcements of radio broadcast.[18]

Before we discuss the possible musical functions of amplification there are footnotes on two sound in space relationships that microphones capture and composers who recreate sonic spaces need to understand. The first is high frequency roll off with distance from the source. Even for direct signals (without any intervening objects between source and listener) the air absorbs higher frequencies preferentially; thus there is an increasing loss of high frequencies with distance (Eargle, 2004, pp. 84–5). This effect is further increased if there are obstacles in the pathway – lower frequencies diffract easily around them compared to higher ones. Secondly, in a reverberant space, source to listener distance changes the direct to reverberant sound level ratio. In theory, if the enclosed space is relatively regular (in the sense that its reflective surfaces are evenly distributed in all directions), then the reverberation level is even throughout, wherever the sound source is placed. Thus as source moves away from microphone (equivalent to listener position), the reverberation level *remains constant* and only the direct sound level falls. If both levels reduce then the sense is of the listener moving away from the space altogether (which may be the desired impression). However John Chowning has suggested an elaborated model in his spatial positioning algorithms in which there is a distinction between *global* and *local* reverberation, the latter being a small additional component in the vicinity of the source, hence a directional/spatial component of reverberation (Chowning, 1977).

As we have seen, microphones have had three complementary and overlapping uses with sound: for *recording*, *transmission* and *projection*. This last is where live performance has traditionally been located, although the other two are increasingly used in 'live mix' and interactive environments. But live use *of the microphone* is what we will discuss next. This is more commonly called 'amplification'. Here we will focus on its relationship to the source of the sound; we shall focus on the output

18 Omnidirectional microphones do not exhibit this proximity effect and some sound engineers advocate their use for close amplification for this reason.

– the loudspeaker – in Chapter 6, although the two depend on each other. What, then, are the *musical* functions of amplification of live sound?

Some Musical Functions of Live Amplification

Of the acousmatic dislocations discussed in Chapter 4 live amplification involves one – dislocation of space. This is often an ambiguous dislocation as the source of the sound is usually present and the direct acoustic sound can often still be perceived. The visual aspect may work in a subtle way.

> Rick Altman has argued that sound in film is subsidiary to image: a 'pure' or unattributed sound is always marked by doubt and mystery until it can be tracked to an synchronized with its source. Thus, Altman can declare '... the sound asks *where?* And the image responds *here!*' ... Sound, and especially the sound of the human voice, is experienced as enigmatic or anxiously incomplete until its source can be identified, which is usually to say, visualized ... (Connor, 2000, pp. 19–20).

The perfect synchronicity of action to sound is one of the major components of ventriloquism. We appear to *relocate* (specifically) a voice source to a dummy human whose lips move in perfect time (Connor, 2000).[19] With instrumental music the location to source has an element of this expectation; the two modes of sight and sound have evolved to reinforce sound location search. The disembodied 'voice' of the instrument has to be brought back into a relationship with its origins. In terms of the ideas discussed in Chapter 4, amplification would normally be a *local* function maintaining that relationship to origin and location, but that need not always be the case. The degree to which spatial dislocation is used can become part of the composer's range of options. But care must be taken to understand the consequences to the perceiver of any time delay between visual and aural cues. As with badly dubbed films even a small delay can result in a strong dislocation of source-to-sound.

I want to distinguish six functions of amplification in live music[20] (focussing in the first instance on traditional instrumental and vocal sources): *Balance*, *Blend*, *Projection (and Spatialization)*, *Perspective*, *Colouration* and *Resonance–Feedback*. These are by no means separate ideas, and overlap and combine in many instances.

Balance

The use of amplification to balance instrumental and vocal forces *changes the relationships* of the mechanical sounding world. Instrumental combinations which

19 As well as the almost unremarked ubiquity of post-recording and synchronising dialogue in film production.

20 Some of the examples which follow are not normally described as 'live electronic' music but they are vital – even central – to any discussion on 'live music requiring electronic technology for its presentation'.

could only have been balanced through performance practice or sheer numbers[21] could easily be brought to some kind of 'equivalence in presence'. The new style known as 'crooning' is a significant early example where an intimate vocal style could be balanced with stronger instrumental forces. The rise of the big band in the 1930s created an imbalance with the solo singer; as Charlie Gillett explains:

> … as a vocalist with Paul Whiteman, he [Bing Crosby] had learned the techniques of singing with a megaphone (necessary before the days of electrical amplification if the singer was to make himself heard above the orchestra). The megaphone produced a curious deadpan and emotionless manner of expression, which was to form the basis of the "crooning" style that developed after microphones and electrical amplification were introduced (Gillett, 1983, p. 5).

So, too, electric guitar pickups and amplification changed the relationship with other instruments in jazz and popular music, allowing a more soloistic function to emerge.

> In a fervent manifesto entitled 'Guitarmen, wake up and pluck!' and published in December 1939 by jazz journal Down Beat, Charlie Christian praised the electric muse by saying things like: *'Electrical amplification has given guitarists a new lease on life … amplifying my instrument has made it possible for me to get a wonderful break.'* He also advocated solo guitar playing: *'So take heart, all you starving guitarists … Practice solo stuff, single string and otherwise, and save up a few dimes to amplify your instrument.'* (Duchossoir, 1998, pp. 16–18 – emphasis original).

Jazz and rock 'n' roll were to have a profound effect on minimalism (at least in its emerging period). Charlie Parker, Dizzie Gillespie, John Coltrane and Miles Davis recur throughout their declared influences.[22] The microphone allows the combination of electrophones (such as the electric organ and electric piano) with acoustic instruments, percussion, and voices which together drive the drones, rhythms and brash 'loudness' of the first decade of this genre. Terry Riley's early solo and electronic works (such as *Poppy Nogood and the Phantom Band* (1967 on Riley, 1971)) are based around the combination of electric organs and soprano saxophone. The Philip Glass ensemble similarly combines electric keyboards and saxophones, from *Two Pages* and *Music in Fifths* (1969) through to *Einstein on the Beach* (1976) (Glass, 1994; 1979). For La Monte Young, amplification is the very basis of his *Dream House* project which, in the (LP) recording of a small part of *The Tortoise, his Dreams and Journeys* (Young, 1973), combines electronic drones and amplified voices and instruments:

---

21 The increasing size of orchestras of the romantic era (compared to the classical) necessitated an increase in the bass sections (strings especially) in greater proportion than the higher sounding sections to preserve balance. This is combined with a vast increase in the range of orchestral instruments available (especially in the brass section): compare Berlioz, Wagner, Strauss and Mahler's orchestra to Haydn's (Carse, 1964).

22 Jazz and rock 'n' roll both contribute to early minimalism's instrumentation (both electric and acoustic) and amplification; they join musics of Africa and Asia as a major influence on its materials.

> By 1962 I had formulated the concept of a Dream House in which a work would be played continuously and ultimately exist in time as a 'living organism with a life and tradition of its own' … in September 1966 I was able to create my first truly continuous electronic sound environment … I maintained an environment of constant periodic sound waveforms almost continuously from September 1966 through January 1970. Marian and I sang, worked and lived in this environment and studied its effects on ourselves and the varied groups of people who were invited to spend time with the frequencies (Young, 1973).

Virtually all the early works[23] of Steve Reich rely on amplification to balance disparate forces. For example in *Drumming* (1971 on Reich, 1974):

> I found that if I used the microphone to make the volume of my voice almost as loud as the drums, but no louder, I could then make some of the resulting patterns very much as if my voice were another set of drums, gradually bringing out one pattern after another (Reich, 2002, p. 64).

The 'resulting patterns' Reich refers to are constructed by the ear of the listener (including the performers) from a kind of hocket between instruments; melodic shapes seem to 'leap out' from the ongoing phasing texture. These can then be reinforced by the vocal 'imitations' (or by the piccolo when glockenspiels are the main instruments).

Blend

One stage further than balance. We have an attempt to integrate timbres for a range of reasons. This would only apply to music within a particular aesthetic, that where *fused sounds*, textures and sound 'blocks' (Erickson, 1975) are important. The dislocation and relocation of the sound in these cases is clear – the aim is to bring different sources into a superimposed integrated relationship to create entirely new timbres in which the constituent elements are indistinguishable. Another possible byproduct (usually intended) is that of psychoacoustic artefacts, sum and difference tones, reinforced harmonics, and sometimes resultant melodies. Here the sum may be considerably greater than the individual parts. Sum and difference tones are formed in the perception system of the listener – they are perceived but not measurable as a physical presence in the air. Resultant melodies are often formed from combinations of sources playing looped melodic patterns, exactly as described by Reich above, except here some of the material is constructed from this 'subjective in the ear' material. Often there is not one such resultant; the listener 'constructs' the melody from within the loops and can change between several alternative hearings. Responses of this kind are more individual and subjective and engage a kind of 'game play' in the listening process. The early works of Philip Glass combine sounds of similar morphology: electric organs, soprano saxophone in *Music in 12 Parts*, for example (Glass, 1989; 1996). Subtle differences in intonation, 'small' differences

---

23 Reich has also remarked that amplification is at the root of his new concept of instrumentation for music theatre, replacing the overblown acoustic forces of 'over 100 years ago' (Reich, 2002, p. 212).

inherent in electronic production,[24] especially at high amplification levels, add 'edge' to the generation of secondary 'melodies' as psychoacoustic by-products:

> What I found happening when we amplified ... was that we were getting psychoacoustical effects – overtones and things that would happen as a result of repetitive structures played rapidly at high volume. You actually hear sounds that nobody is playing, a shiny top to the music (Glass cited in Kozinn, 1997, p. 106).

This is strictly not the same as balance – the relationship may here be *unequal*, the function of one source may be to reinforce just one aspect of another. In Steve Reich's *Music for Mallet Instruments, Voices and Organ* (1973 on Reich, 1974) both balance and blend functions are integral to the work but apply to different sources. The three very contrasting sound types (one by definition loudspeaker produced) were worked out through experiment. Reich had spontaneously sung augmented held notes while working on marimba patterns. There followed a lengthy period of rehearsal with a wide variety of instruments, male and female voices: 'Each instrument and each voice had its own microphone so as to blend all the instrumental and vocal timbres' (Reich, 2002, p. 76). He eventually settled on wood and metal mallet instruments, female voices and electric organ creating 'a constant vocal-instrumental blend as one of the basic timbres of the entire piece' (p. 78).

Projection (and Spatialization)

Projection is the bringing to perceptual foreground or focus of relatively lower amplitude sounds (or constituent components of sounds). While this usually involves 'making the sound louder' this need not necessarily be the case. Making a quiet sound 'available' across a large listening area may involve low level amplification over many loudspeakers. Microphone type, size and position are critical. In general small sound detail (which is usually synonymous with high frequency presence) demands close microphone proximity. The consequent combination of high frequency presence and bass lift engages a general feeling of 'close intimacy' which has become central to much of the aesthetic here. We are not only listening, but feel as if we are *listening in*. Cage's *Cartridge Music* (1960) (Cage, 1960) is his most famous work to exploit the 'amplification of small sounds'. The use of non-air-medium transducers allows far higher levels of amplification to be achieved without

24 Especially analogue production. Recordings of the Philip Glass Ensemble do not indicate makes or types of keyboards used. In Kozinn (1997, p. 105) he describes the keyboards in use in the Glass ensemble in 1980 and the details of their amplification requirements. Tim Page confirms that Farfisa electric organs were the original instruments but that the new recording of *Music in Twelve Parts* 'represents a radical improvement in electronic technology' (details not given). Parts 1–8 of the first version were recorded in 1974–75 (Page, 1997, pp. 99–100). While the sound is clearly 'better' in the later recording, many will prefer the 'edge' of the earlier version (Glass, 1989 and 1996).

feedback[25] – although feedback can and sometimes does occur which is perfectly acceptable to Cage:

> The title *Cartridge Music* derives from the use in its performance of cartridges, that is, phonograph pick-ups into which needles are inserted for playing recordings. Contact microphones are also used. These latter are applied to chairs, tables, wastebaskets etc.; various suitable objects (toothpicks, matches, slinkies, piano wires, feathers, etc.) are inserted in the cartridges. Both the microphones and cartridges are connected to amplifiers that go to loudspeakers, the majority of the sounds produced being small and requiring amplification in order to be heard (Cage cited in Kostelanetz, 1970, p. 144).

Phonograph cartridges are not simple contact microphones, however. Cage contrasts the two, cartridges requiring more active performance. The score is graphic, allowing readings:

> … enabling one to go about his business of making sounds, generally by percussive or fricative means, on the object in a cartridge, changing dial positions on the amplifiers, making 'auxilliary sounds' by use of the objects to which contact microphones are attached, removing an object from a cartridge and inserting another, and, finally, performing 'loops': these are repeated actions, periodic in rhythm (Cage cited in Kostelanetz, 1970, p. 144).

The phonograph needle is a device originally intended to 'trace' a sound wave already physically pressed into vinyl, as such used in many previous of Cage's works from *Imaginary Landscape No.1* (1939) (Cage, 1939) which uses 'phonograph test recordings'. The needle is a mechanical input to an 'electronic synthesizer' (the cartridge), transducing *movement* electromagnetically to voltage variation and hence sound. Here Cage is extending the range of interface objects (replacing the needle) and producing the movement to create sound from performance activity.

One of the most important aspects of Stockhausen's vocal work *Stimmung* (Stockhausen, 1969; 1993b) must be conveyed through reinforcement of the harmonics of a sung vowel.[26] This is achieved through both exaggerated mouth cavity shape control and amplification of the six singers, each to an individual loudspeaker. There is a very real sense in which this is a product of a social concert environment. The Tibetan chant tradition of Buddhist monks and the Mongolian *khoomi* singing technique show a similar focus on the play of harmonics above a held drone[27] but have not (of course) developed with the need for amplification. Amplification techniques are defined by the social definitions of concert hall performance practice in the western tradition, and its consequent acoustic and spatial dispositions. Stockhausen's *Mikrophonie I* (1964) (Stockhausen, 1974; 1995) was briefly mentioned above; it is rare in its exploitation of the microphone as a truly mobile performance instrument in its own right. A large (155cm) tam-tam is played by two 'teams' of two players,

---

25 The waves from loudspeakers are picked up directly by air mics in a 'classic' feedback loop; feedback can occur with contact transducers but the loudspeaker sound has to be strong enough to excite the original source directly (see *Resonance*).

26 Strictly the accurate control of the vowel formants (see the score and Scientific American (1978)).

27 Very substantially suppressed in the case of khoomi.

one on each side of the instrument. In each team, one player excites the tam-tam with a vast variety of materials (cardboard, metal, wood, rubber, plastic) and excitation types (hitting and friction); the excitation implements have themselves secondary resonances (tubes, wine glasses and so forth) which radically effect the sound quality. The second performer wields the microphone in all three dimensions, across the surface of the tam-tam 'exploring' the different sound 'zones' produced, and away from its surface. This latter motion exploits the 'proximity effect' noted above. Small changes of microphone distance can result in very substantial changes in frequency response and hence perspective. The microphone acts as both a smooth envelope shaper and filter at the same time. Each team's sound output is further processed by a third performer who manipulates a band pass filter. The total sound is then projected in discrete 2-channel stereo. The two groups only play together during three short 'moments', otherwise alternating. The part of the microphonist (the second performer in each team) gives indications for two *distances*: first from the point of excitation (executed by the first performer) and second from the surface of the tam-tam. The composer defines a *secondary resonator* to be used by the microphonist: a hollow object open at one end, designated small, medium and large (for example, a glass, mug, plastic flower pot) which is wielded at defined angles to the surface close to the microphone. This acts as a secondary filter: high-low (depending on size) and greater or less effect (depending on angle). The resonator is also used occasionally as a second excitation source:

> … there remains a lot of mystery about the sounds produced directly in the tam-tam itself. They are amplified, enormously amplified; they are filtered; the microphone is moved so the original waveform is continuously transformed. And all we know is what we get from a certain action. This is what I mean in general by microphony, the microphonic process. The microphone is no longer a passive tool for high fidelity reproduction: it becomes a musical instrument, influencing what it is recording (Stockhausen, 1989, p. 80).

Projection is a close relative of spatialization and the two may work in a strong relationship. Projection is not merely the bringing into perceptual foreground but the additional placing of sounds into space. The straightforward amplification of instruments may in addition, perhaps intentionally, add an element of acousmatic dislocation. Extended performance techniques (especially) may produce sounds of perceptually uncertain origin (as discussed in Chapter 4). If these are further spatialized, the image of a performer conjuring up a soundscape 'maybe yet maybe not' related to the instrumental gesture *as seen* can be powerful in its ambiguity. The natural radiation characteristics of instruments may be harnessed.[28] Prepared and extended instruments have also taken this to an extreme. Brass instruments, for example, have been deconstructed such that playing individual valves redirects the sound to separate locations. For example, in Melvyn Poore's *Tubassoon* (for prepared tuba[29] and amplification (1979)) the four valve slides are removed and the

28 *Acoustics and the Performance of Music* by Jörgen Meyer (1978) is one of the only textbooks to publish extensive spatial sound radiation characteristics for traditional western instruments.

29 The instrument is played using a bassoon reed.

apertures close miked and individually routed to surround the audience. The present author's work *Five Spaces* (on Emmerson, 2007) was written for the five stringed electric cello;[30] he constructed a circuit which redirected each string pickup to a separate loudspeaker; thus a performance gesture became strongly spatialized and controllable. In Trevor Wishart's *Anticredos* (1980) (Wishart, 1992) and *Vox* cycle (1980–88) (Wishart, 1990) projection and spatialization are combined. In parts of *Anticredos* voice textures are mixed to two (mono) 'streams' which are panned around the auditorium in independent patterns designed alternately to contrast and separate or to superpose in greater textural density.[31] This was an attempt to create live versions of Wishart's 'soundstream transformation' ideas (see Wishart, 1996) in which musical material, projection and spatial movement are entirely integrated. *Vox 1* is unique to the cycle in requiring a flexible spatialization that is both individual (each of the four voices may be moved individually around the four surround loudspeakers) and 'frame'-based (an entire 'scene' of the four singers must be spatialized and rotated, for example). This was clearly designed with the then emerging ambisonic technology in mind (Malham and Myatt, 1995). In John Cage's performances using his own voice, especially of his *mesostic* works, he commonly used several microphones in a group or line, each routed to a loudspeaker in a different location. The smallest movement of head (mouth) resulted in extraordinary spatial movements.[32]

Perspective

Amplification systems can allow the creation of illusory spaces, changing the depth and breadth of what is evident from the acoustic sound and visual information in the listening space; this is often done with additional use of reverberation and panning (spatial repositioning at or between different loudspeakers). There is therefore the possibility of *playing* perspectives. Composers can create a compositional strategy involving changing the 'normal relations of objects'. There are many instances of this which relate to radiophonic techniques, changing spaces in a theatrical way, referring to real and recognizable spaces. The original version of Luciano Berio's vocal work *A-Ronne* was conceived as 'a radiophonic documentary for five actors on a poem by Edoardo Sanguineti' for Hilversum Radio in 1974; it was never intended for concert performance. In the radio studio artificial spaces could be created for each of the 'characters' in the narrative. In *A-Ronne* ('From A to Z') Sanguinetti's text works through scenes involving characters such as a priest, a demagogic orator, intimate lover and so forth, each having a specific acoustic space projected through

30 Made by Eric Jensen in Seattle for cellist Philip Sheppard who commissioned the work.

31 Two 1-in-to-4-out (Penny and Giles) analogue quadpan potentiometers were used in the live performances.

32 The author attended a concert by Cage and David Tudor at the Royal Albert Hall, London in May 1972 at which Cage used this technique in a performance of *Mesostics re Merce Cunningham* to great effect in such a vast space. A photograph of the microphone set-up for this system taken on the same tour (July 1972 in Pamplona) is available at www.uclm.es/artesonoro/olobo3/Pamplona/Encuentros.html (consulted December 2005).

the amplification. Standard radio-drama techniques of equalization, reverberation and spatial movement were used in this initial recorded production.[33] In 1975 Berio decided to rewrite the work for concert performance for the eight voices of *Swingle II*.[34] The group commissioned electronic control boxes which could be operated by each singer: amplification and reverberation levels could be varied by the singers according to instructions in the score. The aim was to allow local control over the singers 'space' and perspective in the piece. This attempt to recreate 'radiophonic' spaces in performance had rather limited success. The perception of the audience was firmly rooted in the live performers. The lack of an acousmatic listening situation undermined the ideal – it was impossible to suspend disbelief in the face of clear visual cues. In addition the acoustics of the hall interfered with that of the intended artificial spaces and only a vague sense of 'difference' was perceptible.[35]

Footnote Cage (Perspective/Simultaneity/Interpenetration)

The dislocation of space has been exploited in many of John Cage's larger performance works as discussed in Chapter 4. Although not expressly stated as an influence, there is a strong parallel with Zen Buddhism's ideas of 'unimpededness and interpenetration':

> Unimpededness is seeing that in all of space each thing and each human being is at the center and furthermore that each one being at the center is the most honored one of all. Interpenetration means that each one of these most honored ones of all is moving out in all directions penetrating and being penetrated by every other one no matter what the time or what the space (Cage, 1968a, pp. 46–47, original in uppercase throughout).

In the realization of *Variations IV*, made by Cage and David Tudor in Los Angeles in 1964 (Cage (CD-undated)), changes in perspective are taken to an extreme with the projection of one space into another (interpenetration). The score involves the mapping of sound sources onto the performance space. In this version there are microphones above the bar, on the street and in different locations throughout the performance spaces (within the art gallery) which are mixed in the final presentation to undermine (even destroy) any sense of spatial differentiation. The *simultaneity* characteristic of Cage's *musicircus* pieces – especially when using recognizable sources – involves a *relocation* of those sources. The original realization of *Roaratorio* was made as a *Hörspiel* for radio broadcast for the West Deutscher Rundfunk in Cologne in 1979 (Cage, 1994). It was later adapted for live performance (often simultaneously with other works such as *Inlets* (amplified conch shells filled with water, recorded sound of fire) (1977) (Cage, 1977)). This is one of the most

33 The original production has recently become available on CD (Berio, 1990).

34 A vocal ensemble directed by Ward Swingle, this 'second version' was a UK-recruited group which superseded the earlier Paris-based *Swingle Singers* (heard on the original New York Philharmonic recording of Berio's *Sinfonia* (Berio, 1969? – undated). The Swingle II *A-Ronne* recording is Berio (1990).

35 Berio's supervized recording (Berio, 1990) succeeds much better in the acousmatic environment of the studio!

extensive examples of simultaneity and interchangeability of space and time frames. On the tape (16 channel in live performance) recordings of Irish locations (the 1083 places named in Joyce's *Finnegans Wake* (Fetterman, 1996, p. 217)) are *reduced* from landscape to arena. In live sound projection Cage's *mesostic* recitation (in fact a performance within a performance – of *Writing for the second time through 'Finnegans Wake'* (1977) (Cage, 1994)) is *increased* from local event to stage (or larger) level. The everyday life sounds (the 1210 sounds mentioned in Joyce's text) and Irish musicians come and go in an ever changing mosaic of point sounds across the space. In live performance the movement of the audience allows shifts of focus of the individual listener's frame creating a perpetually mobile *stage* (see discussion above). There is clearly no distinction between stage and arena.[36] Both *Hörspiel* and performance seem to externalize an internal theatre of memory.

Colouration

While all amplification 'colours' the source (see the opening discussion), some extreme colouration (even distortion) may deliberately be sought. The most obvious and first to be harnessed consciously was the 'fuzz guitar' sound, a product of overdriven guitar amplifiers. But contact microphones also have very 'coloured' characteristics. The limited frequency response of at least the first generation of contact microphones designed for strings has been deliberately exploited. For his work *Black Angels* (amplified string quartet and ancillary instruments) George Crumb explains that 'the amplification of the stringed instruments is intended to produce a highly surrealistic effect' (Crumb, 1972? – undated). The resulting sound is a claustrophobic, alienated and ugly form of surreality, further enhanced through the use of extended performance techniques, such as the use of 'thimble' tremolo battuto and playing on the wrong side of the strings. The *Pavana Lachrymae* section (movement 6) involves bowing the instruments above the finger stops on the string,[37] results in an imitation of the sound of the viol. The impoverished timbre (with the resonances of the instrument body severely reduced) is amplified through the (band limited) contact microphones to produce a lo-fidelity sound (lacking in high frequencies) as if heard from a great distance. While the composer has not specifically stated the demand for such low fidelity products, the musical aims are clearly stated and would strongly suggest such deliberate practice (let alone issues of a 'historically authentic' performance).

Resonance – Feedback

It is increasingly evident that Cage's innovative use of amplification has tended to overshadow (and perhaps distort) a broader picture of American experimental music of the 1960s and later which has focussed on the exploitation of *resonance*.

36 This is true of any installation art where the listener chooses their own perspective with respect to the object.

37 Played *da gamba* as the viol. The most authentic contemporary recording is Crumb (1972? – undated).

Resonance has a broad and narrow definition. Any object may be said to have 'natural' or resonant frequencies, but a narrower use of the term refers to a phenomenon in which a particular frequency (or narrow band of frequencies) is dominant. A stretched string, a wine glass, a regular tube, a rectangular room produce a series of frequencies when set into motion: these regular shaped objects produce relatively predictable resonances. Irregular shapes do indeed also produce resonant frequencies but these are much more difficult to predict. In fact there is a continuum from regular to irregular shapes. The more regular and exact the shape the more easily the resonant frequencies may be related to the *harmonic series*.[38] Most experimental composers have, however, avoided the regular and predictable and concentrated on the deviant, idiosyncratic and irregular (hence unpredictable) *inharmonic* resonances of objects. Both objects we see and spaces we inhabit have resonances; musical instruments use resonance in two senses: primary resonators (string, wind column, membrane, bar, plate, solid object). Sometimes these produce sufficient air displacement around them to be heard directly; but some (for example, lightweight strings) can hardly be heard unless attached to a *secondary resonator*, usually a hollow object (gourd, wooden body container) or surface (the 'soundboard' in a keyboard instrument). This secondary resonance helps project the sound at higher volume.[39] Generally speaking primary resonances have focused on regular shapes (to generate pitch) and secondary resonances have been more irregular (designed to resonate and project over a *range* of frequencies).[40] Technological resources have opened up all objects to such scrutiny. We may observe environmental sounds as produced from just the same kinds of 'excitation-resonance' models as traditional musical instruments. We may further *generate* such relationships through applications of electronic amplification.

In many pieces this is exploited through *feedback* techniques. In practice each part of the feedback chain acts as a *filter* – having its own characteristic spectrum. The *resonances* of objects and spaces act in exactly this way, colouring the sound as it flows around the loop. Sound energy is focussed within the resonant frequency ranges. Microphones and loudspeakers themselves add their own colour (possessing their own particular resonant characteristics).[41] In Alvin Lucier's *I am sitting in a room* (1969 on Lucier, 1990) recorded speech is played back into the listening

38 All substances deviate from the *idealized* simple harmonic motion description and hence from true harmonic series resonances: thin strings relatively little, metal bars very considerably.

39 For a generation brought up on electricity the term 'amplification' can be misleading: the secondary resonance does not get energy from nowhere: the sound is louder *but lasts a shorter time*. There is the same *total energy*. This explains why a solid body electric bass guitar resonates for longer than its acoustic hollow body relatives which drain energy faster from the string for this additional *loudness*.

40 An exception which helps make the point are the *secondary* resonators of the modern vibraphone which hang beneath the keys – these are *regular* tubes deliberately tuned to the pitch of the note they support.

41 While manufacturers claim to attempt to create the 'perfect' flat frequency response over the audible range, they know that such idealism may not only be impossible but may be misplaced – they simultaneously try to create the concept of 'their' sound. The use of much more subjective descriptions for this is a matter for independent research.

space and re-recorded via a microphone in that space, hence with the reverberant and resonant characteristics of the room. This recording is then itself played back and recorded in the same manner. This process is repeated until the result becomes unintelligible and the room's character (articulated with the frequency and energy contours of the speech) becomes dominant. In addition to the room characteristics, the final sound will also be determined by the noise and bandwidth of the recording and playback media used, and the relative positions of microphone and loudspeaker. This is a kind of 'time delayed' feedback. The room is the instrument which is played by the recorded voice. In the end the room resonance 'speaks'. A local event (speech) is slowly transformed into a field texture.

One of the simplest examples of microphone-loudspeaker resonance use remains Steve Reich's *Pendulum Music* (1968) (Reich, 2002, pp. 30–32). 'Three, four or more' microphones are suspended by their connection cables each above a vertical aiming loudspeaker (to which it is fed via an amplifier). In rehearsal, the amplifiers are set to give feedback when the microphone is directly above but none when it is drawn to the side away from the cone. In the performance the microphones are drawn to one side and set free to swing at the same time, oscillating to and fro, towards and away from the loudspeaker cone, provoking waves of feedback. Slight differences mean the rhythm of the waves will be at slightly different rates for each microphone and will inevitably 'phase'. As the microphone-pendulum oscillations slowly decay, so the feedback bursts become a larger proportion of the cycle time until approaching stationary, when the sound becomes continuous. The timbre of the feedback is determined by the complex interaction of two resonances, that of the microphone-loudspeaker pair and that of the room.

A slightly different kind of resonance feedback is caused when a microphone is brought into close proximity to an air cavity. Especially if regular, the cavity's resonances can easily be excited even when the loudspeaker is relatively distant. The mouth cavity is an interesting case as its shape can be varied and hence (even without further sound produced from within the body) can control the result. Robert Ashley's *The Wolfman* (1964) (solo amplified singer and tape) (Ashley, 1968) is a classic example. Sustained vocal sounds are combined with highly amplified resonance feedback sounds. Ashley defines four variables for the interpreter: *pitch*, *loudness*, *vowel* (controlled by tongue position), and *closure* (jaw position). These are to be considered independent and only one is varied in the course of each 'phrase' of sound (lasting about 10s). The microphone is kept at all times very close to the mouth cavity.

> It is very important that the singer observe the need to produce all of the vocal sounds with the tongue touching at some point along the roof of the mouth. This particular kind of vocal cavity allows a certain amount of acoustical feedback to be present 'within' the sounds produced by the voice, thus, making possible both the characteristic *sound* of the vocal part and the continuity between the vocal phrases and the feedback tones (Ashley, 1968, p. 6).

The relationship between the vocal produced and feedback sounds is complex but closely related: the relative levels interact with the resonances of the vocal cavity, amplification system and room, the vocal sound apparently 'suppressing' and replacing some aspects of the feedback.

In a series of realizations of John Cage's *Fontana Mix* subtitled *Feed*, Max Neuhaus placed contact microphones on a variety of percussion objects but unattached, free to move, with amplification to feedback levels.

> Although the individual intensity of these channels is controlled from the score, the actual sounds that make up the piece are determined by the acoustics of the room and the position of the mikes in relation to the loudspeakers and the instruments at a specific moment (the vibrations cause the mikes to move around) (Neuhaus, 1965).

He remarks that no two performances could be the same even with all other parameters remaining constant.

New Interface Typologies

If the microphone has moved from being observer (though with character) to an active participant, it has moved closer to other instruments and has become a tool for our live music making. But the sound gestures it captures are (with the exception of experimental contact transducer applications) the *results* of physical performance gestures, not the gestures themselves.[42] The first gesture transducer was the musical keyboard. It not only distances the performer from the resonating wind column or string but alters radically the physical relationship of hand action to sounding result. It was a simple matter to replace the purely mechanical leverage of the pipe organ or piano action with the switch detecting circuits of the electronic age.[43] In addition the standard computer interface is a descendent of the typewriter which is the perfect illustration of the conservatism of the universal. Other layouts than QWERTY produce faster and more efficient input – but it's 'too late' to change such a universally accepted layout. Thus most of the first generation of electronic instruments used modifications of keyboard technology as the performer interface: the *Telharmonium*, the *Hammond Organ*, the *Trautonium* and the *Ondes Martenot*[44] for example (Roads, 1996b). The prophetic exception was the *Theremin* which used capacitive proximity methods: two antennas reacted to hand position, controlling pitch and loudness.[45]

42 We commonly refer to 'vocal' and 'instrumental' gestures, of course. But we refer usually to the sound produced. With the emergence of new interfaces we need to distinguish the *sounding gesture* from the *muscle and physical movement gesture* which produced it.

43 The morse-code key had preempted this 60 years before the first serious electric keyboard made for the Telharmonium.

44 Interestingly including an innovative 'continuous glissando' strip, rarely equalled in later designs.

45 http://www.thereminvox.com has many articles on the history and technology of the theremin (consulted November 2005). To summarize, hand proximity changes antenna capacitance which modulates heterodyning (interfering) radio frequency circuits.

Subsequent interface developments[46] fall into two areas: firstly, devices which follow and measure *human physical action*, and secondly those which analyse the *acoustic result* of a performance action.

Action Trackers

Action trackers can be divided into several groups. By far the most common are those which retain physical load or resistance feedback. Although there were examples from the analogue world before 1983, the advent of Midi encouraged the development of other than keyboard controllers. Wind, percussion and guitar controllers measured performance information such as finger position, pressure, velocity and sometimes other switch information and translated these into Midi data. Sound was not usually produced by these devices. More recently games machine technology has furnished many variations of paddles and 'joystick' controllers. In addition membrane surfaces and strings under tension (sometimes multiplied into webs) have been used which combine the actual contact surface with the elastic response. A variant of this approach dispenses with elastic resistance feedback but still requires load and contact. These are devices which detect pressure, for example, built into gloves, pads (used under floor or sometimes on the body) or installed in furniture or sculpture (Bongers, 2000).

A second group requires no direct physical contact with the device: for example, ultrasonic proximity and movement sensors are commonly used in installations. These have given away more recently to video analysis: the detection and tracking of movement, position, size and gestural detail from visual data. In the first instance this relates more to traditions of performance art, dance, movement and installation rather than to those gestures associated with *action on a mechanical object* (as in traditional music instrument performance). Recent research is beginning to unravel the clues we have to the *effort* being made in an action and how this may be mapped to musical result (Tanaka, 2000). Similar movements with and without resistance will produce different visual traces.

Recent developments in interfaces for those with limited motor ability include eye movement detectors[47] which have recently been utilized in music interface designs (Hornof and Sato, 2004). There have been suggestions that these may move into mainstream control possibilities. Some devices appear to 'play empty space'. Don Buchla's *Lightning II* consists of two 'wands' (about the size of bulky percussion beaters) which may be programmed to play the space in the vicinity of the performer (up to about 4 x 3m), mapping different sounds to locations within the space. Position and movement of the wands is measured by infra-red beams between wand and remote controller. The user may define how these map (via

46 Just as we no longer need to separate the 'ear' from 'perception' in this discussion, so here 'interface' bundles together the engineering hardware of transduction with the processing which gives meaningful output. The two are usually strongly integrated.

47 For example a range from Sensormotoric Instruments (Germany/USA), Viewpoint Eyetracker from Arrington Research (USA) and Eyelink from SR Research (Canada).

Midi) to sound production or processing.[48] Michel Waisvisz's *The Hands* (produced at Steim studios in Amsterdam) were likewise performed by hand gesture in empty space (Waisvisz, 1985 describes the first version). Proximity of the hands, inclination in space, switches on the fingers were mapped to a variety of sound producers. In early versions the system was interfaced to the sound synthesis of FM modules, in later versions combined with live sampling software (LiSa, also from Steim) often with audience participation. The move to using video with subsequent analysis to produce similar data has (as with Max/MSP in relation to audio tracking analysis) removed the need for hardware measurement immediately proximate to the performer. Yet the weight of 'the hands' (and the fact that they were not wireless) added a strongly theatrical dimension to a performance. The image of a 'wired up' human has connotations which are unavoidable. Waisvisz's early performances were controlled improvisations which fully integrated this visual aspect. One could see the slow movements controlling slow changes in timbre; fast switch movements (perhaps exaggerated to make the audience aware of them) set sudden and surprising musical boundaries. Remove this visual dimension and an entirely different piece emerges.[49]

Footnote – The Studio Gesture as Action Tracked

We noted in Chapter 1 that 'playing' a group of turntables (as Pierre Schaeffer did while dreaming of a keyboard action to fulfil the function more flexibly) and performing 'fader gestures' on the resulting sound inputs and outputs were performances in their own right. The analogue studio session was full of such short performances, often repeated and the best result chosen (much like classical music recording). The aim however was to make the studio action transparent (that is unperceived as an action 'outside' the sounding result). After Midi was introduced in the early 1980s, 'Midi – usually 'keyboard' – gestures' could be heard in pieces, especially when created on a keyboard, computer sequencer, sampler and synthesis system; the means often 'spoke in the way' of the sounding result.[50] But in contemporary experimental laptop performance, manual cueing of sound, coordinating switches, rotary and linear potentiometer movements have often been retained in ancillary sound sources, local mixers and processors. The versatility of the mouse concept, combining both switch and continuous line function control, temporarily displaced the lightpen and graphics tablet (although now making a comeback). But overall the long predicted disappearance of such simple tactile interfaces has evidently been postponed.

---

48 Don Buchla's *Lightning II* performer is an 'air drummer'. See http://www.buchla.com/lightning/index.html for details.

49 It is probably for this reason that Waisvisz has not formally recorded the series of works composed for The Hands (just two short sections are available on Waisvisz (1987)). If a performance were ever to be recreated using video tracking software (such as Steim's own *BigEye*) the piece would have an entirely different theatre.

50 In creating a 'classic' acousmatic work this is clearly a problem, but it is not to be confused with a *re-engagement* with such characteristics in the form of a reintroduction of pulse and event-based thinking (as discussed in Chapters 3 and 4).

Acoustic Analysers

The earliest devices emerged in the second half of 1960s using analogue technology following on the voltage control revolution. Both pitch and envelope followers were available on the more advanced voltage controlled synthesizers (or as free standing units).[51] These generated 'tracking voltages' which could be used to drive other modules. By the 1980s 'pitch to Midi' converters fulfilled the same function as interfaces to digital production and processing devices[52] (for example, the freestanding Fairlight *Voicetracker* from 1985). All of these were unreliable to an extent – they were not so much *pitch* as *fundamental* trackers. It was known that the perception system perceived pitch from piecing together a variety of clues which could compensate for the low level (even absence) of a *fundamental frequency* in the spectrum – something most devices at this time could not do, often jumping to measuring the second harmonic if it was stronger. Digital technology has brought with it all the possible tools of signal analysis in both time and frequency domains. Control data generated is thus multidimensional. The most comprehensive treatment of this is the collection of papers in Wanderley and Battier (2000).

Combination and Integration

The Steim studio has devised the most comprehensive such interface: a generic device that can in principle be connected to any sound source. The *Sensorlab* can be configured to generate both types of performance information: *physical action* and *acoustic* (Bongers, 2000). Jonathan Impett has developed the *meta-trumpet* using this device[53] with additional customized additions (Impett, 1994). The position of the trumpet in three dimensional space is measured by ultrasound receivers surrounding the instrument. Combined with timing data, both direction and speed of movement can be calculated. The player's physical contact pressure with the instrument is also measured by pressure sensors. The valve technology is slightly modified to include magnetic sensors for valve position. The sound is then analysed for the basic parameters of pitch[54] and volume (on two levels to capture instrumental and 'breath' sounds). There are additional hardware switches for performance instructions to be sent to the software.

The original *hyperinstruments* project directed by Tod Machover at MIT's Medialab also used acoustic analysis in addition to motion and pressure sensing. The first wave of the project involved the measurement of 'virtuosic' performance

51 Moog, Arp (modular) and EMS (free standing) all produced versions.

52 The continuous information of analogue was replaced by the discrete stepped ('seived') values defined for Midi.

53 Each Sensorlab is custom fitted to the instrument or environment desired. It is currently (2006) suspended from production; recent personal computer hardware and software has allowed a reconfiguration of the analysis-data chain as well as a rethink of the Midi-dominated specification.

54 As the information is ultimately converted to Midi format in the Sensorlab environment, pitch is encoded as pitch + pitchbend (in Midi terms) so microtones can be encoded.

parameters. Machover's *Begin Again Again ...* (1991 on Machover, 2003) was written for *hypercello* sensing wrist action, bow pressure and position and left hand fingering position in addition to sound analysis. In an interview with Joel Chadabe he points out the pitfalls of fragmenting the output data into separate parameter streams:

> ... instead of measuring bow position and sending out that as a parameter, I measured types of bowing – pressure, position of the bow, how much bow is being used, how often the bow is changing direction – which is a collection of a bunch of variables together. If you can measure type or style of bowing, that's already much closer to what a musician can feel than if you say, 'Play at this part of the bow to trigger such and such an event' (Chadabe, 1997, p. 219).

More recent developments have moved the project to include the non-music specialist world to develop interfaces related to music games and internet performance.[55]

The first generation of acoustic analysers based on hardware has been superseded by the much more flexible tools available within software environments such as Max/MSP. The ubiquity of the microphone as interface has encouraged composers to focus on the *sound signal*. As previously there is the analysis of the signal to extract basic acoustic parameters such as spectrum and formant information, noise components, pitch and envelope following. But it is now much easier to integrate with this a second generation of information extraction which moves on to answer questions on the 'events' found in the signal. *Event detection* involves the isolation of 'meaningful units' of information, the nature of which must be clearly defined. This may be context dependant (as in speech and language analysis), but is vital in interactive systems or in emerging 'machine tracking and following' software.[56] The parallel shift of performance action analysis to the video domain has its limitations – velocity may be simple to measure at a distance, but not pressure. This emphasizes (by definition) the non-tactile aspects of movement art (its intrinsic forms and expressions) rather than their tactile (operational) aspects on objects or instruments.[57]

Neurological and Biophysical Interfaces

Physiological variables related to the human nervous system have been harnessed to control sound production and modification devices. Six major types of brainwaves are commonly identifiable on an electroencephalogram (EEG): alpha, beta, gamma, delta, theta and a 'sensorimotor' rhythm. In order of frequency range (which is not precisely agreed):[58]

---

55 See http://www.media.edu/hyperins/projects.html (consulted October 2005).

56 See Wanderley and Battier (2000) and recent Proceedings of the NIME conferences (http://www.nime.org/).

57 This can lead to 'conflicts of interest' in the performance act – for example, exaggerated balletic gestures in a performance where this may not be appropriate to the instrument.

58 See Rosenboom (1997) for a discussion and elaboration of these categories.

- *Delta* waves have a frequency range up to 4 Hz and are seen in deep sleep.
- *Theta* waves have a frequency range from 4.5 Hz to 8 Hz. They can be seen during trances, hypnosis, deep day-dreams, lucid dreaming and light sleep and the preconscious state in the transitions between sleep and waking.
- *Alpha* waves have a frequency range from 8.5 Hz to 12 Hz. They are characteristic of a relaxed, alert state of consciousness (and are best detected with the eyes closed).
- *Sensorimotor rhythm* (SMR) is a middle frequency (about 12–16 Hz) wave associated with physical stillness and body presence.
- *Beta* waves have a frequency range above 12 Hz. Low amplitude beta with multiple and varying frequency is often associated with active, busy or anxious thinking and active concentration. Rhythmic beta with a dominant set of frequencies is associated with various pathologies and drug effects.
- *Gamma* waves have a frequency range of approximately 30–80 Hz. Gamma rhythms appear to be involved in higher mental activity, including perception and consciousness.

Current methods of accessing these electrical waves[59] are deemed to be invasive (electrodes attached very closely to shaved parts of the scalp) and are thus subject to rigorous control.[60] Three composers have pioneered and featured such control sources in their work: David Rosenboom, Richard Teitelbaum and Alvin Lucier. There are variations in approach here: one has been described as *biofeedback*. Sometimes the term has been loosely used. Strictly 'feedback' is used to mean that the performer-subject (who is the source of the control information) can modify that information in response to its manifestation as they perceive it, usually in a manner to control and calm.[61] Early purely clinical trials included applications in which subjects could respond to both audio and visual representations of their brain activity and 'learn' to influence it.[62] But there are musical applications where the sonic aspect may be extended to include controlling whole soundworlds not directly produced from the

---

59 They are essentially sine-wave like in form although 'spikes' are encountered which are commonly signs of 'electrical faults' although these are found during sleep states also. They are typically of the order of 100mV on the surface of the scalp and thus require up to 100dB of amplification for display or other functions.

60 At least in the UK; Rosenboom (1997) introduces the nascent technologies for 'No-Contact Electrodes' (pp. 43–46). *Magnetoencephalography* (MEG) and *Functional Magnetic Resonance Imaging* (FMRI) also have great possible potential for music interface control (p. 52; see also the Wikipedia entry on 'Brain-Computer Interface': http://en.wikipedia.org/wiki/Brain_computer_interface).

61 Clinical applications tend to emphasize *negative feedback* where the feedback loop tends to a stable goal (often a calming of system activity), not the more acoustically common *positive feedback* which has an unstable possible outcome – which would presumably be highly dangerous in some clinical situations. Rosenboom (1997) describes the 'goal states' sometimes found in the wider literature; these are not necessarily present in musical objectives.

62 Rosenboom (1997) is keen to stress that the simple minded 'rational control' model is inadequate. 'Rather, the subject must find a way to allow alpha wave production to evolve rather than make it appear.' (p. 8). This is an 'encouraging' rather than a 'driving' paradigm.

source controls. In so far as the performer 'responds to and alters' the sound, there is a feedback of sorts in operation. But in practice this becomes just another set of control functions and the very specific (usually goal-oriented) connotations of 'feedback' are lost. The aim becomes simply to connect the brainwaves directly to the sound production network.

The Moog synthesizer was a development contemporary with the earliest such experiments and was a perfect vehicle for this sonification. The advent of voltage controlled devices in the early-mid 1960s was a major stimulus for such interface development as it allowed sound modules to be 'hooked on' flexibly to produce and modify sound. Before this there was almost literally no sound producing agency that could have been controlled by the EEG waves. Moog and Arp synthesizers all had modules that could be controlled easily by functions produced from biophysical interfaces. The EEG signals were processed through filters and envelope followers (and occasionally further devices including sample-and-hold circuits), which could in turn be connected to control sound synthesis (voltage controlled oscillators of various shapes, and noise generators) and sound processing (voltage controlled filters and amplifiers) (Rosenboom, 1976). An interesting variation (and exception as there was no electronic synthesis as such) was Alvin Lucier's *Music for Solo Performer* of 1965 in which the alpha waves were deliberately overdriven into loudspeakers to produce sound and to resonate percussion instruments (Lucier, 1976).

> I used the alpha to resonate a large battery of percussion instruments including cymbals gongs, bass drums, timpani, and other resonant found objects. In most cases it was necessary physically to couple the loudspeaker to the instrument, although in the case of highly resonant bass drums and timpani, the loudspeaker could be an inch or so away ... I learned that by varying both short bursts and longer sustained phrases of alpha plus making musical decisions as to placement of loudspeakers, choice of resonant instruments or objects, volume control, channelling and mixing, I was able to get a wide variety of sonorities as well as retain the natural physical quality that seemed asked for by the sound source itself (Lucier, 1976, p. 61).

In the same volume Richard Teitelbaum goes on to report on a series of works involving EEG, breath and heartbeat inputs which he composed (many for the live electronics group *Musica Elettronica Viva* based in Rome) from 1967 mostly interfaced to the Moog (Teitelbaum, 1976: see especially Figure 2 (p. 40), the circuit diagram for *Organ Music* (1968)). Teitelbaum and Lucier's works simply present idiosyncratic sonifications of the biofeedback systems. This is very much in the American experimental tradition in which 'the idea' is expressed directly in its sonic manifestation.[63] But David Rosenboom's more elaborate works involve the extension of some of these ideas into the musical syntax itself. Rosenboom has conducted considerable research into a wider range of perception and cognition questions, which includes much more advanced 'meaningful feature extraction' from the EEG data themselves. These are analysed in time and frequency domains to generate streams of 'meaningful' control data in a much more coherent manner than

63 Lucier's *Music for Solo Performer* is dedicated to John Cage who was assistant at the first performance in May 1965.

simply interfacing the original waves.[64] His *On Being Invisible* (1976–77)[65] hooks up two performers to EEG.[66] These are interfaced to (and influence) the 'model of musical perception, the structure generating mechanism and the structure-controlling mechanism' which are all encoded in software (Rosenboom, 1997, p. 34).

64 That is the waves are treated as sources of *information* which require relevant *feature extraction*.

65 Described as an ongoing project, evolving with new technology (Rosenboom, 1997).

66 Theta, alpha and beta wave extraction is required.

CHAPTER SIX

Diffusion-Projection: The Grain of the Loudspeaker

History: Telephones, Horns, Pistons and Baffles

Over recent decades there have been persistent claims that 'perfect reproduction' of a soundfield is within our grasp. But it remains an open question as to whether this is actually an ideal aim. If the soundfield of (say) a concert is 'perfectly' reproduced *without the visual field* then we have a very different experience. In the experience of the live performance, an orchestra may drown the piano solo yet our knowledge of the music and memory of CD recordings may supplement the visual clues to 'reconstruct' the masked signal. Even when film puts visual and sound back together again (usually in post-production – a phrase-word that has become an oxymoron) aspects of the soundfield may have to be made exaggerated, 'hyperreal', in order to appear 'real' (Chion, 1994, especially Chapter 5). However, other less purist traditions play on *differences* and *characteristics* of loudspeakers – their *grain* (after Barthes, 1977) – at its most extreme creating 'loudspeakers' deliberately limited in response and fidelity. To put this rich and sometimes contradictory sweep of approaches into perspective we shall first examine the loudspeaker itself, its principles and history of application.

The invention of the telephone by Alexander Graham Bell in 1875–76 established a linked chain that remains with us today: microphone, transmission, loudspeaker. In the telephone the two transducers, the microphone and the loudspeaker are of roughly the same size. The output loudness resulting is considerably lower than the original sound heard as if close by – even when the ear piece is held close to the ear canal to exclude extraneous sounds and to maximize amplitude at the ear drum. Amplifiers (as we know them) did not exist for a further 30 years after Bell's invention. Relatively high voltage and current handling circuits were needed to counter transmission line losses over distance, originally each unit needing its own battery to furnish the power. By the early twentieth century the importance of improving the three components was recognized and the relationship to radio and recording technologies firmly established. But research in improving them was not always 'in sync'. Before the advent of radio, telephones were a useful way to convey music but were recognized as being of limited quality (in terms both of frequency response and distortion).[1] Following Berliner's invention of the flat disc-based gramophone (in

1 In one of the earliest experiments in stereophony, Clément Ader relayed a performance at the Opéra Garnier to the Paris Electrical Exhibition of 1881 using telephone technology. This was commercialised in France and Britain from the 1890s to the 1920s for theatre and

1887) as a rival to Edison's cylinder phonograph there was a distinct improvement in sound quality even within the all-mechanical world of recording. For recording, a mechanical microphone consisted of a membrane driving a needle acting as a lathe cutter direct onto the wax surface. For playback, a mechanical loudspeaker simply ran this in reverse. Telephone and recording technologies remained broadly separate (as far as public application was concerned) until after 1920.

The low level of production of sound energy from a vibrating diaphragm was recognized quickly. Initially attempts at improvement concentrated on 'reducing the waste' of omnidirectionality. Sound would radiate equally in all directions, away from listeners as well as towards them unless funnelled in some way. There were individual earphones from the earliest days (see the photo of Edison in Copeland, 1991, p. 9) which were very successful in that all the produced sound energy was directed to one (or two) small outlet points. But to listen in a group the horn became a familiar sight resulting in a louder sound over a more limited field. The effect of horns had been known for some time, from brass instruments, the basic use of cupped hands for distance communication and passive megaphones. The shape of the horn became a focus of experimentation and both conical (straight sided) and exponential (flared) horns were tested. Practical research in the last part of the nineteenth century quickly established the superiority of the flared horn.[2] It turns out that exponential horns give a much more efficient coupling of the energy of the source vibration to the surrounding air. The flare 'rate' and absolute size of the horn determines the overall frequency response and (as ever) compromises had to be made in practice (Holland, 2001, pp. 30–37). Horns survived the invention of the baffle-mounted loudspeaker in specialist applications (most notably in increasing high frequency 'tweeter' projection). But telephones were electric devices from the start in all three stages (microphones are discussed in Chapter 5). Even the early Bell telephone receivers (tiny loudspeakers) were built on the *moving iron* electro-magnetic principle. The varying electrical signal in the transmission line fed an electro-magnet. The resultant varying magnetic field caused vibrations in a thin soft iron diaphragm suspended in close proximity which radiated sound. As early as 1898 Sir Oliver Lodge patented a *moving coil* driver in the UK, but it needed higher amplification than was then available to be a realistic option. Here a coil of wire is free to move in a fixed magnetic field. It is fed with the varying signal which establishes a varying magnetic field. This interacts with the fixed field resulting in movement. The coil is attached to a diaphragm, the suspended 'cone' of stiff paper we see and which also holds the coil in position. This vibrates and radiates the sound.

The invention of the thermionic valve by Lee de Forest in 1907 was immediately followed by development of the first valve amplifiers, which led to improved sound quality in transmission and renewed interest in loudspeaker development. A landmark paper published in 1925 by Chester Rice and Edward Kellogg (working at General Electric in the USA) essentially established the moving coil baffle-mounted

---

music relays (http://en.wikipedia.org/wiki/Sterophonic_sound). The *Telharmonium* was originally auditioned using New York's telephone system (Manning, 1993, pp. 1–2).

2 Research on horn size and flare characteristics continued throughout the twentieth century for specialist applications.

loudspeaker in its present form.[3] The first public address systems to be established date from experiments from 1907, but the new generation of amplifiers allowed a big leap forward. Following World War 1 systems were quickly established to relay speech to larger groups of listeners. United States President Wilson addressed 50,000 people in San Diego in 1919.[4]

Three other basic principles have been developed for loudspeakers. The ribbon loudspeaker is the mirror partner to the ribbon microphone. Here the coil and diaphragm are 'rolled into one' in the form of a light and flexible thin metal ribbon. This responds and moves in a magnetic field as the coil does, but it itself also acts as the diaphragm to radiate the sound (Watkinson, 2001, p. 46). Ribbon designs have established a specialist presence for tweeter construction.[5] Similar in this respect is the electrostatic loudspeaker. Here the diaphragm forms one plate of a capacitor. This is a device which stores charge resulting from an applied voltage (see Chapter 5 for principles of the capacitor microphone). The accumulation of charge results in a force between the plates. Suitably mounted and free to move, the diaphragm plate moves in response to the applied voltage and radiates sound.[6] The advantage of both ribbon and electrostatic devices is the reduction in the number of elements in the *mechanical* chain between signal and *radiating surface*. There is bound to be a small time delay between signal change and mechanical movement – the greater, the larger the mass to be moved. This results effectively in phase and transient handling limitations. The ultimate idea might be to set the air in motion directly through electric means – this would mean there were effectively no mechanical moving parts. Only one commercial product has been available, using an *ionisation* principle for this function. A radio frequency oscillator is amplitude modulated by the signal, confined within a quartz cell. This modulates the amplitude of the resulting ionic discharge (spark), displacing the air directly. This is of relatively low amplitude and the cell had to be connected directly to an exponential horn.[7]

The Origins of 'Character'

There are two streams of non-ideal behaviour which mean that all real loudspeakers are approximations. The first involves the basic theory of the *mounted piston*. The moving coil loudspeaker is based on the principle that it drives a piston mounted through a (perfectly sealed) hole in a *baffle*. This is a rigid surface which is assumed not to transmit (radiate) sound. To gain ideal behaviour this baffle is assumed to

3 The only change in design has been the availability of suitable permanent magnets from the late 1930s to replace the original powered electromagnet within the loudspeaker.

4 Steve Schoenherr, 'Recording Technology History', http://history.sandiego.edu/gen/recording/wilson.html (consulted December 2005).

5 See Watkinson (2001), for example the well respected Decca London Ribbon Horn tweeters based on a design by Stanley Kelly.

6 Peter Baxandall (2001) explains these principles in more detail and suggests that seeing the electrostatic loudspeaker 'as a capacitor' has been misleading to its development. A third plate was quickly added with the diaphragm sandwiched between.

7 Produced by Fane (UK) 1951–1968 (Watkinson, 2001, pp. 47–48).

be *infinite*. Thus a first approximation (but it can be made a very good one) is that an *enclosure* may be substituted. Different enclosure designs approximate the ideal to different degrees with different compromises – some are strictly sealed, some vented (there is a pathway open to the outside, sometimes with a transmission line or 'acoustic labyrinth'). Secondly, the appropriate electromagnetic theory assumes a linear relationship between current supplied to the coil and the resulting displacement of the piston. That is, if the electrical wave supplied to the loudspeaker is a perfect replica of the sound wave intended, then so will be the sound wave actually radiated by the piston. However, in practice the size of the piston limits the possible frequencies that can be radiated. Unfortunately we need large pistons for bass frequencies (at any realistic amplitude) and these (by definition larger masses) are not suited to high frequency movement and hence radiation. All of these demands are, of course, not achieved in a single loudspeaker and the history of the subsequent 80 years since the first designs along these lines has been one of improvement rather than radical change. Every manufacturer has attempted to address the problem from a particular point of view. Compromises are optimized for proposed function: studio monitoring, concert use, public address systems, and so forth – and then there are the different demands of each genre of music. Many high quality monitoring loudspeakers combine within one unit (typically) three driver units each optimized for part of the frequency range. However, many systems for venue sound projection separate out the two extremes: 'tweeters' for the high treble (above about 3000 Hz) and 'bass bins' for the lowest material (below about 60 Hz).[8] These two have very different directional characteristics, bass frequencies being virtually omnidirectional (with very high diffraction around objects and obstacles) while high frequencies are extremely directional (and do not 'flow around' obstacles). This is why tweeters are often built to drive small exponential horns which maximize dispersion (rarely reaching greater than a 120 degree funnel).

At another level there are the fragile theories of sound field reproduction. Stereophony, ambisonics and even wavefront synthesis (discussed below) all make assumptions about the loudspeaker being a perfect point source. This is best approximated by earphones; yet the function of the pinna (the outer flesh part of the ear) is to encode and convey vital directional information to the eardrum – we do after all hear a sphere around us from only two sources.[9] However this perception of location is not equally sensitive in all directions. We turn our heads to face sounds we want to (or must) focus on, and if there is subtle ambiguity in location we might move our heads even slightly to see how the information changes. But wearing headphones (as constituted at present) the entire soundfield moves when we do. We are frustrated in applying such a fundamental search method as moving the head. Even if the directional information is encoded in the recording specifically with

8 These are approximate figures – there are great distinctions between lowest frequency units of (say) a three unit monitoring speaker and a concert sub-woofer.

9 Although the role of non-ear perception is increasingly important: reports from non-hearing musicians include a variety of tactile sensations distributed throughout the body. Earphones cannot replace the sensing of bass frequencies directly by the body.

headphone listening in mind[10] (including so-called (HRTF) Head Related Transfer Functions) then the scene still moves with the head. Virtual reality applications will demand there be a fundamental change from 'head-referenced' to 'world-referenced' sound stage presentation (Sherman and Craig, 2003, pp. 164–177).

Thus all loudspeaker playback can be seen as a compromize, but this is unhelpful. We could say more simply that any loudspeaker has its own particular 'character'. We may try to describe this in terms of technical quality – scientifically measurable parameters of frequency response, dynamic range, transient handling, directionality and so forth. Alternatively we may resort to a range of verbal attributes which are much less easy to define, such as 'punch', 'colour', 'clarity', 'warmth' even 'honesty' which seem to convey something of this character. The two approaches relate in a complex manner, although very little research has been carried out into exactly how.[11]

The Spectacle of the Loudspeaker

But is loudspeaker music really 'acousmatic'? The loudspeaker has character and sound systems are judged 'good' or 'bad' as are any performance ensembles. Sometimes we conceal the system (and immerse the listener), as in the cinema and in some club venues, and sometimes we reveal it for all to see, as in the concert hall. Not only that, it can become part of an audio-visual spectacle, dominant, as at a large open air rock concert, or integrated but omnipresent, as in many sound installations (or in Xenakis's *polytopes*). From within the French tradition which invented the idea of acousmatic concert presentation, the element of visual spectacle has never entirely disappeared. Photographs of all the most important installations of the major 'loudspeaker orchestras' show a delight in creating a visual fantasy (which has even included idiosyncratic loudspeaker design) and, quite often, a creative use of historical and 'character' sites. In all cases there is a desire for strong visual presentation through an attention to design detail and lighting. This seems strangely at odds with the developing philosophy of *composition* in this field which apparently stressed the 'transparency' of the technology. There are many views on how loudspeakers may be used to present sound in public and private spaces. We shall examine a variety of such views and some of the many functions of sound projection.

Traditions of 'Sound Projection/Diffusion'

For concert presentations there are two tradition streams of sound projection. There is a clear split between 'idealist' and 'realist' approaches. The idealists believe that the function of concert loudspeaker systems is to present to the listener a soundfield as near as possible to that which the composer heard in the studio during composition

10 Then the signal is not suitable for loudspeaker reproduction.

11 See Toole and Olive (2001). Francis Rumsey has published several papers on verbal attribute analysis with respect to *spatialisation* by loudspeaker (e.g. Berg and Rumsey, 2001).

or – a slightly weaker argument – may be heard on 'very high quality' close field monitors in any studio. The realists however argue that such an ideal cannot exist, or if it does it is meaningless. The studio does not resemble a concert hall: the room acoustic, the available equipment and limitations on its layout, all ensure we can never recreate such an ideal – even if it existed in the first place. The best that can be done is to treat the presentation as *interpretation*. The musical *intentions* of the composer are encoded in the work as 'stored' (in whatever format). Hence the function of sound projection is to present these to the greatest possible effect.[12]

In practice this becomes a contest of two simplifications. Composers and their performers may hold to one or the other, or a confused and uneasy mix of the two. To summarize:

- First the composer's ideal soundfield as heard in the studio of creation. Some composers and performers (the 'idealists') believe that this needs no further interpretation, merely the optimal adjustment of loudspeaker placement and setting the overall sound level;[13]
- Second the composer's 'musical intentions' for the listener. Recognising that the listening space may be radically different from the studio, some composers and performers (the 'realists') believe this demands active interpretation i.e. 'diffusion'.

Both views beg questions of authenticity, especially with historical material where the analogue-to-digital transfer question illustrates this point. Not everyone accepts that the analogue format should be transferred 'dead flat', to sound 'as it did at the time' (tape noise and other limitations included). Recent 'cleaned up' copies of Stockhausen's *Studie I* and *II* (on Stockhausen, 1991) and Berio's *Omaggio a Joyce* (on Berio, 1998) show serious flaws in the process – in *Studie II* the 'pumping' of the tape noise around the sound events contrasts with the 'unnatural' digital silence in the gaps between them; in *Omaggio* the reduction in analogue noise 'reveals' the crudity of the reverberation of 1958. But, *both these transfers were supervized by the composer* – so I beg to differ with the composer. All elements in the recording and reproduction chain are continually being 'improved' (irrespective of format changes). In addition there are changes in both studio and concert presentation *spaces*, some the result of social change. The composer's soundfield in a studio or a performance space of 1960 may not now be achievable. Although we may claim to have 'made it better' in contemporary monitoring environments, this still breaks the 'authentic' ideal. And further we may have endless debates as to the composer's intentions for performance, especially if they are not present or were not written down. Did they have a particular loudspeaker array in mind when producing the final work? Or, like the composer at an orchestral rehearsal, should their opinion be treated as just one input of several? Musical interpretation will evolve and perhaps the composer's view should in time be ignored.

---

12 It easily follows that the sound projectionist can aim to *enhance* these intentions. In practice even the realists can idealise the composer's intentions!

13 Reminiscent of Stravinsky's well-known admonitions concerning the role of the conductor.

Let us look further at the more realist view and its various interpretations. What is the function of active sound diffusion? Denis Smalley argues that the ideal option is hopelessly unrealistic; distinguishing between the *composed space* heard in the studio and the *listening space* of anything subsequent:

> To highlight the relationship ... I have invented the notions of *spatial consonance* and *spatial dissonance*. Composed sound-spaces may be either 'consonant' or 'dissonant' with the listening space, changing the nature of the listening experience to an extent often not contemplated by the composer (Smalley, 1991, p. 121).

Hence the *need* for interpretation – the diffusion of the sound to ensure the presentation of that which is consonant, and hopefully to compensate for the dissonant and possibly thereby to enhance the total experience. There are, in addition, circumstances which are inevitably far from standard and cannot generate the 'everyday' practical experience of diffusion. For large installations such as that for the Philips Pavilion at the Brussels World's Fair (1958) or the German Pavilion at the Osaka World's Fair (1970) there cannot be a studio 'ideal' even approximating to such a site-specific system. Here the ideal (if it exists)[14] must be created in the imagination and experience of the composer and on-site assistants. We shall examine therefore the evolution of the loudspeaker as a musical instrument, more or less actively engaged in interpreting the sounding result.

The Loudspeaker as Instrument

Precursors: The Intonarumori *(noise intoners)*

In March 1913 Luigi Russolo had published *The Art of Noise* in which he described his intention to create a 'Futurist orchestra' designed to produce six 'families of noises' by mechanical means. In May 1913 he described the mechanism of what he now called *intonarumori* (noise intoners):

> ... a single taught diaphragm suitably placed gives, by variation of its tension, a gamut of more than 10 whole tones, with all the passages of semitones, of quarter-tones and also smaller fractions of tones ... Then, by varying the means of excitation of the same diaphragm, one can also obtain a different noise, *in type and in timbre*, always preserving, naturally, the possibility of varying the *tone* (Kirby and Kirby, 1986, pp. 176–177).[15]

The diaphragm was excited either by turning a crank or (in later models) by activating an electric motor; a lever then controlled pitch (in a broad sense). Each instrument was built in a square or rectangular box from which protruded a substantial funnel which acted as a megaphone to project the sound more effectively. The similarity in sound production principles to the acoustic gramophone (then still standard) is striking. The

---

14 Even Cage may have an ideal even if it is not clearly pre-defined and the result of a chance process.

15 The final word *tone* is here used in its American sense of *note* (i.e. *pitch*); *tone* in the sense of *timbre* was not variable on an individual instrument.

groove driven needle was simply replaced by frictional (and other moving) excitation devices. The *intonarumori* were often combined with conventional instruments but also performed as a unique 'noise orchestra' (see photographs in Kirby and Kirby, 1986, pp. 36 and 39):[16] While Pierre Schaeffer was later to claim ignorance of the Futurists' innovations in music in the early years of *musique concrète*, the *Zeitgeist* connections are clear – a 'noise orchestra' and the need for sound projection in live performance:

Description of an Early Performance System for *Musique Concrète*

An anonymous correspondent writing in the New York Times in August 1953 on the 'First International 10 days of experimental music' held in Paris and organized by the *Groupe de Recherches de Musique Concrète* the preceding June, described:

> ... sitting in a small studio which was equipped with four loudspeakers – two in front of one – right and left; one behind one and a fourth suspended above. In the front center were four large loops and an 'executant' moving a small magnetic unit through the air. The four loops controlled the four speakers, and while all four were giving off sounds all the time, the distance of the unit from the loops determined the volume sent out from each. The music thus came to one at varying intensity from various parts of the room, and this 'spatial projection' gave new sense to the rather abstract sequence of sound originally recorded (quoted in Ungeheuer, 1992, p. 152).

This described the experimental *pupitre de relief* (also known as the *pupitre d'espace* or the *potentiomètre d'espace*)[17] designed and built at the GRMC by Jacques Poullin and launched in July 1951 (Chion and Delalande, 1986, p. 259) for a performance of the *Symphonie pour un homme seul.*[18] Hence the desire to move sounds in space was realised in concert some years before being freely available in the studio. For many years the output of the Paris studio was monaural (one track). Davies (1968) lists all works as '1 track' through to as late as 1958, although the GRM's more recent catalogues indicate a few two channel works (such as the electroacoustic *Interpolations* for Varèse's *Déserts* (1954)) (Chion and Delalande, 1986).

---

16 See the score extracts from Francesco Balilla Pratella's *JOY. Trial of a mixed orchestra* and Luigi Russolo's *Awakening of a city* in Kirby and Kirby (1986, pp. 194–195 and 190–191) showing these two approaches.

17 The best photograph is in the accompanying booklet to the CD collection *archives grm* (INA/GRM, 2004, p. 18).

18 The CD note (Schaeffer, 1990) describes Pierre Henry's revised stereo version of 1966 as 'restoring the dimension of cinematic interpretation already anticipated at the time of the first performance of the 11 movement version (1951) ... testing the first "pupitre de relief" owing to J. Poullin'.

Orchestre de Haut-Parleurs: Different Approaches

The 'rise' of multi-loudspeaker sound diffusion within the French tradition is not well documented. Following the re-founding of the *musique concrète* studio and its renaming as the *Groupe de Recherches Musicales* in 1958, concert set-up details are rare for the following eight years. Chion and Reibel (1976) report on the attempt within the newly formed studio to forge a collective spirit through a concentration on group research; this was to feed directly into Schaeffer's monumental *Traité des objets musicaux* of 1966. A unique project emerged in the early 1960s in *Le Concert Collectif* (concluded in 1963). This ambitious project involved finally nine composers[19] and resulted in a 'composite work'[20] for groups of instruments and tape. It threw up many performance problems, including the difficult balancing of live and electroacoustic resources.[21] This contributed to a growing realization that a traditional concert presentation was inadequate for this new music. For the first time a controlled sound environment was conceived for concerts at the GRM, including loudspeakers surrounding the audience and a console for 'spatialization' at the centre of the room. Such a system was launched at the first of an annual series of *Expositions de musique expérimentale* in 1966 (Chion and Reibel, 1976, chapter 3). The expansion of visitor programmes into a full scale *stage pour compositeurs* and the 'export' of new concert ideas through performances outside Paris coincided with an explosion of creativity in general following the Paris 'events' of May 1968. The idea and realization of *un orchestre de haut-parleurs* had arrived but it was only in the 1970s that their formal organization, 'philosophy' and constitution (and their names!) became established. In France the first with an explicit name and agenda was the *Gmebaphone*, the invention of Christian Clozier at the *Groupe de Musique Expérimentale* in Bourges in 1973. But Clozier makes an important distinction:

> The Gmebaphone
> – is not: a loudspeaker orchestra
> – is: an orchestration generator (Clozier, 1998, p. 237).

The early versions of the Gmebaphone were driven with a purpose-built frequency splitting device (the *Gmebahertz*) which subdivided a single signal channel into multiple (band limited) channels – thus 'spatializing' it through frequency

19 Luc Ferrari, François-Bernard Mâche, François Bayle, Edgardo Canton, Bernard Parmegiani, Ivo Malec, Jean-Etienne Marie, Philippe Carson, N'Guyen Van Tuong.

20 Originally intended to be a group work, the sections were finally credited to individuals but some sharing of materials is described in the programme note.

21 Thus *musique mixte* (see Chapter 4) was a major contributor: an *orchestra* of loudspeakers had to balance in all senses an orchestra of instruments.

distribution across several loudspeakers (Figure 6.1).[22] While there was no absolutely standard loudspeaker layout plan, there was a symmetrical 'core' of loudspeakers to which unique bass and treble units were added asymmetrically. While subsequent versions of the *Gmebaphone* have moved away from the literal cross-over filtering of signals, the system retains a much stronger signal processing capability than other such systems. Clozier has always conceived of the system as a real participating 'instrument':

> The Gmebaphone is a processor/simulator of sonic electroacoustic space, as well as a polyphonic acoustic synthesiser of musical spaces. It can generate space, time and timbres. It is an instrument made up of a hierarchical combination of control system, access and operators, and is endowed with a memory, tablatures and combinatory modes of play that give rise to a rich and workable system of interpretation and expression (Clozier, 1998, p. 266).

All six documented stages of development (Clozier, 1998) include signal processing capabilities, the recent versions moving towards fader motion capture and scene automation with crossfade. Clozier has designed the most recent to be software based, and so in principle transportable and useable over the internet (albeit without the 50 loudspeakers considered the 'standard' for the system). It was for this reason renamed the *Cybernéphone* in 1997.

22 It is difficult to match this diagram to a specific generation of *Gmebaphone* (as given in Clozier (1998)). This diagram is from an article by Clozier republished in the Newsletter of the Electroacoustic Music Association of Great Britain in 1981.

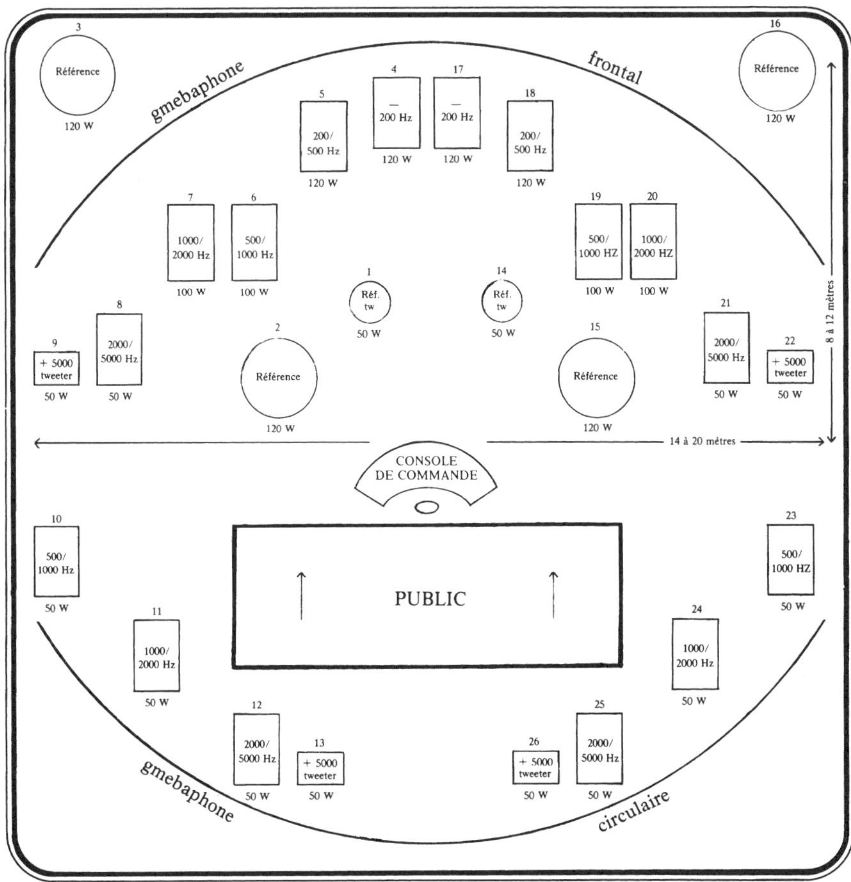

Figure 6.1: Diagram of *Gmebaphone* configuration (late 1970s)

The first *Gmebaphone* was followed in February 1974 by the inauguration of the *Acousmonium* of the GRM. Created for the first Paris performance of François Bayle's *Expérience Acoustique* (Bayle, 1994) and the world première of his *Vibrations Composées* (on Bayle, 1992) in the *Espace Cardin*, the composer's loudspeaker layout diagram sketch and a photograph are juxtposed in his article 'Support/Espace' (Bayle, 1977).[23] A characteristic of his design philosophy is immediately apparent and continues to the present: an *asymmetrical* distribution of loudspeakers. In addition to two (symmetrical) 'soloists', the loudspeakers are described according to tessitura (from *contrebasses*, through *médium/grave*, *médium/neutre*, *médium/aigu*, to *sur-aigus*). Many are, however, grouped together in short diagonal lines across the stage area, the right and left signals being distributed logically along them (each

23 A better version of the photo and sketch is presented in Bayle (1993, plate XIV). The concert at the *Espace Cardin* on the 12 February is always given as the inauguration of the Acousmonium yet a near identical sketch layout and photograph for a concert at the *Eglise St. Séverin* two weeks earlier (30 January) is also presented.

line is thus independently a 'stereo array'). Each group therefore has the complete signal presented with its own characteristic sound depending on loudspeaker type. The diffuser at the console may then choose which 'section of the orchestra' performs which musical phrase or gesture. Subsequent versions of the acousmonium have extended in scope (including to surround the audience) but not changed this principle:

> One will have understood that the principle of the acousmonium consists in an architecture of registers[24] of kinds and colours, liberally deployed inside a sonic space, and continually controlled in reference to a 'normal' image of a smaller dimension. This point is extremely important because subjectivity of hearing is one of the most important difficulties in the conveying of the registration of colours (Bayle 1993, pp. 45–6).

The first systems established in the UK[25] followed these developments closely. Denis Smalley assembled a system along these lines for an 'Arts Council Contemporary Music Network Tour' of 1976 (subsequently establishing such a system and a concert series at the University of East Anglia) and this was followed by Jonty Harrison's founding of BEAST (Birmingham Electro-Acoustic Sound Theatre) in 1980. Since around this time such systems have proliferated throughout the UK, elsewhere in Europe, Canada and (more recently) the United States at centres of production and performance. In most of these systems left-right symmetry has generally been maintained (for stereo works at least). Harrison has described the design 'growth' of the BEAST system (Harrison, 1998). Starting from the premise that simple stereophonic two channel playback cannot address any reasonable sized audience with any degree of equality, he sculpts into the space successive stereo pairs of loudspeakers to address this question. But further, he gives a vast range of alternative possibilities – that turn themselves into performance strategies – in placing additional pairs in a range of configurations throughout the space, each with a different function within the space[26] (Harrison, 1998, pp. 121–3). He distinguishes this philosophy from the acousmonium in that:

> ... a hallmark of many BEAST performances is a tendency to blend loudspeakers in the array rather than to localise sounds in particular boxes, to keep the sound in a constant state of spatial evolution – to sculpt the sound in the space and to sculpt the space with the sound (Harrison, 1998, p. 126).

Harrison describes this approach as 'organic' rather than 'architectonic' – a trait he detects in some other composition and performance philosophies, especially with respect to certain multi-channel works which seek to fix spatial relationships in a 'measured' manner (discussed below).

---

24 'Register' and 'registration', here in the sense of the organ stop, effecting the colour of the overall sound.

25 Loudspeaker orchestras (or looser equivalents) were assembled at several centres throughout Europe, notably Fylkingen and EMS in Stockholm, and Steim in Amsterdam but these lacked the identity with a philosophy of sound projection which a name seems to bring! In France also Pierre Henry assembled his own vast system (see Henry, 1977).

26 The final position may only be determined at installation and in rehearsal.

Immersive Systems[27]

While the loudspeaker orchestras described above can be configured to be 'surround sound' and usually utilize rear auditorium loudspeakers, I make a distinction here with systems explicitly designed to be 'equal' in all directions. These aim to immerse the listener in sound (with the possible exception of 'beneath')[28] to give the total experience of the music. They are sometimes combined with performance spaces in which the listener is free to face in any direction, even in many cases to move around. Not all the systems described below assume this last point but it fundamentally changes the nature of sound diffusion. If you rotate your head 90 degrees, left-right discrimination becomes front-rear with a substantially different sensitivity for the psychoacoustic cues for the perception of space. This will have profound implications for compositional practice – if all directions may be 'forward' for some listeners then no direction can have privileged information.

Geometric Propositions

For performances of his works, Stockhausen has developed a form of idealized sound projection for 2, 4 and recently 8 channel sound. But the earliest work to include space as an integrated part of the composition included an additional (height) channel beyond the then 'cutting edge' four channel machine available. His original conception for the playback of *Gesang der Jünglinge* (1956 on Stockhausen, 1991) was to project the five channels in a square surrounding the audience with the fifth channel above, at the centre of the ceiling.[29] Three years before starting the composition of *Gesang der Jünglinge*, in 1955, Stockhausen had been in Paris at exactly the times of the earliest experiments in spatialisation in *musique concrète* performance.[30] The *pupitre de relief* (discussed above) was launched in 1951 and used at least through 1953, and Messiaen's *Timbres-Durées* (1952 on INA/GRM, 2004), realized by Pierre Henry, was performed in a three channel version (specially constructed by Henry for the concert, designating 'left-centre-right' channels) on the 21 May 1952. Whether Stockhausen was present at this concert, or whether he was shown the *pupitre de relief* (with its centre ceiling loudspeaker) during his

27 In which all directions are considered of equal importance.

28 Bass bins are often perceived as 'low' or 'beneath'. The Sonic Arts Research Centre space at Queens University, Belfast allows placement of loudspeakers beneath the audience which is seated on a 'grid' floor.

29 Extraordinarily reliant on high qualities of tape machine speed maintenance the first performance was from a four track machine plus a mono tape machine *synchronised by hand* (CD notes 1991).

30 Stockhausen was in Paris from the 8 January 1952 mostly to study in Messiaen's composition class, and visited Schaeffer's studio in March through Pierre Boulez. Although he was absent from Paris from the end of June, on his return in October he began studies in *musique concrète*. After preliminary analytical work (and some crude attempts at synthesis) he completed his *Etude* (*musique concrète*) probably in December (as suggested by Kurtz (1992, p. 55) and Toop (1976, p. 296)), although the composer reports 'the first months of 1953' in the CD notes.

stay is not documented.[31] In the event, at the premiere of *Gesang der Jünglinge* in the WDR concert hall in Cologne (on the 30th of May 1956) the fifth channel loudspeaker positioning proved problematic and he was forced to position it centre stage, subsequently mixing it in to the other four channels in what later became the standard 'WDR' 4-channel format.[32]

His next electronic work, *Kontakte* (composed at the WDR studio 1958–1960) is constructed in four channel surround sound. Originally the centre front loudspeaker was maintained; in the first edition of the *performance score*[33] (*Aufführungspartitur*) (Stockhausen, 1966) he defines the loudspeakers in cross formation as 'left, front, right and behind' the audience.[34] The 'floodsounds' characteristic of the work would start at a point and fan out to cover the space:

> In *Kontakte*, I discovered a way of making 'flood sounds'. You have sounds continually starting in speakers behind the listeners, and after a short delay the same sounds appear in speakers at the left and right, and, again a short time later, in the speakers in the front ... The sound really passes from the back to the front like water going over your head – and you're in the water (Cott, 1974, p. 150).

However, in later performances and notes to recordings he explicitly rotates this 45° anticlockwise to the 'traditional' square format[35] – thus reducing the full 'behind-to-front' (or reverse) dramatic effects of the flood sounds to diagonal movements. Stockhausen has consistently proposed severely rectangular geometric 'solutions' to the problem of optimising the soundfield created by loudspeakers, attempting to equalize the experience of spatial sound throughout the auditorium. Each signal channel has a minimum of two loudspeakers set close together but at an angle to project a broadened 'funnel' of sound to the listeners. Figure 6.2 gives in diagramatic form his suggestions for such multichannel projection. But already at the time of

---

31 Richard Toop documents a letter from Stockhausen to Karel Goeyvaerts referring to this concert yet to happen (but only by a short time) (Toop, 1979, p. 382).

32 Channels 1-2-3-4 being a square starting *back left* rotating clockwise (a classic 'rotation' gesture).

33 There are two versions of *Kontakte*, the electroacoustic version and one with additional piano and percussion. There are also two versions of the score, a *realisation* score giving details of the electronic construction of the work, and a *performance* score which combines a graphic representation of the electroacoustic part with the piano and percussion parts. Stockhausen (1968) bundles both together but Stockhausen (1966) is the performance score only with very substantial introduction and performance notes in addition.

34 Also referred to this way when describing the mixdown to 2-channel for broadcast and recording (Stockhausen, 1964a, p. 105). Peter Manning has ascertained that there were two stereo versions mixed for LP: the first (withdrawn) 'collapsed' the original channels literally superimposing two on the left, two on the right (losing most of the rotation movement), the second panning the four channels to retain some sense of this motion (Manning, 2006, p. 88).

35 See the notes to Stockhausen (1993a) which give detailed spatial and projection directions for the version with instruments. The original channel 1 (left) has become channel 1 (left back).

Kontakte he was designing a surround sound auditorium with specialist facilities for depth and height, as well as rotation (discussed below).

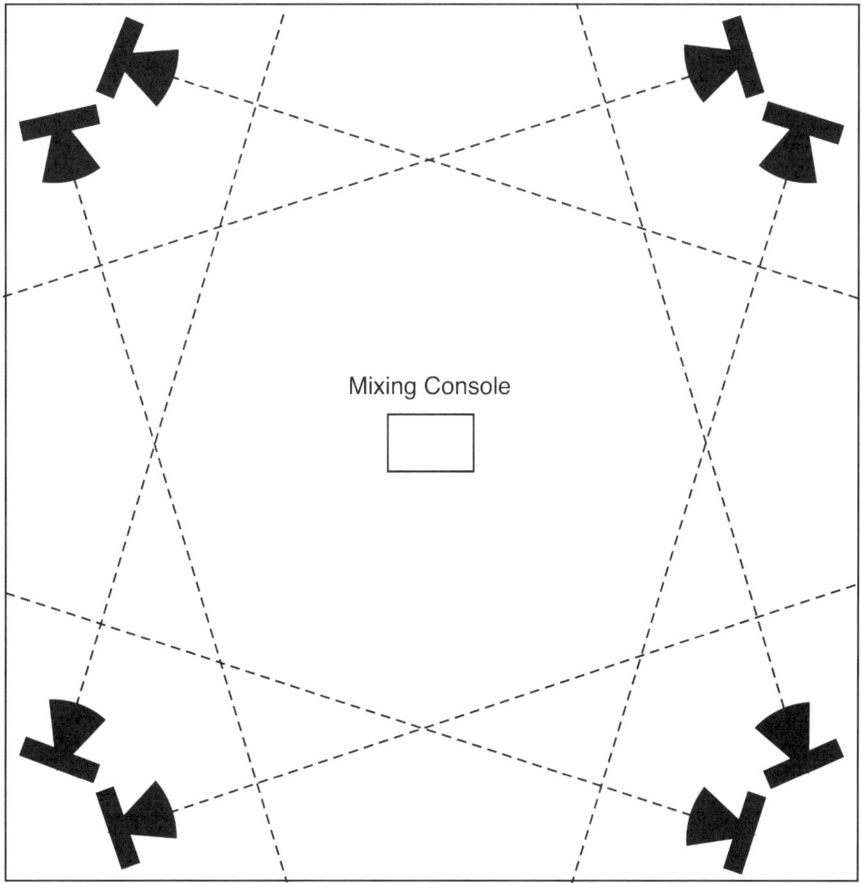

Figure 6.2: Four-channel sound projection (after Stockhausen)

Ideal Octophonics

Jonathan Harvey's *Mortuos Plango, Vivos Voco* (1980) (Harvey, 1999) also designs an ideal cube of eight channels within which the audience 'is projected'. The aim is to produce a play of movement which reinforces the spectral transformations of the piece. These are based on its two fundamental materials, the great tenor bell of Winchester cathedral and the chorister's (his son's) voice. The ideal listener is 'inside' the bell, its partials distributed in space; the boy's voice flies around, derived from, yet becoming the bell sound.[36] The near impossibility of a performance

36 'The walls of the concert hall are conceived as the sides of the bell inside which is the audience and around which (especially in the eight channel version) flies the free spirit of the boy' (Jonathan Harvey: early programme note (1981) in the possession of the present author).

that fulfils these ideals may be overcome if there is developed a new generation of mixing and production techniques for personal listening spaces which will be able to encode height (and perhaps depth beneath) information unambiguously. Stockhausen's *Oktophonie* (1990–91) is similarly constructed for immersive sound in eight channels. Although here strictly this defines a hemisphere – a lower group of four channels are still slightly raised from the floor to give direct pathways to the ears,[37] a second square of 4 is to be placed 14m above these (Stockhausen, 1994a and 1994b).

Multi-Loudspeaker Immersion: Osaka Pavilion

The extraordinary exception to Stockhausen's rectangular conceptions remains his design for the German pavilion at the *Expo 70* (World's Fair) in Osaka in Japan. He had written as early as 1958 on the need for a new type of concert hall wired for spatial sound:

> New halls for listening must be built to meet with demands of spatial music. My idea would be to have a spherical chamber, fitted all around with loudspeakers. In the middle of this spherical chamber, a platform, transparent to both light and sound, would be hung for the listeners. They could hear music ... coming from above, from below and from all directions (Stockhausen, 1959, p. 69).

In Osaka this vision was almost exactly realized. A total of 50 loudspeakers were constructed in seven circles.[38] Three of the circles are below a suspended transaudient floor for the performers and listeners. His specially constructed projection console included two 'rotation mill' potentiometers which could be flexibly patched to ten loudspeakers to produce a variety of rotation shapes and even a kind of spiral motion (Stockhausen, 1971, pp. 153–187 and 1973 (diagrams)). There is evidently a potential conflict between active spatial sound projection on such a system and the best presentation of studio-prepared spatial movement.[39] The Osaka diffusion system invites a playful, experimental approach best suited to those pieces which do not demand a fixed sound image. Stockhausen's *intuitive music* texts and the '+/-' scores (including *Spiral*, *Pole* and *Expo* (Stockhausen 1973; 1975) which were composed for the Osaka residency) were performed regularly throughout the season, along with some fixed image works.[40]

37 This remains a major problem for 'beneath' sound. By definition there can be no direct loudspeaker to ear sound pathway and hence there will be high absorption of sound, especially at high frequencies which severely reduces directional information; hence many systems confine beneath floor loudspeakers to bass information which is less directional.

38 An additional low frequency loudspeaker in the centre below the floor makes a total of 51.

39 To which Stockhausen has returned in all his multi-channel works since this time.

40 Stockhausen has given his own 'Resumé' of the works performed (Stockhausen, 1971, pp. 183–4).

Polytopes – Clouds of Loudspeakers

> Goethe said that 'architecture was music become stone'. From the composer's point of view the proposition could be reversed by saying that 'music is architecture in movement'. On the theoretical level the two statements may be beautiful and true, but they do not truly enter into the intimate structures of the two arts (Xenakis quoted in Le Corbusier, 1968, p. 326).

In 1958 Xenakis crystallized his thoughts on the integration of the arts of sound and sight in an article, published a year later in French as 'Notes sur un "Geste Electronique"' (reprinted in Xenakis, 1976). He extols the contemporary trend towards abstraction:

> In effect, the play of forms and colours detached from their concrete context implies conceptual networks of a superior level ... Through abstraction, these two arts [painting and sculpture] approach a philosophy of essences which calmly shows itself in mathematics and in logic (Xenakis, 1976, p. 143).

He goes on to suggest that the advent of cinema (with its time component) has not only allowed a new possibility but demands it. 'We realise that this need for a 'cinematic painting' is not a luxury but a vital need for the art of colour and forms' (p. 144). To this effect he abolishes the 'small screen' and envisages an enormous surface (irregular with varying curvatures) on which to project this new art. This he imagines includes 'coloured ambiences coming forth in rhythmic jets ... which ... would transform the spatial configurations of the irregular surfaces' (p. 145). He describes the Philips Pavilion at the Brussels World's Fair of 1958 as 'a first experience of this synthesis' (p. 150). Thus the idea of *polytope* was effectively suggested here before the name emerged.

The Pavilion was constructed according to the same geometric model which helped construct his work *Metastasis* five years earlier (as discussed in Chapter 2): about 325 loudspeakers were distributed on the inside surface of the space (Treib, 1996, p. 250).[41] Sound and film were displayed in timed sequences with the short electroacoustic work *Concret PH* (1958) by Xenakis (Xenakis, 1997) acting as 'transition' music as groups of visitors moved on and were replaced. Details of the sound distribution system have only recently been published in a clear form (Treib, 1996). Prompted by load bearing problems for such an enormous number, Xenakis suggested dividing the loudspeakers into two kinds with higher (and lighter) units set in the relatively thin walls and lower frequency units at floor level (p. 205). The entire audio-visual show (including spatialization of the sound) was controlled from synchronized tapes controlling amplifiers (pp. 202–07). In fact the visual side of the event was outside Xenakis's control and he found it disappointing.[42]

---

41 In his meticulous account of the entire Philips Pavilion project, Marc Treib (1996) uses the phrase '… the army of speakers (reported as being anywhere from 300 to 450, with 325 being a reasonable estimate) ...' (p. 250).

42 The entire show was called *La Poème Electronique*, within which Varèse's piece of virtually the same name (*Poème Electronique*) was performed; Xenakis suggests the visuals were directed by Le Corbusier who had in fact delegated it to the film maker Philippe Agostini

The loudspeaker was a key building block in Xenakis's increasingly complex *polytopes* – an absolute point in space from which an individual soundstream would contribute to the statistical whole. In principle there was always a strong relationship with a visual equivalent – strobe lights on steel cables (*Polytope de Montréal*, 1967), points of light (torches) held by moving people (*Persepolis*, 1971), strobe lights and lasers (*Polytope de Cluny*, 1972; *Diatope*, 1978), search lights, torches[43] (*Polytope de Mycenae*,[44] 1978) (Revault d'Allonnes, 1975; Matossian, 1986). Xenakis contrasts two types of 'stereophony'.[45] He defines first a 'static stereophony' which maps a straightforward fixed Euclidian space in acoustic terms. But secondly:

> We could equally construct an acoustic line with the help of movement, a sound which displaces itself in a line of loudspeakers. The notions of acoustic speed and acceleration are introduced here. All the geometric curves and all the surfaces can be transposed cinematically with the help of the definition of the sound point. We shall call this stereophony, 'cinematic stereophony' (Xenakis, 1976, p. 148).

Here the loudspeaker becomes an agent in a mass of agents, its character subsumed into the essential group activity. This engages perfectly with Xenakis's interest in granular synthesis: the loudspeaker here acts not as a virtual source of a 'stereo image' but as an individual source within a mass of sources. Outside the polytope series but similarly performed in a 'spectacular' space was *Hibiki-Hana-Ma* a 12-track tape work (Xenakis, 1997)[46] which was commissioned for the Japanese Steel Federation Pavilion at the Osaka Expo (1970) and:

> ... used 800 loudspeakers, scattered in the air and in the ground. They were divided into approximately 150 independent groups. The sounds were designed to traverse these groups according to various kinematic diagrams. After the Philips Pavilion at the 1958 Brussels World's Fair, the Steel Pavilion was the most advanced attempt at placing sounds in space. However only twelve independent magnetic tracks were available (two synchronised six-track tape recorders) (Xenakis, 1992, p. 379).

(Treib, 1996). The Philips Pavilion project precipitated the break between Xenakis and Le Corbusier (Treib, 1996; Matossian, 1986).

43 At one point a herd of 200 goats with bells and lights were released to roam on the mountainside (the performance was after dark).

44 While not in Xenakis's official list of works the *Polytope de Mycenae* took place in 1978 and was reviewed (Schiffer, 1978).

45 'Stereo' is derived from the Greek for 'solid'; the French language tends to preserve this general use – thus (unlike in English) *stereophonic* sound means any spatialized sound in any number of channels above one (mono) which is how Xenakis uses the term here.

46 '... in conjunction with a laser show designed by the sculptor Keiji Usami' (Matossian, 1986, p. 219).

Loudspeaker-Performer-Processor

David Tudor's *Rainforest* was an evolving project which existed in at least four distinct incarnations (Rogalsky, 2006). In an interview/article written in 1972 he explains:

> One of the ideas in my *Rainforest* series is that loudspeakers should be individuals, they should be instruments. So if you need a hundred of them to fill a hall, each one should have its own individual voice ... After all what is a loudspeaker? At present it's a reproducing instrument, but my feeling all along has been that you should regard it as a generating instrument ... Why shouldn't there be a thousand or more ways of building loudspeakers? ... Suppose you build one which only responds to the frequencies between 100 and 200? ... If you put sine waves through it, then you get quite a different sound emerging ... The loudspeaker is transforming what goes into it, instead of reproducing it (Tudor, 1972, p. 26).

Rainforest focused on principles of feedback and resonance of objects.[47] In *Rainforest IV* – the original version of 1973 was a group creation working to Tudor's basic circuit and ideas – a vast range of objects was collected and tested for resonant properties. Each object had (at least) two attached transducers. One was a *driver*, feeding a pre-recorded signal into the object. The second was a pickup transducer fed on to mixing, amplification and sound projection. There was thus a kind of 'orchestra of resonating objects'. The driver signals included a collection of animal sound recordings:[48] these are thus not heard directly but solely filtered through the resonance of the object to which they are fed. Most of these sources could be described as landscape sounds, although they might only be perceived as such when played as an ensemble; and each individually was 'small' in the sense used by Cage. Thus a remote and imaginary landscape was fragmented, resonated through objects, filtered and reassembled in the real performance space through which performers and audience could move at will (Tudor, 1998).

Collective and Personal Immersion

The ever expanding sound systems of rock music followed the social trends of music listening in ever larger numbers in the 1960s and 1970s. An experiment such as *Pink Floyd*'s quintaphonic PA system of the mid-1970s was an early example of 'surround sound' experimentation in a large space.[49] Discos (1960s/70s) and clubs (1980s/90s) take us into amniotic immersion, an all-embracing sonic fluid – the system must be good but not intrusively seen. In fluids, the pressure (*of the fluid alone*) at any given

---

47 For a detailed history of this extraordinary work see Rogalsky (2006).

48 Originally made for a project in the Pepsi Pavilion at the Osaka World's Fair in 1970 (Rogalsky, 2006).

49 Constructed for *Pink Floyd*'s tour of 1975 ('Wish You Were Here') including the Knebworth Festival (where the author was present), the five separated surround sound stacks were intended for delay and echo effects around the audience but were only partially successful on this occasion. A definitive and accurate history of rock music PA is sorely needed.

point is not directional while sound propagated in the fluid remains directional. However in some totally immersive environments, sonic directionality is deliberately reduced to omnidirectionality through many loudspeakers and high sound levels. This reinforces the impression of the sound as being omnipresent – almost *becoming* the fluid that surrounds the listener.

Headphones are simply small loudspeakers; all the current methods of loudspeaker transduction are found in headphone design. But there are several areas where headphone and loudspeaker listening differ. Two are of particular importance to electroacoustic music. The perception of frequency can be qualitatively different and – if the same signal that was created for loudspeaker listening is used – localisation is very often confined to 'within the head'. Close-to-ear loudspeakers were in effect invented with the telephone, and straps to attach one or two to the head appeared shortly after in telephone exchanges and dictation machines. Although a singular date for invention is not helpful, commercially available headphones for home listening 'take off' with the 'personal stereo' from about 1979. Poldy (2001) distinguishes three kinds of coupling of transducer to ear: *circumaural* (cushion surrounding the outer ear), *supra-aural* (foam cushion lying on the outer ear) and *intra-aural* (small in-ear devices) (p. 595).[50] The ideal 'isolation' of the sound from neighbours is limited by design, as for acoustic reasons there needs to be some 'leakage' of sound. This is because in-ear devices need to limit low frequency response through acoustic resistances 'leaking' back to the outside world (pp. 621–23). Thus the notoriously unpopular leakage of personal stereo sound is inevitable; with the proximity effect working in reverse, low frequency sounds progressively 'roll off' leaving only the 'high hat' sounds for close neighbours to enjoy. Researchers also report an anomaly between headphone and loudspeaker listening to bass frequencies. It appears that headphone listeners require up to 10 dB additional sound pressure level *for the same subjective sensation* of bass sound (below about 300 Hz) (Poldy, 2001, pp. 653–4). No firm explanation has been agreed, although suggestions that other parts of the body will be perceiving and contributing to the subjective impression of loudness have been advanced. In any case there is an actual physiological difference between (say) an immersive club space and a personal stereo space in the absence of these 'total body' components. They would need to be included if the reproduction of the *psychology* of the former was the aim.

But even given an adequate flat frequency response for the headphone the experience remains very different to listening to loudspeakers: the signal on the headphone effectively bypasses sound diffraction due to the head. High frequencies especially are effected by this 'head related transfer function' (HRTF). The mechanisms of sound localization – how only two ears can decode the entire sphere of sound around us – include head and pinna (the outer ear) effects and excluding these contributes to the collapse of spatial realism in headphone listening. The image can become flat. Some reverberant spaces retain a certain sense of depth but rarely to the realistic degree of their loudspeaker equivalent.

---

50 It is possible to add 'canalphones' which reside truly inside the ear canal; some hearing aids and recent PA foldback applications use these. Standard earphones are placed on the outer aperture of the canal.

There are 'cones of confusion' and possible front/rear ambiguities in localisation which are often resolved in practice by even the slightest head movement. The perception system can decode a *difference* fast enough to 'fix' a location ambiguity. But headphone listening does not allow this to happen – the entire sound-scene moves with the head. We are always 'listening straight ahead' at the sound image. The 'earphone space' created by the smallest of loudspeakers returns full circle to one of Edison's own listening methods. Early attempts to record suitable signals for headphone listening which restored depth and 'outside head' sensations were centred on ideas of binaural ('dummy head') recording which included (real) head and pinna processing of the signal.[51] The recent availability of software to mimic HRTF functions may not only recreate this but be used positively to enhance at least some of directional and soundscape information.[52]

New Objectivity: from Ambisonics to Wavefront Synthesis

Much of what we have discussed so far rests on different responses to the creation and re-presentation of soundfields which are based on – or extensions of – Alan Blumlein's technique of capturing the stereophonic sound image (Borwick, 1990, pp. 118–120). This hovers clearly yet precariously between two (or more) loudspeakers. Of course practitioners are aware of the fundamental fact and limitation that such theory and practice presupposes a 'sweet spot'. Move too far from a position equidistant between the two sources and as far from each as they are from each other (an equilateral triangle is considered optimum) and the image collapses towards the source closest to the listener. John Chowning's surround sound extension to this theory, giving reverberation and Doppler-shift calculations for realistic movement in a two dimensional plane, was also only 'true' for a fixed central listening location (Chowning, 1977).[53]

A major claim towards overcoming this problem was made by the developers of *ambisonics*. In principle this involves recording (or synthesising) a complete three-dimensional soundfield. By combining three coincident figure-of-eight and an omnidirectional capsule in a single microphone unit an entire *periphonic* soundfield may be captured. Suitable manipulation of these components gives the apparently extraordinary ability *electronically* to change the forward direction – to tumble,

---

51 In-ear microphones (such as those from OKM) are an example. The sound recordist's head and pinna directly effect the signal and encode into it some of the directional time delay (phase) and level information.

52 The contribution of head movement within a real space has been mimicked in virtual reality applications (including both sound and vision) but these are not yet commonly available. There is no reason why audio only applications along these lines should not exist, fixing the sound space to an external reference. Such a 'world-referenced' sound stage has been referred to above (Sherman and Craig, 2003, pp. 164–177).

53 And (often misunderstood) Chowning defines a space outside the four loudspeakers. It should also be noted that traditional 'quad' loudspeaker positioning in a square has a 90 degree angle between any two loudspeakers from the listener's point of audition, greater than the optimum for a phantom image and often resulting in a 'hole in the middle'.

tilt and rotate the entire image. The signal is suitably decoded onto an array of loudspeakers, the layout of which can in principle be decided for individual set-ups although this will need to be programmed into the decoder. The image created is claimed to be substantially more robust than that for previous surround sound systems (Malham and Myatt, 1995).[54]

Doppler Reproduction Paradox

Such sound imaging systems however cannot handle fast moving sounds in a way which allows *Doppler shift* to be heard correctly *at more than one location*. To describe Doppler shift is easy if we refer to a commonplace everyday experience. Imagine a motor bike travelling in a straight line from far to your left, passing directly in front of you, then receding far away to the right. It is travelling at constant speed and *to the rider* the pitch of the engine is constant. But to you, the listener, the pitch of the engine changes as the bike passes. You hear a near steady pitch as it approaches in the distance; then as it goes by there is a rapid glissando down and a lower near steady pitch is heard as the bike recedes into the distance once more.[55] Without need of mathematical treatment, the soundwaves are 'compressed' closer together (and hence higher pitched) forward of the bike, and 'stretched' apart (and hence lower pitched) in the trail of the bike; to either side of the bike the waves retain the wavelength of the sound as emitted by the engine. Thus the bike sounds different from different directions. This can be simulated for a particular listener (of course, usually the one at the 'sweet spot' in the centre), by varying the pitch of the recorded sound coordinated with its amplitude between loudspeakers. But as the real sound source of the recording (the loudspeaker) is not itself moving, this effect will not be correctly timed for any other position in the listening space (Figure 6.3).

54 For a comparison with other systems and a critique of current practice see Malham (2001).

55 The length of the glissando down depends on how far you are away from the line of travel. If the bike brushes your coat, the change is near instantaneous!

Figure 6.3: Doppler reproduction paradox

Wave Field Synthesis (WFS)

The most radical answer to this paradox has come from the development of *Wave Field Synthesis* (WFS) (Baalman, 2004; Sporer, 2004). This has returned to an idea based on the principle put forward by Christiaan Huygens in 1690. This states that each point on a wavefront may be considered to act as an individual point source of an ongoing wave. Subsequent wavefronts may thus be built from summing the results of these point sources. Originally developed for optics, the principle applies equally to any wave phenomenon and is here applied to sound. Point sources may be interpreted as loudspeakers. While Huygens's theory in principle requires an infinite number of such point sources for absolute fidelity, small efficient loudspeakers 17cm apart produce (it is claimed) acceptably low errors and limitations. The ideal extension of such a system may be in development – a 'surface' acting as a continuous loudspeaker. In addition to claiming a high degree of spatial definition – even *within* the space, in front of the loudspeakers – the system so far developed claims to have solved the Doppler paradox. A fast moving sound is effectively played back over many successive loudspeakers which will create a naturally Doppler-shifted pattern of waves, the loudspeakers acting as successive 'real sources' not relying on the phantom images of stereo. The most revolutionary aspect of this development is, however, in its conceptualization of 'real-time' performance on such a system. At present a multichannel format requires a mix onto that specific number of channels (4, 8, 5.1, 7.1, for example); any change requires a new mix. WFS is 'object-oriented'; individual sound objects or attributes (reverberation, for example) may be defined along with their spatial positions and trajectories. It is then up to the playback software to 'allocate' these to the individual loudspeakers of the specific array (which may vary from place to place). In other words the composer's specifications contain no loudspeaker (track or channel) information.[56] This is directly related to the rapid development and application of the MPEG-4 encoding standard which allows '3-D Audio Profiles'.[57] While currently being intensively developed for film and video sound projection (Sporer, 2004), compositional applications are rapidly following (Baalman, 2004). This shift of thinking may indeed be easier for composers than for sound engineers. It relates directly to the earliest experiments of the *potentiomètre d'espace* discussed above and to Stockhausen's 'rotating loudspeaker' used in the production of *Kontakte*[58] and 'coffee mill' sound spatializer for the Osaka Pavilion. The functioning of such devices was easy to grasp but impossible to notate. Even with the most advanced track-based software an option to switch to 'rotary pot' thinking has only recently been implemented (in, for example, the software for 5.1-format mixing options). But this approach does rely on specified objects and their manipulation; there are real limits to the amount that present computing power can handle: the greater the number of objects and complexity of parameter manipulation, and the greater the number of loudspeakers, the sooner such limits are reached.[59]

Audio Beam

The dream of 'tight' sound beaming is diametrically opposite to that of Wave Front Synthesis. Any wave phenomenon diffracts – that is bends around objects or spreads out into the 'acoustic shadow'. This is increasingly true at low frequencies (longer wavelengths). Low sound is very difficult to locate for this reason as it flows out in all directions and round corners. High frequencies are increasingly directional, the 'direct' sound on axis from the bell of a trumpet is brighter, 'tweeters' have a tight throw of their sound – hence the coupling to a tiny exponential horn to increase dispersion. Thus ultrasound (high frequencies beyond human hearing) is in fact

56 Track and channel information can be stored and manipulated within WFS systems but as objects in their own right (Sporer, 2004).

57 Not to be confused with MPEG-7 which is a 'multimedia content description standard' working on metadata which will move towards agreed 'auditory scene descriptors'.

58 See the *realisation score* of *Kontakte* (Stockhausen, 1968, p. 3).

59 The development of this technology will probably be driven by commercial forces: Sporer (2004) calculates that a typical two hour film could be encoded (all sound streams 'unmixed') ready for WFS rendering, and reduced by compression to something approaching the limits of today's commercial storage devices (DVD-based). Composers, however, can be fussy about lossy compression.

highly directional and may be directed in a tightly controlled beam. From the 1960s onwards researchers have suggested the possibility of using ultrasound as a carrier for sound. Inherent transmission properties of the air cause the ultrasound to distort and produce audible frequencies.[60] Thus the aim became to modulate the ultrasound carrier in some way by the required perceivable signal such that the distortion acted as a decoder. Early attempted implementations (through to the 1980s) failed to understand the full effect of the distortion and the results were limited and development (commercially) abandoned. Solutions and consequent rival systems have emerged from the late 1990s. Two of these have resulted in commercially available products: from American Technology Corporation[61] (Woody Norris's 'HyperSonic Sound Technology') and Holosonics Research Labs[62] (Joseph Pompei's 'Audio Spotlight'). Both have managed to lock together a better understanding of so-called 'non-linear acoustics' (applied to the distortion of ultrasound in air) with a suitable software coder,[63] and the engineering of a new transducer to produce a first generation of 'tight beam' loudspeakers. The transducer is a relatively flat and thin (up to 10cm) disc or rectangle which may accurately be aimed at recipients. Typical 'usable ranges' are given as 20–30m but both companies claim a much higher range under 'ideal conditions'. There must be a clear path from transducer to listener (or via a specified reflector panel)[64] thus ceiling mounted experiments have featured strongly. The bass response of such systems is, however, severely limited by the theory and practice of this kind of sound propagation.[65]

The radical reappraisal of sound spaces that this suggests has hardly been considered. The individualized space of the headphones has effectively been liberated into the real space surrounding the body as it moves. The consequences of this integration cannot be predictable. The existing applications suggest that composers might consider this a 'point source' technology of extraordinary versatility, allowing – for example, using many such units – a 'spatialized' installation where sounds could be placed with near pinpoint accuracy within a real space.[66]

---

60 *Not* – as anecdotally reported by many people – through interference patterns.

61 http://www.atcsd.com/index.html (consulted May 2006). This website has a comprehensive documentation section including an 'HSS Technology White Paper' giving an excellent historical and theoretical summary.

62 http://www.holosonics.com (consulted May 2006). This includes a BBC Television *Tomorrow's World* video demonstration.

63 Detailed knowledge of the distortion characteristic allows us to programme a kind of 'correction mirror' to this process in the encoder, thus the 'distortion-decoder' of the natural air generates the original signal. Demonstrations current at the time of writing indicate that bass frequencies are not yet fully handled.

64 Both companies suggest the possibility of 'projected audio' – deliberately reflecting the beam for increased flexibility (and also) greater dispersion. Spatial (stereo) aspects of the individual sound stream have not so far been discussed. They appear at this stage to be monaural.

65 ATC gives a typical HSS bandwidth as 400 Hz – 16 kHz.

66 Were such a technology to have been universally implemented for the Hayward Gallery's Sonic Boom exhibition (2000) there would have been gain in ability to focus but a loss of holistic immersion and some beautiful 'crossfades' between sonic environments.

Acousmatic Acousmatic Music: 'Seeing (or not seeing) the Loudspeaker; seeing (or not seeing) the Music'

Many listeners feel – with Stockhausen – that it is *necessary* to close the eyes when listening to acousmatic music, to avoid the distraction of the physical world.[67] Indeed as Jonathan Harvey comments: 'He wants us not to be conscious *of* the music (dualistic) but to be conscious *as* the music (non-dualistic). *We are the music*' (Harvey, 1999, p. 21). He goes on to quote Stockhausen himself:

> I even said we should become the sound. If the sound moves upward I also move upward; if it moves downwards, I go down too. If it becomes quieter, so do I. If the sound divides itself into two, I follow suit, and meet myself again when the sound reunites, etc. This means that one is completely swallowed up in the process of listening… (cited in Harvey, 1999, p. 21).

But whereas Stockhausen perceives one possible sound experience, Francisco Lopez takes the same philosophy further for a different aim – the widest possible range of interpretations:

> I always do my live performances in complete darkness and providing blindfolds for the audience, in order to promote a profound listening and immersion into the sound matter, and also to avoid the classic annoying distractions of scenic presence of the artist and his technology. When you've done hundreds of performances you usually have a collection of weird anecdotes, including people crawling on the floor, crying, feeling as carried up to heaven by angels or down to hell by demons, and the like. What I find encouraging is not the extreme examples of this, but the astonishing variety of individual experiences/reactions to the same sonic material. I interpret this [as] a sign of openness in the content of the sonic creation, and this is also one of my main concerns: to work towards the development of a 'blank' sonic universe (Lopez, 2004).

However, I have decided to make a personal statement to contribute to this discussion. I am a heretic, in that I maintain my eyes wide open during performances of such (acousmatic) music. I wish to see clearly the loudspeakers as sound sources[68] as well as the environment in which they are set. In a darkened auditorium I maintain this stance and mentally reconstruct the real space around me from memory (and any residual visual clues). The state of readiness to perceive sound and music requires my ear/brain to be in an ultra-attentive mode which is (for me) only possible when all senses are on full alert and active. I guess that for others the hearing sense is accentuated with the eyes closed but for me this is simply not the case.[69] In addition I clearly perceive 'images of the music'. These are at least as far away from me as the loudspeakers. They are not superimposed as a separate landscape, but somehow integrated and even at times interacting with it: a real-imaginary symbiosis. Music – good music – does indeed take me 'somewhere else', although 'here' (the real

67 He announces this before most of the acousmatic concerts he presents.

68 I have even been known to change from my reading glasses to my long distance glasses for an electroacoustic concert.

69 To tell the truth I might fall asleep if I'm not careful.

space I am in) is still perceived clearly but reduced in 'presence'. How I interpret these images is not separate from how I interpret the music – they are indissoluble. The images I perceive are not strictly synaesthesic.[70] The acousmatic condition deliberately reduces information on source and cause which we[71] (products of evolution) attempt to 'fill in'. For me – and I believe many others – that process has a visual component. The imagination constructs a quasi-visual mindscape with many of the characteristics of 'real' vision. There are also interesting cross-references to other sense modes, most notably that I might be able to 'feel' sound textures and even sense heat – though at a distance, much as one might when viewing a volcano from a distance.

If I try to introspect about the kind of images that occur, my instinct is to assume that (say) a relatively 'abstract' spectromorphological composition might produce a different kind of mindscape than (say) a 'true' soundscape recording. But, interestingly, this is not always so. I was surprised in listening to a soundscape compositon by UK sound artists (led by Gregg Wagstaff) of sheep shearing in the Outer Hebrides Islands off the west coast of the Highlands of Scotland,[72] at the degree to which the absolute clarity and accuracy of the recording flipped my imagination *away* from a 'literal' image of sheep and human. It appeared that the acousmatic experience, far from provoking a source/cause search by my perception, created instead a three-dimensional tactile 'world' of textures, shapes and colours. Hyperreality quickly became 'unreality' – or at least a very personal inner reality. But what I have described could be equally present whether my eyes were open or closed. It was clear to me I wanted my eyes open for the experience to be optimized.

Conclusion – Synthesis?

Perhaps loudspeaker space not only allows but encourages my visual 'interpretation'. Loudspeakers are not a distraction. I am not joining that substantial group who always want some visual activity with the music and cannot bear to see an 'empty stage' or to 'stare at loudspeakers'. And I do not always feel the need to participate in the form of dancing. The sound remains, at all times, the focus of attention. But then there are increasingly common combinations with other arts to consider. If I go to a modern dance production with electroacoustic music,[73] then I often find this imaginary world I have described collapses completely. I find I have focused on watching the movement for a while and have little recollection of the music, or *vice versa*. So here the visual element is a serious distraction – conflicting with my own imaginary construction. It is the visual equivalent of Denis Smalley's description of audio-spatial 'dissonance' (above). While not always the case, the sight of the body (like the sound of the voice carried within it) has a strong focal pull on the attention.

---

70 In the sense that Messiaen saw colours associated with sounds and their combinations (Bernard, 1995).

71 Perhaps it would be better to say 'some of us': of course, Schaefferian purists attempt to 'bracket this process out'.

72 Issued as the CD 'TESE – The Sounds of Harris and Lewis' (TESE, 2002).

73 Often described in a hardly Freudian slip as 'accompaniment'.

Of course this is a pessimistic view – the aim remains that dance and music could have a symbiotic and mutually supporting function; but for some kinds of musician this will require a different kind of perceiving and appreciation.[74] For video/film with electroacoustic music my response depends on the content, but there is often less distraction than with actually present dance/human movement. There is greater probability that the 'real' visuals might complement, even meld in ('consonantly') with my aural-visual world – hopefully enhancing my response. I thus have to make a more complex comparison of the sound/image conjunction: it becomes the relationship of 'sound-image' to 'visual image'.

In the final analysis, eyes closed or open, there is a space to be filled, senses and sensualities to be aroused. Music and sound flow out beyond their physiological boundaries to resonate with all the other senses to a greater or lesser extent. Perhaps all we can conclude is that, while there are no boundaries, each of us has a unique 'sense resonance' pattern.

Footnote – Authenticity?

The desire to hear now 'what was it really like then' is a recurrent theme in music. 'Authentic' performances aim to recreate a 'sound' or 'technique'. European art music has recently seen successive centuries of the tradition 'made authentic', from mediaeval, renaissance, through baroque to classical (and beyond). Jazz and popular music also have many such authentic recreation streams. The process has also been under way in music made through technology. This has been most marked since the rapid transition to digital technology in the last two decades of the twentieth century. Such phenomena as the desire for analogue sound, the vinyl renaissance, valve amplifiers, or the use of lo-tech interfaces are well established demands. There does not appear to be an equivalent in 'authentic' loudspeaker demands. This is possibly because the loudspeaker has evolved more slowly – there has been no quantum leap in technology since its invention (effectively) in the 1920s. It is therefore not so immediately obvious that the 'loudspeaker sound' of studio and concert hall has changed profoundly in 50 years.[75] Changes (improvements) in loudspeaker quality are also to an extent masked by other 'analogue noise': mixers, recording devices, amplifiers and sound processors contributed considerably to this. Nonetheless an 'authentic sound' from any of the last eight decades would demand attention to loudspeaker construction of that time.

---

74 Similarly for those dancers and choreographers who consider the music secondary.

75 Personal and home listening is a similar story as studio quality has progressively been moved 'down market' in this time, culminating in '5.1' home systems that are in many cases superior to the cinema experience.

References

Books and articles

Agawu, Kofi (1991), *Playing with Signs – A Semiotic Interpretation of Classic Music*, Princeton: Princeton University Press.

Ake, David (2002), *Jazz Cultures*, Berkeley: University of California Press.

Alvarez, Javier (1989), 'Rhythm as motion discovered', *Contemporary Music Review*, 3(1), pp. 203–231.

Apollonio, Umbro (ed.) (1973), *Futurist Manifestos*, London: Thames and Hudson.

Ashley, Robert (1968), 'The Wolfman', *Source – music of the avant garde*, 2(2) (Issue 4), pp. 5–6.

Attali, Jacques (1985), *Noise – The Political Economy of Music*, Manchester: Manchester University Press.

Avraamov, Arseni (1992), 'The Symphony of Sirens (1923)', in Kahn, Douglas and Whitehead, Gregory (eds), *Wireless Imagination – Sound, Radio and the Avant-Garde*, pp. 245–252, Cambridge, MA: MIT Press.

Baalman, Marije (2004), 'Application of Wave Field Synthesis in electronic music and sound installations', *Proceedings of the 2nd International Linux Audio Conference (Karlsruhe 2004)*, Karlsruhe: ZKM (www.zkm.de/lac/2004).

Backus, John (1977), *The Acoustical Foundations of Music*, New York: Norton.

Bailey, Derek (1992), *Improvisation – its nature and practice in music*, London: The British Library National Sound Archive.

Barthes, Roland (1977), *Image-Music-Text* (tr. Stephen Heath), London: Fontana.

Bartok, Bela (1976), *Essays* (ed. Benjamin Suchoff), London: Faber and Faber.

Baxandall, Peter (2001), 'Electrostatic loudspeakers', in Borwick, John (ed.), *Loudspeaker and Headphone Handbook* (3rd Edition), pp. 108–195, Oxford: Focal Press.

Bayle, François (1977), 'Support/Espace', *Cahiers recherche/musique 5 (Le concert pourquoi? Comment?)*, pp. 13–39, Paris: INA/GRM.

Bayle, François (1993), *Musique acousmatique – propositions ... positions*, Paris: Buchet/Chastel.

Berg, Jan and Rumsey, Francis (2001), 'Verification and correlation of attributes used for describing the spatial quality of reproduced sound', *Proceedings of the AES 19th International Conference (June 2001)*, pp. 233–251, New York: Audio Engineering Society.

Berio, Luciano (1958a), 'Poesia e Musica – un'esperianza', *Incontri Musicali*, III, Milan: Suvini Zerboni.

Bernard, Jonathan (1987), *The Music of Edgard Varèse*, New Haven: Yale University Press.

Bernard, Jonathan (1995), *Colour*, in Hill, Peter (ed.), *The Messiaen Companion*, pp.203–219, London: Faber and Faber.

Blacking, John (1973), *How Musical is Man?*, Seattle: University of Washington Press.

Bongers, Bert (2000), 'Physical Interfaces in the Electronic Arts – Interaction Theory and Interfacing Techniques for Real-time Performance', in Wanderley, Marcelo and Battier, Marc (eds), *Trends in Gestural Control of Music*, CD-ROM, Paris: IRCAM.

Borges, Jorge Luis (1964), *Labyrinths*, London: Penguin Books.

Borwick, John (1990), *Microphones – Technology and Technique*, London: Focal Press.

Borwick, John (ed.) (2001), *Loudspeaker and Headphone Handbook* (3rd Edition), Oxford: Focal Press.

Bosma, Hannah (2000), 'Who creates electro-vocal music? (authors, composers, vocalists and gender)', in *Ctrl+Shift Art – Ctrl+Shift Gender*, Amsterdam: Axis v/m. Republished on www.hannahbosma.nl (consulted December 2005).

Boulez, Pierre (1971), *Boulez on Music Today* (translated by Susan Bradshaw and Richard Rodney Bennett), London: Faber and Faber.

Boulez, Pierre (1975), *Pierre Boulez: conversations with Célestin Deliège*, London: Eulenburg Books.

Boulez, Pierre (1991), *Stocktakings from an Apprenticeship*, Oxford: Oxford University Press.

Bregman, Albert (1990), *Auditrory Scene Analysis: the perceptual organisation of sound*, Cambridge, MA: MIT Press.

Cage, John (1968a), *Silence*, London: Marion Boyars.

Cage, John (1968b), *A Year from Monday*, London: Marion Boyars.

Campbell, Murray and Greated, Clive (1987), *The Musician's Guide to Acoustics*, London: Dent.

Carse, Adam (1964), *The History of Orchestration*, New York: Dover.

Cascone, Kim (2000), 'The Aesthetics of Failure: "Post-Digital" Tendencies in Contemporary Computer Music', *Computer Music Journal*, 24(4), pp. 12–18.

Cascone, Kim (2003), 'Grain, Sequence, System: Three Levels of Reception in the Performance of Laptop Music', *Contemporary Music Review*, 22(4), pp. 101–104.

Casserley, Lawrence (1998), 'A Digital Signal Processing Instrument for Improvised Music', *Journal of Electroacoustic Music*, 11, pp. 25–29.

Casserley, Lawrence (2001), '*Plus ça change:* Journeys, Instruments and Networks, 1966–2000', *Leonardo Music Journal*, 11, pp. 43–49.

Chadabe, Joel (1997), *Electric Sound – The Past and Promise of Electronic Music,* Upper Saddle River, NJ: Prentice Hall.

Chanan, Michael (1994), *Musica Practica: The social practice of western music from Gregorian chant to postmodernism*, London: Verso.

Chanan, Michael (1995) *Repeated Takes: A Short History of Recording and its Effects on Music*, London: Verso.

Chion, Michel (1983), *Guide des objets sonores – Pierre Schaeffer et la recherche musicale*, Paris: Buchet/Chastel.

Chion, Michel (1994), *Audio-Vision*, New York: Columbia University Press.

Chion, Michel and Delalande, François (eds) (1986), 'Recherche Musicale au GRM', *Revue Musicale*, 394–397 (Quadruple numero).

Chion, Michel and Reibel, Guy (1976), *Les musiques électroacoustiques*, Paris: INA-GRM/Edisud.

Chowning, John (1977), 'The Simulation of Moving Sound Sources', *Computer Music Journal*, 1(3), pp. 48–52.

Clozier, Christian (1998), 'Composition, diffusion and interpretation in electroacoustic music', *Proceedings (Volume III) of the Académie Internationale de Musique Electroacoustique, Bourges June 1997*, pp. 52–101 (French) and 233–281 (English), Bourges: Mnémosyne.

Collins, Nick; McClean, Alex; Rohrhuber, Julian; Ward, Adrian (2003), 'Live coding in laptop performance', *Organised Sound*, 8(3), pp. 321–330.

Connor, Steven (2000), *Dumbstruck – a Cultural History of Ventriloquism*, Oxford: Oxford University Press.

Copeland, Peter (1991), *Sound Recordings*, London: The British Library.

Cott, Jonathan (1974), *Stockhausen – Conversations with the composer*, London: Robson.

Cox, Christoph and Warner, Daniel (2004), *Audio Culture – Readings in Modern Music*, New York: Continuum.

Cross, Ian (1999), 'Is music the most important thing we ever did? Music, development and evolution', in Suk Won Yi, (ed.), *Music, Mind and Science*, pp. 10–39, Seoul: Seoul National University Press.

Cross, Ian (2003), 'Music and evolution: causes and consequences', *Contemporary Music Review*, 22(3), pp. 79–89.

Cutler, Chris (2000), 'Plunderphonics', in Emmerson, Simon (ed.), *Music, Electronic Media and Culture*, pp. 87–114, Aldershot: Ashgate.

Dalmonte, Rossana and Varga, Bálint András (1985), *Luciano Berio – Two Interviews*, London: Marion Boyars.

Davies, Hugh (1968), *Répertoire International des Musiques Electroacoustiques – International Electronic Music Catalog*, Cambridge, MA: MIT Press.

Debussy, Claude (1962), 'Monsieur Croche the Dilittante Hater', in *Three Classics in the Aesthetic of Music*, pp. 1–71, New York: Dover.

Diamond, Jared (1998), *Guns, Germs and Steel – A Short History of Everybody for the Last 13,000 Years*, London: Vintage.

Duchossoir, André R. (1998), *Gibson Electrics – The Classic Years*, Milwaukee: Hal Leonard.

Eargle, John (2004), *The Microphone Book* (Second edition), Oxford: Focal Press.

Emmerson, Simon (1976a), 'Luciano Berio talks to Simon Emmerson', *Music and Musicians* (London), 24(6) (Issue 282, February 1976), pp. 26–28.

Emmerson, Simon (ed.) (1986a), *The Language of Electroacoustic Music*, Basingstoke: Macmillan.

Emmerson, Simon (1986b), 'The Relation of Language to Materials', in Emmerson, Simon (ed.), *The Language of Electroacoustic Music*, pp. 17–39, Basingstoke: Macmillan.

Emmerson, Simon (1991), 'Live electronic music in Britain: three case studies', *Contemporary Music Review*, 6(1), pp. 179–195.

Emmerson, Simon (1994a), "Live' versus 'real-time'", *Contemporary Music Review*, 10(2), pp. 95–101.

Emmerson, Simon (1994b), "Local/field': towards a typology of live electroacoustic music', *Proceedings of the International Computer Music Conference 1994*, pp. 31–34, San Francisco: International Computer Music Association.

Emmerson, Simon (1998a), ' Acoustic/Electroacoustic: The Relationship with Instruments', *Journal of New Music Research*, 27(1–2), pp. 146–164.

Emmerson, Simon (1998b), 'Aural landscape: musical space', *Organised Sound*, 3(2), pp. 135–140.

Emmerson, Simon (1999). '"Body and Soul": two meditations on the 50th birthday of *musique concrète*', *Proceedings (Volume IV) of the Académie Internationale de Musique Electroacoustique, Bourges June 1998*, pp. 76–78 (French) and 198–200 (English), Bourges: Mnémosyne.

Emmerson, Simon (ed.) (2000), *Music, Electronic Media and Culture*, Aldershot: Ashgate.

Emmerson, Simon (2001a), 'From *Dance! To "Dance"*: Distance and Digits', *Computer Music Journal*, 25(1), pp. 13–20.

Emmerson, Simon (2001b), 'The Electroacoustic Harpsichord', *Contemporary Music Review*, 20(1), pp. 35–58.

Erickson, Robert (1975), *Sound Structure in Music*, Berkeley: University of California Press.

Fetterman, William (1996), *John Cage's Theatre Pieces – Notations and Performances*, Amsterdam: Harwood Academic Publishers.

Field, Ambrose (2000), 'Simulation and reality: the new sonic objects', in Emmerson, Simon (ed.), *Music, Electronic Media and Culture*, pp. 36–55, Aldershot: Ashgate.

Forsyth, Michael (1985), *Buildings for Music – The Architect, the Musician, and the Listener from the Seventeenth Century to the Present Day*, Cambridge: Cambridge University Press.

Gerzso, Andrew (1984), 'Reflections on *Répons*', *Contemporary Music Review*, 1(1), pp. 23–34.

Gibson, James (1966), *The Senses Considered as Perceptual Systems*, London: Unwin.

Gibson, James (1979), *The ecological approach to visual perception*, Boston: Houghton Mifflin.

Gillett, Charlie (1983), *The Sound of the City*, London: Souvenir Press.

Goldberg, RoseLee (1988), *Performance Art*, London: Thames & Hudson.

Gordon, Mel (1992), 'Songs from the Museum of the Future: Russian Sound Creation (1910–1930)', in Kahn, Douglas and Whitehead, Gregory (eds), *Wireless Imagination – Sound, Radio and the Avant-Garde*, pp. 197–243, Cambridge, MA: MIT Press.

Griffiths, Paul (1984), *Bartok*, London: Dent and Sons.

Handel, Stephen (1989), *Listening: An Introduction to the Perception of Auditory Events*. Cambridge, MA: MIT Press.

Harley, Maria Anna (1997), 'An American in Space: Henry Brant's "Spatial Music", *American Music*, 15(1), pp. 70–92.

Harrison, Jonty (1998), 'Sound, space, sculpture: some thoughts on the 'what', 'how' and 'why' of sound diffusion', *Organised Sound*, 3(2), pp. 117–127.

Harvey, David (1990), *The Condition of Postmodernity*, Cambridge MA: Blackwell.

Harvey, Jonathan (1999), *In Quest of Spirit – Thoughts on Music*, Berkeley: University of California Press.

Hayward Gallery (2000), *Sonic Boom – The Art of Sound*, London: Hayward Gallery Publishing.

Heikinheimo, Seppo (1972), *The Electronic Music of Karlheinz Stockhausen*, Helsinki: Suomen Musiikitieteellinen Seura.

Helmholtz, Hermann (1954), *On the Sensations of Tone*, New York: Dover.

Hempel, Carl and Oppenheim, Paul (1960), 'Studies in the logic of explanation', in Madden, E. H. (ed.), *The Structure of Scientific Thought*, Buffalo: Buffalo University Press.

Henry, Pierre (1977), 'Dispositifs techniques de quelques concerts de Pierre Henry', *Cahiers recherche/musique 5 (Le concert pourquoi? Comment?)*, pp. 195–212, Paris: INA/GRM.

Hewish, Antony; Bell, S. Jocelyn; Pilkinton, J.D.; Scott, P.F and Collins, R.A. (1968), 'Observation of a Rapidly Pulsating Radio Source', *Nature*, 217, pp. 709–713.

Holland, Keith (2001), 'Principles of sound radiation', in Borwick, John (ed.), *Loudspeaker and Headphone Handbook* (3rd Edition), pp. 1–43, Oxford: Focal Press.

ten Hoopen, Christiane and Landy, Leigh (1992), 'La musique électroacoustique', *Les Cahiers du CIREM*, 22–23 (Numéro double: 'François-Bernard Mâche'), pp. 79–96.

ten Hoopen, Christiane (1994), 'Issues in Timbre and Perception', *Contemporary Music Review*, 10(2), pp. 61–71.

Hornof, Anthony and Sato, Linda (2004), 'EyeMusic: Making Music with the Eyes', *Proceedings of the 2004 Conference on New Interfaces for Musical Expression (NIME04)*, pp. 185–188, http://www.nime.org/2004/ (consulted May 2006).

Howat, Roy (1983), *Debussy in Proportion – A musical analysis*, Cambridge: Cambridge University Press.

Huberman, Anthony (2004), Interview with Kaffe Matthews, *Bomb* magazine, 89 (Fall 2004), republished on www.annetteworks.com, (consulted September 2005).

Impett, Jonathan (1994), 'A Meta-Trumpet(-er)', *Proceedings of the International Computer Music Conference 1994*, pp. 147–150, San Fransisco: International Computer Music Association.

Ingold, Tim (2000), *The Perception of the Environment – Essays in livelihood, dwelling and skill*, London: Routledge.

James, Jamie (1995), *The Music of the Spheres*, London: Abacus.

Jencks, Charles (1986), *What is Post-Modernism?*, London: Academy Editions.

Kahn, Douglas and Whitehead, Gregory (eds) (1992), *Wireless Imagination – Sound, Radio and the Avant-Garde*, Cambridge, MA: MIT Press.

Kahn, Douglas (1999), *Noise, Water, Meat – A History of Sound in the Arts*, Cambridge, MA: MIT Press.

Kirby, Michael and Kirby, Victoria Nes (1986), *Futurist Performance*, New York: PAJ Publications.

Kostelanetz, Richard (1970), *John Cage*, London: Allen Lane The Penguin Press.

Kostelanetz, Richard (1989), *Conversing with Cage*, London: Omnibus Press.

Kozinn, Allan (1997), 'The Touring Composer as Keyboardist', in Kostelanetz, Richard (ed.), *Writings on Glass – Essays, Interviews, Criticism*, pp. 102–108, Berkeley: University of California Press.

Kurtz, Michael (1992), *Stockhausen: A Biography* (tr. Richard Toop), London: Faber and Faber.

Landy, Leigh (1991), *What's the Matter with Today's Experimental Music? – Organized Sound Too Rarely Heard*, Chur: Harwood Academic Publishers.

Le Corbusier (Charles Edouard Jeanneret) (1968), *Modular 2* (tr. Peter de Francia and Anna Bostock), Cambridge, MA,.: MIT Press.

Lewis, George (2000), 'Two Many Notes: Computers, Complexity and Culture in *Voyager*', *Leonardo Music Journal*, 10, pp. 30–39.

Lockspeiser, Edward (1978), *Debussy, His Life and Mind (Volume II: 1902–1918),* Cambridge: Cambridge University Press.

Lopez, Francisco (2004), Interview for db magazine (Adelaide, Australia) by Lenin Simons (June 2004), available on http://www.franciscolopez.net/int_db.html (consulted December 2005).

Lucier, Alvin (1976), 'Statement on: Music for Solo Performer', in Rosenboom, David (ed.), *Biofeedback and the Arts: results of early experiments*, pp. 60–61, Vancouver: A.R.C. Publications.

Mâche, François-Bernard (1992), *Music, Myth and Nature or The Dolphins of Arion*, (tr. Susan Delaney), Chur: Harwood Academic Publishers.

Maconie, Robin (1990), *The Works of Karlheinz Stockhausen* (Second Edition), Oxford: Oxford University Press.

Malham, David and Myatt, Anthony (1995), '3-D Sound Spatialization using Ambisonic Techniques', *Computer Music Journal*, 19(4), pp. 58–70.

Malham, David (2001), 'Toward Reality Equivalence in Spatial Sound Diffusion', *Computer Music Journal*, 25(4), pp. 31–38.

Mandelbrot, Benoît (1982), *The Fractal Geometry of Nature*, New York: W.H. Freeman.

Manning, Peter (1993), *Electronic and Computer Music* (Second Edition), Oxford: Oxford University Press.

Manning, Peter (2006), 'The significance of *techné* in understanding the art and practice of electroacoustic composition', *Organised Sound*, 11(1), pp. 81–90.

Matossian, Nouritza (1986), *Xenakis*, London: Kahn and Averill.

McClary, Susan (1991), *Feminine Endings – Music, Gender, and Sexuality*, Minnesota: University of Minnesota Press.

McMillen, Keith (1994), 'ZIPI: Origins and Motivations', *Computer Music Journal*, 18(4), 47–41.

McNabb, Michael (1981), 'Dreamsong: The Composition', *Computer Music Journal*, 5(4), pp. 36–53.

Mellor, Hugh (1968), 'Models and analogies in science: Duhem versus Campbell?', *ISIS*, 59, pp. 282–90.

Meyer, Jürgen (1978), *Acoustics and the Performance of Music*, Frankfurt am Main: Verlag Das Musikinstrument.

Miller, Simon (ed.) (1993), *The last post – Music after modernism*, Manchester: Manchester University Press.

Moore, F. Richard (1988), 'The Dysfunctions of MIDI', *Computer Music Journal*, 12(1), pp. 19–28.

Nattiez, Jean-Jacques (1990), *Music and Discourse* (tr. Carolyn Abate), Princeton: Princeton University Press.

Nattiez, Jean-Jacques (ed.) (1993), *The Boulez-Cage Correspondance* (translated and edited by Robert Samuels), Cambridge: Cambridge University Press.

Neill, Ben (2004), 'Breakthrough Beats: Rhythm and the Aesthetics of Contemporary Electronic Music', in Cox, Christoph and Warner, Daniel (eds), *Audio Culture – Readings in Modern Music*, pp.386–391, New York: Continuum.

Nettl, Bruno (1983), *The Study of Ethnomusicology – Twenty-nine Issues and Concepts*, Urbana: University of Illinois Press.

Nietzsche, Friedrich (1956), *The Birth of Tragedy* and *The Genealogy of Morals*, (tr. Francis Golffing), New York: Anchor/Doubleday

Nietzsche, Friedrich (1974), *The Gay Science*, (tr. Walter Kaufmann), New York: Vintage Books.

Nochlin, Linda (1968), 'The Invention of the Avant-Garde: France, 1830–80', in Hess, Thomas B. and Ashbery, John (eds), *Avant-Garde Art*, London: Collier Macmillan.

Norman, Katharine (1996), 'Real-World Music as Composed Listening', *Contemporary Music Review*, 15(1–2), pp. 1–27.

Norman, Katharine (2000a), 'Stepping outside for a moment: narrative space in two works for sound alone', in Emmerson, Simon (ed.), *Music, Electronic Media and Culture*, pp. 217–244, Aldershot: Ashgate.

Norman, Katharine (2004), *Sounding Art – Eight Literary Excursions through Electronic Music*, Aldershot: Ashgate.

Nyman, Michael (1999), *Experimental Music – Cage and Beyond* (Second Edition), Cambridge: Cambridge University Press.

Osmond-Smith, David (1991), *Berio*, Oxford: Oxford University Press.

Page, Tim (1997), 'Music in 12 Parts', in Kostelanetz, Richard (ed.), *Writings on Glass – Essays, Interviews, Criticism*, pp. 98–101, Berkeley: University of California Press.

Paradiso, Joseph and O'Modhrain, Sile (2003), 'Current Trends in Electronic Music Interfaces', *Journal of New Music Research*, 32(4), pp. 345–9.

Pauli, Hansjörg (1971), *Für wen komponieren Sie eigentlich?*, Frankfurt am Main: Fischer.

Poggioli, Renato (1968), *The Theory of the Avant-Garde*, Cambridge, MA: Harvard University Press.

Poldy, Carl A. (2001), 'Headphones', in Borwick, John (ed.), *Loudspeaker and Headphone Handbook* (3rd Edition), pp. 585–692, Oxford: Focal Press.

Popper, Karl (2002a), *The Poverty of Historicism,* London: Routledge.

Popper, Karl (2002b), *Conjectures and Refutations: The Growth of Scientific Knowledge*, London: Routledge.

Potter, Keith (2000), *Four Musical Minimalists*, Cambridge: Cambridge University Press.

Prévost, Edwin (1995), *No Sound Is Innocent*, Harlow: Copula.

Pritchett, James (1993), *The Music of John Cage*, Cambridge: Cambridge University Press.

Proust, Marcel (1983), *Remembrance of Things Past* (3 vols), (tr. C.K. Scott Moncrieff and Terence Kilmartin), Harmondsworth: Penguin Books

Rehfeldt, Philip (1977), *New Directions for Clarinet*, Berkeley: University of California Press.

Reich, Steve (2002), *Writings on Music 1965–2000 (ed. Paul Hillier)*, New York: Oxford University Press.

Revault d'Allonnes, Olivier (1975), *Xenakis – Les Polytopes*, Paris: Balland.

Rietveld, Hillegonda (1998), *This is our House – House Music, Cultural Spaces and Technologies*, Aldershot: Ashgate.

Roads, Curtis (1996a), *The Computer Music Tutorial*, Cambridge, MA: MIT Press.

Roads, Curtis (1996b), 'Early Electronic Music Instruments: Time Line 1899–1950', *Computer Music Journal*, 20(3), pp. 20–23.

Robindoré, Brigitte (1998), 'Luc Ferrari: Interview with an Intimate Iconoclast', *Computer Music Journal*, 22(3), pp. 8–16.

Rogalsky, Matthew (2006), *Idea and Community: The Growth of David Tudor's* Rainforest, *1965–2006*, PhD thesis, City University, London.

Rosenboom, David (ed.) (1976), *Biofeedback and the Arts: results of early experiments*, Vancouver: A.R.C. Publications.

Rosenboom, David (1997), 'Extended Musical Interface with the Human Nervous System', *Leonardo Monograph 1*, San Francisco: ISAST.

Sachs, Curt (1962), *The Wellsprings of Music*, New York: Da Capo Press.

Schaeffer, Pierre (1952), *A la recherche d'une musique concrète*, Paris: du Seuil

Schaeffer, Pierre (1966), *Traité des objets musicaux*, Paris: du Seuil.

Schaeffer, Pierre (1973), *La Musique Concrète*, Paris: Presses Universitaires de France.

Schafer, R. Murray (1969), *The New Soundscape*, London: Universal Edition.

Schafer, R. Murray (1970), *The Book of Noise*, Wellington: Price Milburn.

Schafer, R. Murray (1977), *The Tuning of the World*, New York: Knopf.

Schafer, R. Murray (ed.) (1978), *The Vancouver Soundscape*, Vancouver: ARC Publications.

Schiffer, Brigitte (1978), 'Xenakis's 'Polytope de Mycenae'', *Tempo*, 127 (December 1978), pp. 44–45.

Schoenberg, Arnold (1975), *Style and Idea*, London: Faber and Faber.

Scientific American (1978), *The Physics of Music*, San Francisco: Freeman.

Sherman, William and Craig, Alan (2003), *Understanding Virtual Reality – Interface, Application, and Design*, San Francisco: Morgan Kaufmann Publishers.

Small, Christopher (1998), *Musicking – The meanings of performing and listening*, Hanover: Wesleyan University Press.

Smalley, Roger (1974a), ''Momente': material for the listener and composer – 1', *The Musical Times*, 115(1571), January 1974, pp. 23–28.

Smalley, Roger (1974b), ''Momente': material for the listener and performer – 2', *Musical Times*, 115(1574), April 1974, pp. 289–95.

Smalley, Denis (1986), 'Spectro-morphology and Structuring Processes', in Emmerson, Simon (ed.), *The Language of Electroacoustic Music*, pp.61–93, Basingstoke: Macmillan.

Smalley, Denis (1991), 'Spatial experience in electro-acoustic music', in Dhomont, Francis (ed.), *L'Espace du Son II*, pp. 121–124, Ohain: Musiqes et Recherches.

Smalley, Denis (1992a), 'The listening imagination: listening in the electroacoustic era', in Paynter, John; Howell, Tim; Orton, Richard; Seymour, Peter (eds), *Companion to Contemporary Musical Thought*, pp.514–554, London: Routledge.

Solymar, Laszlo (1999), *Getting the Message – A history of communications*, Oxford: Oxford University Press.

Sporer, Thomas (2004), 'Wave Field Synthesis – Generation and Reproduction of Natural Sound Environments', *Proceedings of the 7th International Conference on Digital Audio Effects, Naples, October 2004*, pp. 133–138.

Stockhausen, Karlheinz (1958), 'Actualia', *Die Reihe*, 1, pp. 45–51.

Stockhausen, Karlheinz (1959), 'Music in Space', *Die Reihe*, 5, pp. 67–82.

Stockhausen, Karlheinz (1963), *Texte Band 1 – Texte zur elektronischen und instrumentalen Musik*, Köln: DuMont Schauberg.

Stockhausen, Karlheinz (1964a), *Texte Band 2 – Texte zu eigenen Werken – zur Kunst Anderer – Aktuelles*, Köln: DuMont Schauberg.

Stockhausen, Karlheinz (1964b), 'Music and Speech', *Die Reihe*, 6, pp. 40–64.

Stockhausen, Karlheinz (1971), *Texte Band 3 – Texte zur Musik 1963–1970*, Köln: DuMont Schauberg.

Stockhausen, Karlheinz (1989), *Stockhausen on Music –Lectures and Interviews Compiled by Robin Maconie*, London: Marion Boyars.

Stockhausen, Karlheinz; Aphex Twin; Scanner; Pemberton, Daniel (2004),

'Stockhausen vs. the "Technocrats"', in Cox, Christoph and Warner, Daniel, *Audio Culture – Readings in Modern Music*, pp. 381–385, New York: Continuum.

Tamm, Eric (1989), *Brian Eno: His Music and the Vertical Color of Sound*, Boston: Faber and Faber.

Tanaka, Atau (2000), 'Musical Performance Practice on Sensor-based Instruments', in Wanderley, Marcelo and Battier, Marc (eds), *Trends in Gestural Control of Music*, CD-ROM, Paris: IRCAM.

Tate Gallery (1974), *Turner – 1775–1852* (exhibition catalogue, authors unattributed), London: Tate Gallery Publications.

Teitelbaum, Richard (1976), 'In Tune: Some Early Experiments in Biofeedback Music (1966–74)' in Rosenboom, David (ed.) *Biofeedback and the Arts: results of early experiments*, pp. 35–56, Vancouver: A.R.C. Publications.

Thoreau, Henry David (1986), *Walden* and *Civil Disobedience*, London: Penguin.

Tingen, Paul (2004), 'Autechre – Recording Electronica', *Sound on Sound*, 19(6) (April 2004), pp. 96–102.

Toole, Floyd and Olive, Sean (2001), 'Subjective evaluation', in Borwick, John (ed.), *Loudspeaker and Headphone Handbook* (3rd Edition), pp. 565–584, Oxford: Focal Press.

Toop, David (1995). *Ocean of Sound: aether talk, ambient sound and imaginary worlds*, London: Serpent's Tail.

Toop, David (2004), *Haunted Weather – music, silence and memory*, London: Serpent's Tail.

Toop, Richard (1976), 'Stockhausen'*s Konktrete Etude*', *Music Review*, XXXVII (November 1976), pp. 295–300.

Toop, Richard (1979), 'Stockhausen and the Sine-Wave: The Story of an Ambiguous Relationship', *Musical Quarterly*, LXV (July 1979), pp. 379–391.

Treib, Marc (1996), *Space Calculated in Seconds – The Philips Pavilion, Le Corbusier, Edgard Varèse*, Princeton: Princeton University Press.

Truax, Barry (1994), 'Discovering Inner Complexity: Time-Shifting and Transposition with a Real-time Granulation Technique', *Computer Music Journal*, 18(2), pp. 38–48.

Truax, Barry (1996), 'Soundscape, Acoustic Communication and Environmental Sound Composition', *Contemporary Music Review*, 15(1–2), pp. 49–65.

Truax, Barry (ed.) (1999), *Handbook for Acoustic Ecology* (CD-ROM Edition), Vancouver: Cambridge Street Publishing.

Tudor, David (1972), 'From piano to electronics', *Music and Musicians* (London), XX, August 1972, pp. 24–26.

Turing, Alan (1950), 'Computing machinery and intelligence', *Mind*, LIX (no.236), pp. 433–460, republished at www.abelard.org/turpap/turpap.htm (consulted December 2005).

Ungeheuer, Elena (1992), *Wie die elektronische Musik 'erfunden' wurde: Quellenstudie zu Werner Meyer-Epplers Entwurf zwischen 1949 und 1953*, Mainz: Schott.

Viñao, Alejandro (1989), 'An old tradition we have just invented', *Electro-Acoustic Music* (EMAS Journal), 4(1–2), pp. 33–43.

Wagner, Richard (1977), *Wagner on Music and Drama*, (tr. H. Ashton Ellis), Goldman, Albert and Sprinchorn, Evert (eds), London: Victor Gollancz.

Waisvisz, Michel (1985), 'The Hands, a set of remote Midi controllers', *Proceedings of the International Computer Music Conference 1985*, pp. 313–318, San Francisco: International Computer Music Association.

Wanderley, Marcelo and Battier, Marc (eds) (2000), *Trends in Gestural Control of Music*, CD-ROM, Paris: IRCAM.

Warburton, Dan (2001), 'Keith Rowe – Interview by Dan Warburton', *Paris Transatlantic Magazine* (January 2001) archived at www.paristransatlantic.com/magazine/interviews/rowe.html (consulted December 2005).

Waters, Simon (2000), 'Beyond the acousmatic: hybrid tendencies in electroacoustic music', in Emmerson, Simon (ed.), *Music, Electronic Media and Culture*, pp. 56–83, Aldershot: Ashgate.

Watkinson, John (2001), 'Transducer drive mechanisms', in Borwick, John (ed.), *Loudspeaker and Headphone Handbook* (3rd Edition), pp. 44–107, Oxford: Focal Press.

Watson, James D. (1970), *The Double Helix*, Harmondsworth: Penguin

Windsor, Luke (2000), 'Through and around the acousmatic: the interpretation of electroacoustic sounds', in Emmerson, Simon (ed.), *Music, Electronic Media and Culture*, pp. 7–35, Aldershot: Ashgate.

Wishart, Trevor (1978), *Red Bird: A Document*, York: Wishart and London: Universal Edition.

Wishart, Trevor (1979), *Book of Lost Voices*, York: Wishart.

Wishart, Trevor (1986), 'Sound Symbols and Landscapes', in Emmerson, Simon (ed.), *The Language of Electroacoustic Music*, pp.41–60, Basingstoke: Macmillan.

Wishart, Trevor (1988), 'The Composition of *Vox-5*', *Computer Music Journal*, 12(4), pp. 21–27.

Wishart, Trevor (1996), *On Sonic Art*, Amsterdam: Harwood Academic Publishers.

Worby, Robert (2000), 'Cacophony', in Emmerson, Simon (ed.), *Music, Electronic Media and Culture*, pp. 138–163, Aldershot: Ashgate.

Wörner, Karl (1973), *Stockhausen, life and work*, London: Faber and Faber.

Xenakis, Iannis (1976), *Musique Architecture*, Tournai: Casterman.

Xenakis, Iannis (1985), *Arts/Sciences: Alloys – The Thesis Defense of Iannis Xenakis*, New York: Pendragon Press.

Xenakis, Iannis (1992), *Formalized Music – Thought and Mathematics in Composition*, Stuyvesant: Pendragon Press.

Young, Rob (1995), 'Transparent Messages – Aphex Twin', *The Wire*, 134 (April 1995), pp. 28–31.

Young, Rob (ed.) (2002), *Undercurrents – The Hidden Wiring of Modern Music*, London: Continuum.

Scores and recordings

Recordings are identified by album title, if there is one, as found on the spine of the media covering (for example, '*Isostasie*'). Failing a title, recordings usually list the works on the spine instead; this is here used as identifier with the individual works separated by a dash (for example, '*Zyklus – Refrain – Kontakte*'). Double or triple CD albums are indicated 'CD(2)', 'CD(3)' and so forth. '(1968?)' means media undated, date of publication estimated. '(1971*)' (for example) means that the CD reissue of this works retains the copyright date of the original (LP) issue, no other date is given. In the text, a date given immediately after a work's title refers to its date of composition, not of its publication; thus Stockhausen's *Gesang der Jünglinge* (1956) is referenced as Stockhausen (1991).

Alvarez, Javier (1992), *Papalotl - Transformaciones Exoticas*, CD, Saydisc: CD-SDL 390.

AMM (1989), *AMMMusic 1966*, CD, ReR Megacorp/Matchless Recordings: AMMCD.

AMM (2001), *Fine*, CD, Matchless Recordings: MRCD46.

Aphex Twin (1994), *Selected Ambient Works Volume II*, CD(2), Warp Records WARP021.

Aphex Twin (1995), *I care because you do*, CD(2), Warp Records WARP030.

Aphex Twin (2001), *drukqs*, CD(2), Warp Records: WARP092.

Barrett, Natasha (2002), *Isostasie*, CD, Empreintes Digitales: IMED 0262.

Bayle, François (1992), *Grande Polyphonie*, CD, Magison: MG CB 0392.

Bayle, François (1994), *L'Expérience Acoustique*, CD(2), INA/GRM: INA E 5009.

Berio, Luciano (1968?), *Thema (Omaggio a Joyce)*, LP, Vox Turnabout: TV34177S.

Berio, Luciano (1967), *Visage*, LP, Vox Turnabout: TV 34046S.

Berio, Luciano (1969?), *Sinfonia*, LP, CBS Masterworks: MS7268.

Berio, Luciano (1990), *A-Ronne*, CD, Decca: 425 620–2.

Berio, Luciano (1998), *Luciano Berio - Many More Voices*, CD, BMG Classics: 09026-68302-2.

Boulez, Pierre (1998), *Répons - Dialogue de l'ombre double*, CD, Deutsche Grammophon: 457 605–2.

Cage, John (1951), *Imaginary Landscape No. 4*, score, New York: Henmar Press (Edition Peters): P6718

Cage, John (1960a), *Imaginary Landscape No.1*, score, New York: Henmar Press (Edition Peters): P6716.

Cage, John (1960b), *Cartridge Music*, score, New York: Henmar Press (Edition Peters): P6703.

Cage, John (1961) *Music for Carillion No. 4*, score, New York: Henmar Press (Edition Peters): P6727.

Cage, John (CD undated – recorded 1965), CD, Legacy International: LEGACY CD439.

Cage, John (1966), *Variations VI*, score, New York: Henmar Press (Edition Peters): P6802.

Cage, John (1975), *Etudes Australes*, score, New York: Henmar Press (Edition Peters): P6816a-d.

Cage, John (1977), *Inlets*, score, New York: Henmar Press (Edition Peters): P66787.

Cage, John (1978), *Etudes Boreales*, score, New York: Henmar Press (Edition Peters): 66327.

Cage, John (1994), *Roaratorio – Writing for a second time through 'Finnegans Wake'*, CD, Wergo: WER 6303-2.

Crumb, George (1972? – undated), *Black Angels*, LP, CRI: SD 283.

Emmerson, Simon (1993), *Dreams, Memories and Landscapes*, CD, Continuum Records: CCD 1056.

Emmerson, Simon (2007), *Spaces and Places*, CD, Sargasso SCD28055.

Eno, Brian (1975), *Discreet Music*, LP, Island Records: obscure no.3.

Ferrari, Luc (1969?), *Luc Ferrari: Und so weiter, Music Promenade*, LP, WERGO: 60046.

Ferrari, Luc (1980), *Presque Rien*, LP, INA/GRM: 9104 fe.

Ferrari, Luc (1995), *Presque Rien*, CD, INA/GRM-MUSIDISC: 254172.

Ferrari, Luc (2005), *Son Mémorisé*, CD, Sub Rosa SR252.

Glass, Philip (1979*), *Einstein on the Beach*, CD(4), CBS Masterworks: M4K 38875.

Glass, Philip (1989), *Music in Twelve Parts*, CD(3), Virgin Records America: 91311-2.

Glass, Philip (1994), *Two Pages – Contrary Motion – Music in Fifths – Music in Similar Motion*, CD, Elektra Nonesuch: 7559-79326-2.

Glass, Philip (1996), *Music in Twelve Parts*, CD(3), Nonesuch: 79324-2.

Globokar, Vinko (1970s?), *Fluide – Ausstrahlungen – Atemstudie*, LP, Harmonia Mundi (Musique Vivante): HMU933.

Globokar, Vinko (1978), *Echanges – Res/As/Ex/Ins-spirer – Discours IV*, LP, Harmonia Mundi: 1C 065-99 712.

Harrison, Jonty (1996a), *Articles indéfinis*, CD, Empreintes Digitales: IMED 9627.

Harrison, Jonty (1996b), *EQ,* on *Klang*, CD, NMC Recordings: NMC D035.

Harrison, Jonty (2000), *Évidence matérielle*, CD, Empreintes Digitales: IMED 0052.

Harvey, Jonathan (1999), *Mortuos Plango*, Vivos Voco, CD, Sargasso: SCD 28029.

Henry, Pierre (1987), *Variations/Voile d'Orphée*, CD, Harmonia Mundi: HMC905200.

Henry, Pierre (1991), *Des Années 50*, CD(3), Mantra Records: Mantra 032.

Henry, Pierre and Colombier, Michel (1997), *Métamorphose – Messe pour le temps présent*, CD, Philips 456 640-2.

INA/GRM (2004), *archives grm*, CD(5), INA/GRM: 276512-276552.

Kagel, Mauricio (1973*), *1898 – Music for Renaissance Instruments*, CD, Deutsche Grammophon: 459 570-2.

Levinas, Michael (1978), *Froissements d'ailes*, LP, INA/Collection GRM: AM 821.10.

Lucier, Alvin (1990), *I am sitting in a room*, CD, Lovely Music: LCD 1013.

Mâche, François-Bernard (1990), *Korwar*, on *Rhythm Plus*, CD, ADDA: 581233.

Mâche, François-Bernard (1994), *Korwar*, score, Paris: Durand.

Machover, Tod (2003), *Hyperstring Trilogy*, CD, Oxingale: OX2003.

Maderna, Bruno (1967), *Musica su due dimensioni*, on *elektron 3*, LP, Sugar Music: esz 3.

Matthews, Kaffe (1997), *cd-Ann*; (1998), *cd-Bea*; (2000), *cd-dd*; (2003), *cd-eb + flo*, CDs, Annette Works (UK).

McNabb, Michael (1983), *Computer Music*, CD, Mobile Fidelity Sound Lab: MFCD818.

McNabb, Michael (1989), *Invisible Cities*, CD, Wergo: WER 2015–50.

Méfano, Paul (1981), *Traits suspendu*, LP, Le Chant du Monde: LDX 78700.

Moore, Adrian (2000), *Traces*, CD, Empreintes Digitales: IMED 0053.

Nelson, Gary Lee (1992), *Fractal Mountains*, on *Computer Music Currents 10*, CD, Wergo: WER 2030–2.

Neuhaus, Max (1965), *Electronics and Percussion – Five Realizations by Max Neuhaus*, LP, Columbia Masterworks: MS 7139.

Nono, Luigi (1970s?), *Non Consumiamo Marx*, LP, Philips: 6521 027.

Nono, Luigi (2000), *A floresta è jovem e cheja de vida*, CD, mode records: mode 87.

Nono, Luigi (1992), *Luigi Nono*, CD, Wergo: WER 6038–2.

Norman, Katharine (1991), *Trying to Translate*, score, London: BMIC.

Norman, Katharine (2000b), *Transparent things*, CD, Metier: MSV CD92054.

Normandeau, Robert (1990), *Lieux inouïs*, CD, Empreintes Digitales: IMED-9002-CD.

Parker, Evan *et al.* (Evan Parker Electro-Acoustic Ensemble) (1999), *Drawn Inward*, CD, ECM Records: ECM 1693 547 209-2.

Plastikman (1993), *sheet one*, CD, Mute Records: NoMu CD 22.

Reich, Steve (1974*), *Drumming – Six Pianos – Music for Mallet Instruments, Voices and Organ*, CD(2), Deutsche Grammophon: 427 428-2.

Reich, Steve *et al.* (1999), *Reich Remixed*, CD, Nonesuch: 79552.

Riley, Terry (1971*), *A Rainbow in Curved Air – Poppy Nogood and the Phantom Band*, CD, Columbia 477849 2.

Scanner (1995), *Sulphur*, CD, Sub Rosa: subrosa vista2 sr95.

Schaeffer, Pierre (1990), *Pierre Schaeffer – l'œuvre musicale intégrale*, CD(4), INA. GRM: INA C 1006-1009.

Smalley, Denis (1992b), *Impacts intérieurs*, CD, Empreintes Digitales: IMED-9209-CD.

Smalley, Denis (2000), *Scources/scènes*, CD, Empreintes Digitales: IMED 0054.

Squarepusher (2001), *Go Plastic*, CD, Warp Records: WARPCD85.

Stockhausen, Karlheinz (1966), *Kontakte*, performance score, Vienna: Universal Edition: UE14246.

Stockhausen, Karlheinz (1968), *Kontakte*, realisation score/performance score, Vienna: Universal Edition: UE13678.

Stockhausen, Karlheinz (1969), *Stimmung*, score, Vienna: Universal Edition: 14805.

Stockhausen, Karlheinz (1970), *From the Seven Days – Aus den sieben Tagen*, score, Vienna: Universal Edition 14790 E.

Stockhausen, Karlheinz (1973), *Spiral*, score, Vienna: Universal Edition: 14957.

Stockhausen, Karlheinz (1974), *Mikrophonie I*, score, Vienna: Universal Edition: 15138.

Stockhausen, Karlheinz (1975), *Pole – Expo*, score, Kürten: Stockhausen Verlag.

Stockhausen, Karlheinz (1976), *Für kommende Zeiten*, score, Kürten: Stockhausen Verlag.

Stockhausen, Karlheinz (1977), *Sternklang*, score, Kürten: Stockhausen Verlag.

Stockhausen, Karlheinz (1991), *Elektronische Musik 1952–1960*, CD, Stockhausen Verlag: CD 3.

Stockhausen, Karlheinz (1992), *Sternklang*, CD(2), Stockhausen Verlag: CD 18.

Stockhausen, Karlheinz (1993a), *Zyklus – Refrain – Kontakte*, CD, Stockhausen Verlag: CD 6.

Stockhausen, Karlheinz (1993b), *Stimmung*, CD(2), Stockhausen Verlag: CD 12.

Stockhausen, Karlheinz (1994a), *Oktophonie*, score, Kürten: Stockhausen Verlag.

Stockhausen, Karlheinz (1994b), *Oktophonie*, CD, Stockhausen Verlag: CD 41.

Stockhausen, Karlheinz (1995), *Mikrophonie I – II – Telemusik*, CD, Stockhausen Verlag: CD 9.

TESE (2002), *TESE – Touring Exhibition of Sound Environments (2002) –The Sounds of Harris & Lewis*, CD(3), Earminded: www.earminded.org/tese.

Tudor, David (1998), *Rainforest*, CD, mode records: mode 64.

Truax, Barry (1991) *Pacific*, on *Pacific Rim*, CD, Cambridge Street Records: CSR-CD 9101.

Vaggione, Horacio (1988), *Tar*, on *Cultures Electroniques 3*, CD(2), Le Chant du Monde: LDC 278046/47.

Viñao, Alejandro (1990). *Son Entero – Triple Concerto*, CD, Wergo: WER 2019-50.

Waisvisz, Michel (1987), *The Hands* (extracts), CD, Wergo: WER 2010-50.

Wehinger, Rainer (1970), *Ligeti – Artikulation*, aural score, Mainz: Schott 6378.

Westerkamp, Hildegard (1995), *Der Verlust der Stille*, CD, Baden: Evangelische Akademie Baden.

Westerkamp, Hildegard (1996), *Transformations*, CD, Empreintes Digitales: IMED 9631.

Wishart, Trevor (1990), *VOX*, CD, Virgin: VC 7 91108-2.

Wishart, Trevor (1992), *Red Bird – Anticredos*, CD, October Music: Oct 001.

The Wizard of Oz (1939), DVD, Warner Brothers 65123.

World Soundscape Project (1997), *The Vancouver Soundscape 1973 – Soundscape Vancouver 1996*, CD(2), Cambridge Street Records: CSR-2CD 9701.

Xenakis, Iannis (1997), *Electronic Music*, Electronic Music Foundation: EMF CD 003.

Xenakis, Iannis (2002), *Persepolis Remixes – Edition I*, CD, Ashodel: LTD 2005.

Young, La Monte (1973), *La Monte Young – Marian Zazeela – The Theatre of Eternal Music*, LP, Shandar (France): 83.510.

Zapruda Trio (2000), *Live at Smallfish*, CD, Visionofsound VSZAPCD 1.

Index